THE FORCEFUL YOGA

The Forceful Yoga

Being the Translation of
Haṭhayoga-Pradīpikā, Gheraṇḍa-Saṁhitā
and Śiva-Saṁhitā

Translated into English by
PANCHAM SINH
RAI BAHADUR SRISA CHANDRA VASU

Romanised and Edited by
DR. G.P. BHATT

MOTILAL BANARSIDASS PUBLISHERS
PRIVATE LIMITED • DELHI

2nd Reprint : Delhi, 2014
First revised, corrected and enlarged edition: Delhi, 2004

ISBN : 978-81-208-2054-8 (Cloth)
ISBN : 978-81-208-2055-5 (Paper)

MOTILAL BANARSIDASS
41 U.A. Bungalow Road, Jawahar Nagar, Delhi 110 007
8 Mahalaxmi Chamber, 22 Bhulabhai Desai Road, Mumbai 400 026
203 Royapettah High Road, Mylapore, Chennai 600 004
236, 9th Main III Block, Jayanagar, Bangaluru 560 011
Sanas Plaza, 1302 Baji Rao Road, Pune 411 002
8 Camac Street, Kolkata 700 017
Ashok Rajpath, Patna 800 004
Chowk, Varanasi 221 001

Printed in India

by RP Jain at NAB Printing Unit,
A-44, Naraina Industrial Area, Phase I, New Delhi–110028
and published by JP Jain for Motilal Banarsidass Publishers (P) Ltd,
41 U.A. Bungalow Road, Jawahar Nagar, Delhi-110007

Contents

Prologue

We herewith offer a combined edition of three most popular Sanskrit texts (Romanized) with English translation, on Haṭhayoga, of the post-classical, that is, Post-Patañjali period, namely, *Haṭha yoga-Pradīpikā* or *Haṭha-Pradīpikā, Gheraṇḍa-Saṁhitā* and *Śiva-Saṁhitā* of 14th-18th centuries C.E., being a completely revised and edited version of the editions of the three works published by the Panini Office, Allahabad long ago in 1914-15.

Out of the three, *Haṭhayoga-Pradīpikā* is the best known manual. The text gives the name of the author as Svātmārāma Yogin. Georg Feuerstein, an eminent contemporary authority and propounder of Yoga assigns fourteenth century C.E. as the date of the work. It contains (in the present version) a total of 383 *ślokas* divided into four *Upadeśas* (instructions or lessons) including 69 of the first, 78 of the second, 123 of the third and 113 of the fourth lesson. The first lesson discusses mainly the Yogic Postures (Āsanas), the second Prāṇāyāma, the third Mudrā and the fourth Samādhi, the final goal of Yoga-sādhanā. Incidentally the proper environment for the practice of Yoga, the exercises for the purification of the Nāḍīs *(ṣaṭkarmāṇi)*, certain moral requirements as preliminaries and the line of teachers of the system are also discussed. The work appears to be a compilation of passages from prior works, notably those attributed to Gorakṣanātha, rather than an original work.

The second, *Gheraṇḍa-Saṁhitā*-is a work of 351 *Ślokas* (in the present version) divided into seven *Upadeśas* or lessons each dealing with one stage of the seven-stage system of Haṭhayoga comprising: (1) six purificatory acts, (2) postures, (3) Mudrās, (4) Pratyāhāra or withdrawal of senses, (5) Prāṇāyāma, (6) Dhyāna or meditation and (7) Samādhi. The date assigned to the work by Feuerstein is late seventeenth century, being later than Haṭhayoga-

Pradīpikā from which several ślokas have been borrowed. The work is in the form of a dialogue between a teacher, Gheraṇḍa, and a disciple, Caṇḍakāpāli.

The third text, *Śivasaṁhitā* or the collection of the teachings of god Śiva, contains (in the version included here) 517 Ślokas (96+54+97+58+212) in five chapters called *Paṭalas*. It contains Advaita ideas and Tāntrika material also and is supposed to have been compiled in late seventeenth or early eighteenth century C.E. The first chapter exhorts one to realise the unity of the individual with the universal soul and realise the true nature of reality by piercing the veil of *Māyā*. The second chapter discusses the human subtle bodily matrix. The third one deals with Āsana and Prāṇāyāma. The fourth one is concerned with Mudrā. The last chapter, which is the largest, includes discussion of six major Cakras and four varieties of Yogas viz. Mantra, Haṭha, Laya and Rāja Yoga.

Now Haṭhayoga being a variety of Yoga, it is natural for one to ask how it differs from other varieties, especially from Rājayoga, and still more to know what Yoga is and what its origin is. In view of the wide popularity and currency that Yoga has gained internationally today we can proudly say that Yoga is a unique contribution of India in the field of spirituality and is on a par with other Indic contributions like zero in mathematics. Yoga has its origin far back in the pre-historic times, as recent archaeological evidence has shown. It was quite in vogue in the ancient Indus-Sarasvatī Culture formerly designated as Indus Valley Civilization going back to 3000 B.C.E. It aimed at transcending the human condition. In the words of Georg Feuerstein, "Yoga is indeed the technology of ecstatic transcendence."

The word *Rājayoga* is a late coinage used for Patañjali's Classical Yoga Systeṁ of eight limbs in 16th century C.E. Several explanations are possible, e.g., that it was practised by kings like the 10th century King Bhoja or as referring to the transcendental self which is the ruler or King of the body-mind complex or which in 'luminous' or 'resplendent' *(rājate)* or that it refers to the Lord or God recognized by Patañjali as a special Self in contrast to the Sāṁkhya system of Kapila with which Patañjali's system has a special affinity.

As contrasted with Rājayoga which has Yama, Niyama, Āsana,

Prāṇāyāma, Pratyāhāra, Dhāraṇā, Dhyāna and Samādhi as the eight limbs, Haṭhayoga has seven limbs, viz., *Ṣaṭkarmāṇi* or six purificatory exercises, e.g., Neti, Dhauti etc., Āsana, Mudrā and Bandha, Pratyāhāra, Prāṇāyāma, Dhyāna and Samādhi.

Haṭhayoga or "forceful yoga" is a post-classical or medieval development of Yoga under the influence of Tantra and Nāthism involving belief in practices relating to mystic entities like subtle body, Cakras, Nāḍīs, Kuṇḍalinī, etc. and aiming at Siddhis or paranormal powers. While ignoring the moral requirements implied by the practice of Yama, Niyama etc., Haṭhayoga involves a shift of focus from spirit to body, to mastery over the physical nature. The body had traditionally been despised as an inflated bladder of skin full of filth like urine, faeces, pus, blood, bones, marrow etc. Haṭhayoga rejecting this model which was more a strategy to wean people, especially spiritual seekers, from materialistic inclinations than a statement of truth, aims to transmute the body into a "divine body", or "adamantine body" which would guarantee "immortality in the manifest realms." As Feuerstein states, "The psycho-spiritual technology of Haṭhayoga is particularly focused on developing the body's potential so that the body can withstand the onslaught of transcendental realization."

For a fuller and excellent treatment of the subject the reader is advised to read profitably:

1. Georg Feuerstein, *The Yoga Tradition,* Hohm Press Prescot, Arizona 86302.
2. Mikel Burley, *Haṭha Yoga,* Motilal Banarsidass Publishers Private Limited, Delhi.

No. 1 is the most authoritative and exhaustive work that has appeared in print so far on the complete subject of Yoga and is a must. No. 2 has a limited scope as it treats of Haṭhayoga only, yet its quality is excellent.

— G.P. Bhatt

Introduction

There exists at present a good deal of misconception with regard to the practices of the Haṭha Yoga. People easily believe in the stories told by those who themselves heard them second-hand, and no attempt is made to find out the truth by a direct reference to some good treatise. It is generally believed that the six practices, (Ṣaṭkarma) in Haṭha Yoga are compulsory for the student and that besides being dirty, they are fraught with danger to the practitioner. This is not true, for these practices are necessary only in case there exist impurities in the Nāḍīs, and not otherwise.

There is also a lot of misunderstanding with regard to Prāṇāyāma. People put their faith implicitly in the stories told about the dangers attending the practice without ever taking the trouble of ascertaining the facts themselves. We have been breathing in and breathing out air since our birth, and will continue to do so till death; and this is done without the help of any teacher. Prāṇāyāma is nothing but a properly regulated form of the otherwise irregular and hurried flow of air, without using much force or undue restraint; and if this is accomplished by patiently keeping the flow slow and steady, there can be no danger. It is the impatience for the Siddhis which causes undue pressure on the organs and thereby causes pain in the ears, eyes, chest, etc. If the three *Bandhas* be carefully performed while practising Prāṇāyāma, there is no possibility of any risk.

There are two classes of students of Yoga: (1) those who study it theoretically; (2) those who combine the theory with practice.

Yoga is of very little use, if studied theoretically. It was never meant for such a study. In its practical form, however, the path of the student is beset with difficulties. The books on Yoga give instructions so far as it is possible to express the methods in word, but all persons, not being careful enough to follow these instructions to the very letter, fail in their object. Such persons require a teacher versed in the practice of Yoga. It is easy to find a teacher who will explain the language of the books, but this is far from satisfactory. For instance, a Paṇḍita wihtout any knowledge of the science of Materia Medica will explain *kaṇṭakāriḥ* as *kaṇṭakasya ariḥ* or an enemy of thorns, *i.e.*, shoes, while it is in reality the name of a medicinal plant.

The importance of a practical Yogī as a guide to a student of Yoga cannot be overestimated; and without such a teacher it is next to impossible for him to achieve anything. The methods followed by the founders of the system and followed ever afterwards by their followers, have been wisely and advisedly kept secret; and this is not without a deep meaning. Looking to the gravity of the subject and the practices which have a very close relation with the vital organs of the human body, it is of paramount importance that the instructions should be received by students of ordinary capacity through a practical teacher only, in order to avoid any possibility of mistake in practice. Speaking broadly, all men are not equally fitted to receive the instructions on equal terms. Man inherits at birth his mental and physical capacities, according to his actions in past births, and has to develop them by practice, but there are, even among such, different grades. Hence, one cannot become a Yogī in one birth, as says Śrī Kṛṣṇa

> *bahūnāṁ janmanām ante jñānavān māṁ prapadyate /*
>
> (BG VII.19)

and again

> *manuṣyāṇāṁ sahasreṣu kaścid yatati siddhaye /*
> *yatatām api siddhānāṁ kaścin māṁ vetti tattvataḥa //*
>
> (BG VII. 3)

There are men who, impelled by the force of their actions of previous births, go headlong and accomplish their liberation in a single attempt; but others have to earn it in their successive births. If the student belongs to one of such souls and being earnest, desires from his heart to get rid of the pains of birth and death, he will find the means too. It is well-known that a true Yogī is above temptations and so to think that he keeps his knowledge secret for selling it to the highest bidder is simply absurd. Yoga is meant for the good of all creatures, and a true Yogī is always desirous of benefitting as many men as possible. But he is not to throw away this precious treasure indiscriminately. He carefully chooses its recipients, and when he finds a true and earnest student who will not trifle with this knowledge, he never hesitates in placing his valuable treasure at the disposal of the man. What is essential in him is that he should have a real thirst for such knowledge—a thirst which will make him restless till satisfied, the thirst that will make him blind to the world and its enjoyments. He should be, in short, fired with *Mumukṣutva* or desire for emancipation. To such a one there is nothing dearer than the accomplishment of this object. A true lover will risk his very life to gain union with his beloved like Tulasīdāsa. A true lover will see everywhere, in every direction, in every tree and leaf, in every blade of grass his own beloved. The whole of the world, with all its beauties, is a dreary waste in his eyes, without his beloved. And he will court death, fall into the mouth of a gaping grave, for the sake of his beloved. The student whose heart burns with such intense desire for union with Paramātmā, is sure to find a teacher, and through him he will surely find Him. It is a tried experience that Paramātmā will try to meet you halfway, with the degree of intensity with which you go to meet Him. Even He Himself will become your guide, direct you on to the road to success, or put you on the track to find a teacher, or lead him to you.

Well has it been said:

> *jina ḍhūm̐ḍhā tina pāiyām̐ gahare pānī paiṭhi /*
> *maim̐ bāvari ḍhūm̐ḍhana calī rahī kināre baiṭhi //*

It is the half-hearted who fail. They hold their worldly pleasures dearer to their hearts than their God, and therefore He in His turn does not consider them worthy of His favours. Says Muṇḍaka Upaniṣad (III.2.3):

> *nāyamātmā pravacanena labhyo na medhayā na bahunā śrutena /*
> *yamevaiṣa vṛṇute tena labhyas tasyaiṣa ātmā vivṛṇute tanuṁ svām //*

The Ātmā will choose you as its abode only if it considers you worthy of such a favour, and not otherwise. It is therefore neccessary that one should first make oneself worthy of His acceptance. Having prepared the temple (your heart) well fitted for His installation there, having cleared it of all the impurities which stink and make the place unsuitable for the highest personage to live in, and having decorated it beautifully with objects as befit that Lord of the creation, you need not wait long for Him to adorn this temple of yours which you have taken pains to make worthy of Him. If you have done all this, He will shine in you in all His glory. In your difficult moments, when you are embarrassed, sit in a contemplative mood, and approach your Parama Guru submissively and refer your difficulties to Him, you are sure to get the proper advice from Him. He is the Guru of the ancients, for He is not limited by Time. He instructed the ancients in bygone times, like a Guru, and if you have been unable to find a teacher in human form,enter your inner temple and consult this Great Guru who accompanies you everywhere, and ask Him to show you the way. He knows best what is best for you. Unlike mortal beings, He is beyond the past and the future, will either send one of His agents to guide you or lead you to one and put you on the right track. He is always anxious to teach earnest seekers, and waits for you to offer Him an opportunity to do so. But if you have not done your duty and prepared yourself as worthy of entering His door, and try to gain access to His presence, laden with your unclean burden, stinking with Kāma, Krodha, Lobha, and Moha, be sure He will keep you off from Him.

The Āsanas are a means of gaining steadiness of position and help to gain success in contemplation, without any distraction of the mind. If the position be not comfortable, the slightest inconvenience will draw the mind away from the lakṣya (aim), and so no peace of mind will be possible till the posture has ceased to cause pain by regular practice.

Of all the various methods for concentrating the mind, repetition of *Praṇava* or *Ajapā japa* and contemplation on its meaning is the best. It is impossible for the mind to remain idle even for a single moment, and, therefoe, in order to keep it well occupied and to keep other antagonistic thoughts from entering it, repetition of *Praṇava* should be practised. It should be repeated till Yoga Nidrā is induced which, when experienced, should be encouraged by slackening all the muscles of the body. This will fill the mind with sacred and divine thoughts and will bring about its one-pointedness without much effort.

Anāhata Nāda is awakened by the exercise of Prāṇāyāma. A couple of weeks' practice with 80 Prāṇāyāmas in the morning and the same number in the evening will cause distinct sounds to be heard; and, as the practice will go on increasing, varied sounds become audible to the practitioner. By hearing these sounds attentively one gets concentration of the mind and there Sahaja Samādhi. When yoga sleep is experienced the student should give himself up to it and make no effort to check it. By and by these sounds become subtle and they become less and less intense, so the mind loses its waywardness and becomes calm and docile; and, on this practice becoming well-established, Samādhi becomes a voluntary act. This is, however, the highest stage and is the lot of the favoured and fortunate few only.

During contemplation one sees, not with his eyes as he does the objects of the world, various colours , which the writers on Yoga call the colours of the five elements. Sometimes stars are seen glittering, and lightning flashes in the sky. But these are all fleeting in their nature.

At first these colours are seen in greatly agitated waves which show the unsteady condition of the mind; and as the practice increases and the mind becomes calm, these colour-waves become steady and motionless and appear as one deep ocean of light. This is the ocean in which one should dive and forget the world and become one with his Lord—which is the condition of highest bliss.

Faith in the practice of Yoga, and in one's own powers to accomplish what others have done before, is of great importance to insure speedy success. I mean "faith that will move mountains," will accomplish anything, be it howsoever difficult. There is nothing which cannot be accomplished by practice. Says Śiva in Śiva-Saṁhitā (IV. 9-11):

> *abhyāsāj jāyate siddhir abhyāsān mokṣam āpnuyāt //*
> *saṁvidaṁ labhate' bhyāsād yogā' bhyāsāt pravartate /*
> *mudrāṇāṁ siddhir abhyāsad abhyāsād vāyusādhanam //*
> *kālavañcanam abhyāsāt tathā mṛtyuñjayo bhavet /*
> *vāksiddhiḥ kāmacāritvaṁ bhaved abhyāsayogataḥ //*

Through practice success is obtained; through practice one gains liberation. Perfect consciousness is gained through practice; Yoga is attained through practice; success in *Mudrās* comes by practice. Through practice is gained success in *Prāṇāyāma*. Death can be evaded through practice, and man becomes the conqueror of death by practice. And then let us gird up our loins, and with a firm resolution engage in the practice, having faith in *karmaṇyevādhikāras te mā phaleṣu kadācana,* and the success must be ours. May the Almighty Father be pleased to shower His blessings on those who thus engage in the performance of their duties.

— PANCHAM SINGH

Section I

HAṬHA-YOGA-PRADĪPIKĀ

CHAPTER 1

On Āsanas

Prathamopadeśaḥ

śrīādināthāya namo'stu tasmai yenopadiṣṭā haṭhayogavidyā /
vibhrājate pronnatarājayogam āroḍhum icchor adhirohiṇīva// 1 //

Salutation to Ādinātha (Śiva) who expounded the knowledge of Haṭha Yoga, which like a staircase leads the aspirant to the high-pinnacled Rāja Yoga.

praṇamya śrīgurum nātham svātmārāmeṇa yoginā /
kevalam rājayogāya haṭhavidyopadiśyate // 2 //

Yogī Svātmārāma, after saluting first his Guru Śrīnātha, explains Haṭha Yoga as a preparation for the attainment of Rāja Yoga only.

bhrāntyā bahumatadhvānte rājayogam ajānatām /
haṭhapradīpikām dhatte svātmārāmaḥ kṛpākaraḥ // 3 //

Owing to the darkness arising from the multiplicity of opinions people are unable to know Rāja Yoga. Compassionate Svātmārāma composes the Haṭha Pradīpikā (like a torch) to dispel it.

haṭhavidyām hi matsyendragorakṣādyā vijānate /
svātmārāmo'thavā yogī jānīte tatprasādataḥ // 4 //

Matsyendra, Gorakṣa, etc., knew Haṭha Vidyā, and by their favour Yogī Svātmārāma also learnt it from them.

śrīādināthamatsyendraśābarānandabhairavāḥ /
cauraṅgīmīnagorakṣavirūpākṣabileśayāḥ // 5 //

The following Siddhas (masters) are said to have existed in former times :

Śrī Ādinātha (Śiva), Matsyendra, Śābara, Ānanda, Bhairava, Cauraṅgī, Mīna, Gorakṣa, Virūpākṣa, Bileśaya,

manthāno bhairavo yogī siddhir buddhaśca kanthaḍiḥ /
koraṇṭakaḥ surānandaḥ siddhipādaś ca carpaṭiḥ // 6 //

Manthāna, Bhairava, Siddhi, Buddha, Kanthaḍi, Koraṇṭaka, Surānanda, Siddhipāda, Carpaṭi,

kānerī pūjyapādaś ca nityanātho nirañjanaḥ /
kapālī bindunāthaś ca kākacaṇḍīśvarāhvayaḥ // 7 //

Kānerī, Pūjyapāda, Nityanātha, Nirañjana, Kapālī, Bindunātha, Kākacaṇḍīśvara,

allāmaḥ prabhudevaśca ghoḍācolī ca ṭiṇṭiṇiḥ /
bhānukī nāradevaśca khaṇḍaḥ kāpālikas tathā // 8 //

Allāma, Prabhudeva, Ghoḍācolī, Ṭiṇṭiṇi, Bhānukī, Nāradeva, Khaṇḍa, Kāpālika, etc.

ityādayo mahāsiddhā haṭhayogaprabhāvataḥ /
khaṇḍayitvā kāladaṇḍaṁ brahmāṇḍe vicaranti te // 9 //

These and other Mahāsiddhas (great masters), breaking the sceptre of death by the power of Haṭha Yoga, are roaming in the universe.

aśeṣatāpataptānāṁ samāśrayamaṭho haṭhaḥ /
aśeṣayogayuktānām ādhārakamaṭho haṭhaḥ // 10 //

Like a house protecting one from the heat of the sun, Haṭha Yoga protects its practitioner from the burning heat of the three Tāpas (types of suffering); and, similarly, it is the supporting tortoise, as it were, for those who are constantly devoted to the practice of Yoga.

haṭhavidyā paraṁ gopyā yoginā siddhim icchatā /
bhaved vīryavatī guptā nirvīryā tu prakāśitā // 11 //

A Yogī desirous of success should keep the knowledge of Haṭha Yoga secret; for it becomes potent when concealed, and ineffective when exposed.

surājye dhārmike deśe subhikṣe nirupadrave /
dhanuḥ pramāṇaparyantaṁ śilāgnijalavarjite /
ekānte maṭhikāmadhye sthātavyaṁ haṭhayoginā // 12 //

A Yogī should practise Haṭha Yoga in a small room, situated in a solitary place, measuring four cubits square, and free from stones, fire, water, disturbances of all kinds, and in a country where justice is properly administered, where good people live, and food can be obtained easily and plentifully.

alpadvāram arandhragartavivaraṁ nātyuccanīcāyataṁ /
samyaggomayasāndraliptam amalaṁ niḥśeṣajaṁtūjjhitam //
bāhye maṇḍapavedikūparuciraṁ prākārasaṁveṣṭitam /
proktaṁ yogamaṭhasya lakṣaṇam idaṁ siddhair haṭhābhyāsibhiḥ//13//

The room should have a small door, be free from holes, hollows, neither too high nor too low, well plastered with cowdung and free from dirt, filth and insects. On its outside there should be bowers, raised platform (cabūtarā), a well, and a compound. These characteristics of a room for Haṭha Yogīs have been described by adepts in the practice of Haṭha.

evaṁvidhe maṭhe sthitvā sarvacintāvivarjitaḥ /
gurūpadiṣṭamārgeṇa yogam eva samabhyaset // 14 //

Having seated in such a room and free from all anxieties, he should practise Yoga, as instructed by his *Guru*.

alpāhāraḥ prayāsaś ca prajalpo niyamāgrahaḥ /
janasaṅgaś ca laulyaṁ ca ṣaḍbhir yogo vinaśyati // 15 //

Yoga is destroyed by the following six causes : Over-eating; exertion; talkativeness; adhering to rules, e.g., cold bath in the morning, eating at night or eating fruits only; company of men; and unsteadiness.

utsāhāt sāhasād dhairyāt tattvajñānāc ca niścayāt /
janasaṅgaparityāgāt ṣaḍbhir yogaḥ prasiddhyati // 16 //

The following six bring speedy success : enthusiasm, courage or daring, perseverance, correct understanding, determination, and aloofness from company of people.

atha yamaniyamāḥ :
ahiṁsā satyam asteyaṁ brahmacaryaṁ kṣamā dhṛtiḥ //
dayārjavaṁ mitāhāraḥ śaucaṁ caiva yamā daṣa // 17 //

Yamas and Niyamas

The ten Yamas or Restraints are: Ahiṁsā (non-injuring), truth, non- stealing, continence, forgiveness, endurance, compassion, meekness, moderate diet and cleanliness.

tapaḥ santoṣa āstikyaṁ dānam īśvarapūjanam /
siddhāntavākyaśravaṇaṁ hrīmatī ca tapo hutam /*
niyamā daśa samproktā yogaśāstraviśāradaiḥ // 18 //

The ten Niyamas (Obseravances) mentioned by those proficient in the knowledge of Yoga are : austerity, contentment, belief in God, charity, adoration of God, hearing discourses on the principles of religion, shame, intellect, Tapa and Yajña.

atha āsanam:
haṭhasya prathamāṅgatvād āsanaṁ pūrvam ucyate /
kuryāt tadāsanaṁ sthairyam ārogyaṁ cāṅgalāghavam // 19 //

Being the first accessory of Haṭha Yoga, Āsana is described first. It should be practised for gaining steady posture, health and lightness of body.

Āsanas

vasiṣṭhādyaiś ca munibhir matsyendrādyaiś ca yogibhiḥ /
aṅgīkṛtānyāsanāni kathyante kānicin mayā // 20 //

I am going to describe certain Āsanas which have been adopted by Munis like Vasiṣṭha, etc., and Yogīs like Matsyendra, etc.

Svastika-āsana

jānūrvor antare samyak kṛtvā pādatale ubhe /
ṛjukāyaḥ samāsīnaḥ svastikaṁ tat pracakṣate // 21 //

Having kept both the soles under both the thighs, with the body erect, when one sits calmly in this posture, it is called Svastika.

Gomukha-āsana

savye dakṣiṇagulphaṁ tu pṛṣṭhapārśve niyojayet /
dakṣiṇe'pi tathā savyaṁ gomukhaṁ gomukhākṛti // 22 //

Placing the right ankle on the left side and the left ankle on the right side, makes Gomukha-āsana, having the appearance of a cow's face.

Vīrāsana

ekaṁ pādam athaikasmin vinyased ūruṇi sthitam /
itarasmiṁs tathā coruṁ vīrāsanam itīritam // 23 //

* The last two words, according to commentator Brahmānanda, are *'japo vratam'* meaning muttering prayers or repeating divine names and observing vows.

One foot is to be placed on the thigh of the opposite side; and so also the other foot on the opposite thigh. This is called Vīrāsana.

Kūrma-āsana

gudaṁ nirudhya gulphābhyāṁ vyutkrameṇa samāhitaḥ /
kūrmāsanaṁ bhaved etad iti yogavido viduḥ // 24 //

Placing the right ankle on the left side of anus, and the left ankle on the right side of it makes what the Yogīs call Kūrma- āsana.

Kukkuṭa-āsana

padmāsanaṁ tu saṁsthāpya jānūrvor antare karau /
niveśya bhūmau saṁsthāpya vyomasthaṁ kukkuṭāsanam // 25 //

Taking the posture of Padmāsana and carrying the hands under the thighs, when the Yogī raises himself above the ground, with his palms resting on the ground, it becomes Kukkuṭa-āsana.

Uttāna Kūrma-āsana

kukkuṭāsanabandhastho dorbhyāṁ saṁbadhya kandharām /
bhavet kūrmavad uttāna etad uttānakūrmakam // 26 //

Having assumed Kukkuṭāsana, when one grasps his neck by crossing his hands behind his head, and lies in this posture with his back touching the ground, it becomes Uttāna Kūrma-āsana, from its appearance like that of a tortoise.

Dhanur-āsana

pādāṅguṣṭhau tu pāṇibhyāṁ gṛhītvā śravaṇāvadhi /
dhanurākarṣaṇaṁ kuryād dhanurāsanam ucyate // 27 //

Having caught the toes of the feet with both the hands and carried them to the ears by drawing the body like a bow, it becomes Dhanurāsana.

Matsya-āsana

vāmorumūlārpitadakṣapādaṁ jānor bahir veṣṭitavāmapādam /
pragṛhya tiṣṭhet parivartitāṅgaḥ śrīmatsyanāthoditam āsanaṁ syāt// 28//

matsyendrapīṭhaṁ jaṭharapradīptiṁ
pracaṇḍarugmaṇḍalakhaṇḍanāstram /
abhyāsataḥ kuṇḍalinīprabodhaṁ candrasthiratvaṁ
ca dadāti puṁsām //29//

Having placed the right foot at the root of the left thigh, let the toe be grasped with the right hand passing over the back, and having placed the left foot on the right thigh at its root, let it be grasped with the left hand passing behind the back. This is the āsana, as explained by Śrī Matsyanātha. It increases appetite and is an instrument for destroying the group of the most deadly diseases. Its practice awakens the Kuṇḍalinī, and gives people steadiness of the moon, i.e. stops the nectar shedding from the moon in people.

Paścimatāna

prasārya pādau bhuvi daṇḍarūpau dorbhyāṁ padāgradvitayaṁ gṛhītvā /
jānūparinyastalalāṭadeśo vased idaṁ paścimatānam āhuḥ // 30 //

Having stretched the feet on the ground, like a stick, and having grasped the toes of both the feet with both the hands, when one sits with his forehead resting on the thighs, it is called Paścimatāna.

iti paścimatānam āsanāgryaṁ pavanaṁ paścimavāhinaṁ karoti /
udayaṁ jaṭharānalasya kuryād udare kārśyaṁ arogatām ca puṁsām//31//

This Paścimatāna carries the air from the front to the back part of the body(i.e., to Suṣumṇā). It kindles gastric fire, reduces obesity and cures all diseases of men.

Mayūra-āsana

dharām avaṣṭabhya karadvayena tatkūrparasthāpitanābhipārśvaḥ /
uccāsano daṇḍavad utthitaḥ san mayūram etat pravadanti pīṭhaṁ// 32//

Place the palms of both the hands on the ground, and place the navel on both the elbows and balancing thus, the body should be stretched backward like a stick. This is called Mayūra-āsana.

harati sakalarogān āśu gulmodarādīn abhibhavati ca doṣān āsanaṁ śrīmayūram /
bahu kadaśanabhuktaṁ bhasmakuryād aśeṣaṁ janayati jaṭharāgniṁ jārayet kālakūṭam // 33 //

This Āsana quickly destroys all diseases, and removes abdominal disorders, and also those arising from irregularities of phlegm, bile and wind, digests unwholesome food taken in excess, increases appetite and destroys the most deadly poison.

Śava-āsana

uttānaṁ śavavad bhūmau śayanaṁ tat śavāsanam /
śavāsanaṁ śrāntiharaṁ cittaviśrāntikārakam // 34 //

Lying down on the ground, like a corpse, is called Śava-āsana. It removes fatigue and gives rest to the mind.

***

caturaśītyāsanāni śivena kathitāni vai /
tebhyaś catuṣkam ādāya sārabhūtaṁ bravīmyaham // 35 //

Śiva taught 84 āsanas. Of these the first four are essential ones; I am going to explain them here.

siddhaṁ padmaṁ tathā siṁhaṁ bhadraṁ ceti catuṣṭayam /
śreṣṭhaṁ tatrāpi ca sukhe tiṣṭhet siddhāsane sadā // 36//

These four are : Siddha, Padma, Siṁha and Bhadra. Even of these, Siddha-āsana, being very comfortable, should always be practised.

Siddhāsana

yonisthānakam aṅghrimūlaghaṭitaṁ kṛtvā dṛḍhaṁ vinyaset /
meḍhre pādam athaikameva hṛdaye kṛtvā hanuṁ susthiram //
sthāṇuḥ saṁyamitendriyo'caladṛśā paśyed bhruvor antaram /
hyetan mokṣakapāṭabhedajanakaṁ siddhāsanaṁ procyate // 37//

Press firmly the heel of the left foot against the perineum, and the right heel above the male organ. With the chin pressing on the chest, one should sit calmly, having restrained the senses, and gaze steadily at the space between the eyebrows. This is called the Siddha-āsana, the opener of the door of salvation.

matāntare tu :
meḍhrād upari vinyasya savyaṁ gulphaṁ tathopari /
gulphāntaraṁ ca nikṣipya siddhāsanam idaṁ bhavet // 38 //

This Siddhāsana is performed also by placing the left heel on Meḍhra (above the male organ), and then placing the right one on it.

etat siddhāsanaṁ prāhur anye vajrāsanaṁ viduḥ /
muktāsanaṁ vadantyeke prāhur guptāsanaṁ pare // 39 //

Some call this Siddhāsana, some Vajrāsana. Others call it Mukta-āsana or Gupta-āsana.

yameṣviva mitāhāra ahiṁsā niyameṣviva /
mukhyaṁ sarvāsaneṣvekaṁ siddhāḥ siddāsanaṁ viduḥ // 40 //

Just as moderation in food is chief among Yamas, and Ahiṁsā chief among Niyamas, so is Siddhāsana called by adepts the chief of all the Āsanas.

caturaśītipīṭheṣu siddham eva sadābhyaset /
dvāsaptatisahasrāṇāṁ nāḍīnāṁ malaśodhanam // 41 //

Out of the 84 Āsanas Siddhāsana should always be practised, because it cleanses the impurities of 72,000 Nāḍīs.

ātmadhyāyī mitāhārī yāvad dvādaśavatsaram //
sadā siddhāsanābhyāsād yogī niṣpattim āpnuyāt // 42 //

By contemplating on oneself, by eating moderately, and by practising Siddhāsana for 12 years, a Yogī obtains success.

kim anyair bahubhiḥ pīṭhaiḥ siddhe siddhāsane sati /
prāṇānile sāvadhāne baddhe kevalakuṁbhake // 43 //

Other postures are of no use, when success has been achieved in Siddhāsana, and Prāṇa Vāyu has become calm and restrained by Kevala Kumbhaka.

utpadyate nirāyāsāt svayam evonmanī kalā /
tathaikasminneva dṛḍhe siddhe siddhāsane sati /
bandhatrayam anāyāsāt svayam evopajāyate // 44 //

Success in one Siddhāsana alone becoming firmly established, one gets Unmanī at once, and the three bonds (Bandhas) are accomplished automatically with ease.

nāsanaṁ siddhasadṛśaṁ na kumbhaḥ kevalopamaḥ /
na khecarīsamā mudrā na nādasadṛśo layaḥ // 45 //

There is no Āsana like Siddhāsana and no Kumbhaka like Kevala. There is no Mudrā like Khecarī and no Laya like Nāda (Anāhata Nāda).

Padmāsana

atha padmāsanam :
vāmorūpari dakṣiṇaṁ ca caraṇaṁ saṁsthāpya vāmaṁ tathā /
dakṣorūpari paścimena vidhinā dhṛtvā karābhyāṁ dṛḍham /
aṅguṣṭhau hṛdaye nidhāya cibukaṁ nāsāgram ālokayet ;
etad vyādhivināśakāri yamināṁ padmāsanaṁ procyate // 46 //

Place the right foot on the left thigh and the left foot on the right thigh, and grasp the toes with the hands crossed over the back. Press the chin against the chest and gaze on the tip of the nose. This is called Padmāsana, the destroyer of the diseases of the Yamīs.

uttānau caraṇau kṛtvā ūrusaṁsthau prayatnataḥ /
ūrumadhye tathottānau pāṇī kṛtvā tato dṛśau // 47 //

Place the feet on the thighs, with the soles turned upwards, and place the hands on the thighs, with the palms turned upwards.

nāsāgre vinyased rājadantamūle tu jihvayā /
uttaṁbhya cibukaṁ vakṣasyutthāpya pavanaṁ śanaiḥ // 48 //

Gaze on the tip of the nose, keeping the tongue pressed against the root of the teeth of the upper jaw, and the chin against the chest, and raise the air up slowly, i.e., pull the Apāna-Vāyu gently upwards.

idaṁ padmāsanaṁ proktaṁ sarvavyādhivināśanam /
durlabhaṁ yena kenāpi dhīmatā labhyate bhuvi // 49 //

This is called Padmāsana, the destroyer of all diseases. It is difficult of attainment by everybody, but can be learnt by intelligent people in this world.

kṛtvā saṁpuṭitau karau dṛḍhataraṁ badhvā tu padmāsanaṁ
gāḍhaṁ vakṣasi sannidhāya cibukaṁ dhyāyaṁś ca tat cetasi /
vāraṁ vāram apānam ūrdhvam anilaṁ protsārayan pūritaṁ
nyañcan prāṇam upaiti bodham atulaṁ śaktiprabhāvān naraḥ// 50//

Having kept both the hands together in the lap, performing Padmāsana firmly, keeping the chin fixed to the chest, and contemplating on Him in the mind, by drawing the Apāna-Vāyu up (performing Mūla Bandha) and pushing down the air after inhaling it, joining thus Prāṇa and Apāna in the navel, one gets the unequalled knowledge by awakening the Śakti (Kuṇḍalinī) thus.

N.B.: When Apāna Vāyu is drawn gently up and after filling in the lungs with the air from outside, Prāṇa is forced down by and by so as to join both of them in the navel, they both enter then Kuṇḍalinī and, reaching Brahma Randhra(the great hole), they make the mind calm. Then the mind can contemplate on the nature of the Ātman and can enjoy the highest bliss.

padmāsane sthito yogī nāḍīdvāreṇa pūritam /
mārutaṁ dhārayed yastu sa mukto nātra saṁśayaḥ // 51 //

A Yogī who, sitting with Padmāsana, can control breathing, is undoubtedly free from bondage.

Siṁhāsana

atha siṁhāsanam :
gulphau ca vṛṣaṇasyādhaḥ sīvanyāḥ pārśvayoḥ kṣipet /
dakṣiṇe savyagulphaṁ tu dakṣagulphaṁ tu savyake //52 //

Press the heels on both sides of the seam of perineum, in such a way that the left heel touches the right side and the right heel touches the left side of it.

hastau tu jānvoḥ saṁsthāpya svāṅgulīḥ saṁprasārya ca /
vyāttavaktro nirīkṣeta nāsāgraṁ susamāhitaḥ //53 //

Place the hands on the thighs, with stretched fingers, and keeping the mouth open and the mind collected, gaze on the tip of the nose.

siṁhāsanaṁ bhaved etat pūjitaṁ yogipuṅgavaiḥ /
bandhatritayasandhānaṁ kurute cāsanottamam //54 //

This is Siṁhāsana, held sacred by the best of Yogīs. This excellent Āsana effects the completion of the three Bandhas (Mūlabandha, Kaṇṭha or Jālandhara Bandha and Uḍḍīyāna Bandha).

Bhadrāsana

atha bhadrāsanam :
gulphau ca vṛṣaṇasyādhaḥ sīvanyāḥ pārśvayoḥ kṣipet /
savyagulphaṁ tathā savye dakṣagulphaṁ tu dakṣiṇe //55 //

pārśvapādau ca pāṇibhyāṁ dṛḍhaṁ badhvā suniścalam /
bhadrāsanaṁ bhaved etat sarvavyādhīvināśanam //56 //

Place the heels on either side of the seam of perineum, keeping the left heel on the left side and the right one on the right side, hold the feet firmly joined to one another with both the hands. This Bhadrāsana is the destroyer of all the diseases.

gorakṣāsanam ityāhur idaṁ vai siddhayoginaḥ /
evam āsanabandheṣu yogīndro vigataśramaḥ // 57 //

Expert Yogīs call this Gorakṣa Āsana. By sitting with this Āsana, a Yogī gets rid of fatigue.

abhyasen nāḍikāśuddhiṁ mudrādipavanakriyām /
āsanaṁ kumbhakaṁ citraṁ mudrākhyaṁ karaṇaṁ tathā //58 //

The Nāḍīs should be cleansed of their impurities by performing the Mudrās, etc. (which are the practices relating to the air), Āsanas, Kumbhakas and various curious Mudrās.

atha nādānusandhānam abhyāsānukramo haṭhe /
brahmacārī mitāhārī tyāgī yogaparāyaṇaḥ /
abdād ūrdhvaṁ bhavet siddho nātra kāryā vicāraṇā // 59 //

By regular and close attention to Nāda (Anāhata Nāda) in Haṭha Yoga, a Brahmacārī, moderate in diet, unattached to objects of enjoyment, and devoted to Yoga, gains success, no doubt, within a year.

susnigdhamadhurāhāraś caturthāṁśavivarjitaḥ /
bhujyate śivasaṁprītyai mitāhāraḥ sa ucyate // 60 //

Moderate feeding is that in which $^3/_4$ of hunger is satisfied with food, well cooked with ghee and sweets, and eaten with the offering of it to Śiva.

Foods Injurious to a Yogī

kaṭvamla-tīkṣṇa-lavaṇoṣṇa-haritaśāka-
sauvīra-taila-tila-sarṣapa-madya-matsyān /
ājādi-māṁsa- dadhi- takra-kulattha- kola-
piṇyāka-hiṁgu-laśunādyam apathyam āhuḥ //61//

Bitter, sour, pungent, saltish, hot, green vegetables, fermented, oily, mixed with Tila seed, rape seed, intoxicating liquors, fish, meat, curds, buttermilk, Kulattha pulses, plums, oil-cake, asafoetida (Hiṅga), garlic, onion, etc., should not be eaten.

bhojanam ahitaṁ vidyāt punarapyuṣṇīkṛtaṁ rukṣam /
atilavaṇam amlayuktaṁ kadaśanaśākotkaṭaṁ varjyam /
vahnistrīpathisevānām ādau varjanam ācaret // 62 //

Food heated again, dry, having too much salt, sour, minor grains, and vegetables that cause burning sensation should not be eaten. Fire, women, travelling, etc. should be avoided while beginning (Yoga practice).

tathāhi gorakṣavacanam :
varjayed durjanaprāntaṁ vahni-strī-pathi- sevanam /
prātaḥsnānopavāsādi kāyakleśavidhiṁ tathā //63 //

godhūma-śāli-yava-ṣāṣṭika-śobhanānnam /
kṣīrājyakhaṇḍa-navanīta- sitāmadhūni /
śuṇṭhīpaṭolakaphalādikapañcaśākam /
mudgādidivyam udakaṁ ca yamīndrapathyam // 64 //

puṣṭaṁ sumadhuraṁ snigdhaṁ gavyaṁ dhātuprapoṣaṇam /
manobhilaṣitaṁ yogyaṁ yogī bhojanam ācaret // 65 //

As said by Gorakṣa, one should keep aloof from the society of the evil-minded, fire, women, travelling, early morning bath, fasting, and all kinds of bodily exertion.
Wheat, rice, barley, Ṣāṣṭika (a kind of rice), good corns, milk, ghee, sugar, butter, sugarcandy, honey, dried ginger, Parwal (a vegetable), the five vegetables, Moong, pure water—these are very beneficial to those who practise Yoga.
A Yogī should eat tonics (things giving strength), well-sweetened, greasy (made with ghee), milk, butter, etc., which may increase humors of the body, according to his desire.

yuvā vṛddho'tivṛddho vā vyādhito durbalo'pi vā /
abhyāsāt siddhim āpnoti sarvayogeṣvatandritaḥ // 66 //

Whether young, old or too old, sick or lean, one who discards laziness, gets success if he practises Yoga.

kriyāyuktasya siddhiḥ syād akriyasya kathaṁ bhavet /
na śāstrapāṭhamātreṇa yogasiddhiḥ prajāyate // 67 //

Success comes to him who is engaged in the practice. How can one get success without practice; for by merely reading books on Yoga, one can never get success.

na veṣadhāraṇam siddheḥ kāraṇaṁ na ca tatkathā /
kriyaiva kāraṇaṁ siddheḥ satyam etan na saṁśayaḥ // 68 //

Success cannot be attained by adopting a particular dress (Veṣa). It cannot be gained by telling tales. Practice alone is the means to success. This is true, there is no doubt.

pīṭhāni kumbhakāś citrā divyāni karaṇāni ca /
sarvāṇyapi haṭhābhyāse rājayogaphalāvadhi // 69 //

Āsanas (postures), various Kumbhakas, and other divine means, all should be practised in Haṭha Yoga, till the fruit—Rāja Yoga—is obtained.

iti haṭhapradīpikāyāṁ prathamopadeśaḥ //1//

End of Chapter 1, On Āsanas.

CHAPTER 2

On Prāṇāyāma

Dvitīyopadeśaḥ

athāsane dṛḍhe yogī vaśī hitamitāśanaḥ /
gurūpadiṣṭamārgeṇa prāṇāyāmān samabhyaset // 1 //

Posture having become established, a Yogī, master of himself, eating salutary and moderate food, should practise Prāṇāyāma, as instructed by his Guru.

cale vāte calaṁ cittaṁ niścale niścalaṁ bhavet /
yogī sthāṇutvam āpnoti tato vāyuṁ nirodhayet // 2 //

Respiration being disturbed, the mind becomes disturbed. By restraining respiration, the Yogī gets steadiness of mind.

yāvad vāyuḥ sthito dehe tāvaj jīvanam ucyate /
maraṇaṁ tasya niṣkrāntis tato vāyuṁ nirodhayet //3 //

So long as the (breathing)air stays in the body, it is called life. Death consists in the passing out of the (breathing) air. It is, therefore, necessary to restrain the breath.

malākulāsu nāḍīṣu māruto naiva madhyagaḥ /
kathaṁ syād unmanībhāvaḥ kāryasiddhiḥ kathaṁ bhavet // 4//

Breath does not pass through the middle channel (Suṣumṇā), owing to the impurities of the Nāḍīs. How can then success be attained, and how can there be the *Unmanī Avasthā*.

śuddhim eti yadā sarvaṁ nāḍīcakraṁ malākulam /
tadaiva jāyate yogī prāṇasaṅgrahaṇe kṣamaḥ // 5 //

When the whole system of Nāḍīs which is full of impurities, is cleaned, then the Yogī becomes able to control the Prāṇa.

prāṇāyāmaṁ tataḥ kuryān nityaṁ sāttvikayā dhiyā /
yathā suṣumṇānāḍīsthā malāḥ śuddhiṁ prayānti ca // 6 //

Therefore, Prāṇāyāma should be performed daily with Sāttvika *Buddhi* (intellect free from Rajas and Tamas or activity and sloth), in order to drive out the impurities of Suṣumṇā.

Method of Performing Prāṇāyāma

baddhapadmāsano yogī prāṇaṁ candreṇa pūrayet /
dhārayitvā yathāśakti bhūyaḥ sūryeṇa recayet // 7 //
prāṇam sūryeṇa cākṛṣya pūrayed udaraṁ śanaiḥ /
vidhivat kumbhakaṁ kṛtvā punaś candreṇa recayet // 8 //

Sitting in Padmāsana posture the Yogī should fill in the air through the left nostril (closing the right one); and, keeping it confined according to one's ability, it should be expelled slowly through the Sūrya (right nostril). Then, drawing in the air through the Sūrya (right nostril)slowly, the belly should be filled, and after performing Kumbhaka as before, it should be expelled slowly through the Candra (left nostril).

yena tyajet tena pītvā dhārayed avirodhataḥ /
recayec ca tato'nyena śanair eva na vegataḥ // 9 //

Inhaling thus through the one, through which it was expelled, and having retained it there, till it is possible, it should be exhaled through the other, slowly and not forcibly.

prāṇaṁ ced iḍayā piben niyamitaṁ bhūyo'nyayā recayet /
pītvā piṅgalayā samīraṇam atho badhvā tyajed vāmayā /
sūryācandramasor anena vidhinā'bhyāsaṁ sadā tanvatām /
śuddhā nāḍigaṇā bhavanti yamināṁ māsatrayād ūrdhvataḥ // 10 //

If the air be inhaled through the left nostril, it should be expelled again through the other, and filling it through the right nostril, confining it there, it should be expelled through the left nostril. By practising in this way, through the right and the left nostrils alternately, the whole of the collection of Nāḍīs of the Yamis (practitioners) becomes clean, i.e., free from impurities, after 3 months and over.

prātarmadhyandine sāyam ardharātre ca kumbhakān /
śanair aśītiparyantaṁ caturvāraṁ samabhyaset // 11//

Kumbhaka should be performed gradually 4 times during day and night (i.e., morning, noon, evening and midnight), till the number of Kumbhakas for one time is 80 and for day and night together it is 320.

kanīyasi bhavet svedaḥ kampo bhavati madhyame /
uttame sthānam āpnoti tato vāyuṁ nibandhayet // 12 //

In the beginning there is perspiration, in the middle stage there is quivering, and in the last or the third stage one obtains steadiness; and then the breath should be made steady or motionless.

jalena śramajātena gātramardanam ācaret /
dṛḍhatā laghutā caiva tena gātrasya jāyate // 13 //

The perspiration exuding from exertion of practice should be rubbed on the body (and not wiped), as by so doing the body becomes strong.

abhyāsakāle prathame śastaṁ kṣīrājyabhojanam /
tato'bhyāse dṛḍhībhūte na tādṛṅ niyamagrahaḥ // 14 //

During the first stage of practice food consisting of milk and ghee is wholesome. When the practice becomes established, no such restriction is necessary.

yathā siṁho gajo vyāghro bhaved vaśyaḥ śanaiḥ śanaiḥ /
tathaiva sevito vāyur anyathā hanti sādhakam // 15 //

Just as lions, elephants and tigers are controlled by and by, so the breath is controlled by slow degrees, otherwise (i.e., by being hasty or using too much force) it kills the practitioner himself.

prāṇāyāmādiyuktena sarvarogakṣayo bhavet /
ayuktābhyāsayogena sarvarogasamudbhavaḥ // 16 //

When Prāṇāyāma, etc., are performed properly, they eradicate all diseases; but improper practice generates diseases.

hikkā śvāsaś ca kāsaś ca śiraḥkarnākṣivedanāḥ /
bhavanti vividhā rogāḥ pavanasya prakopataḥ // 17 //

Hiccough, asthma, cough, pain in head, ears, and eyes : these and other various kinds of diseases are generated by the disturbance of breath.

yuktaṁ yuktaṁ tyajed vāyuṁ yuktaṁ yuktaṁ ca pūrayet /
yuktaṁ yuktaṁ ca badhnīyād evaṁ siddhim avāpnuyāt // 18 //

The air should be expelled with proper tact and should be filled in skilfully; and when it has been kept confined properly it brings success.

N.B.: The above caution is necessary to warn the aspirants against omitting any instruction; and, in their zeal to gain success or Siddhis early, to begin the practice, either by using too much force in filling in, confining and expelling the air, or by omitting any instructions, it may cause unnecessary pressure on their ears, eyes,&c., and cause pain. Every word in the instructions is full of meaning and is necessarily used in the Ślokas, and should be followed very carefully and with due attention. Thus there will be nothing whatsoever to fear. We are inhaling and exhaling the air throughout our lives without any sort of danger, and Prāṇāyāma being only a regular form of it, there should be no cause to fear.

yadā tu nāḍīśuddhiḥ syāt tadā cihnāni bāhyataḥ /
kāyasya kṛśatā kāntis tadā jāyeta niścitam // 19 //

When the Nāḍīs become free from impurities, and there appear the outward signs of success, such as lean body and glowing colour, then one should feel certain of success.

yatheṣṭadhāraṇaṁ vāyor analasya pradīpanam /
nādābhivyaktir ārogyaṁ jāyate nāḍiśodhanāt // 20 //

By removing the impurities, the air can be retained according to one's wish and the appetite is increased; the divine sound is awakened; and the body becomes healthy.

medaḥśleṣmādhikaḥ pūrvaṁ ṣaṭkarmāṇi samācaret /
anyas tu nācaret tāni doṣāṇāṁ samabhāvataḥ // 21 //

If there be excess of fat or phlegm in the body, the six kinds of Kriyās (acts) should be performed first. But others, not suffering from the excess of these, should not perform them.

dhautir bastis tathā netis trāṭakaṁ naulikaṁ tathā /
kapālabhātiś caitāni ṣaṭkarmāṇi pracakṣate // 22 //

The six kinds of acts are : Dhauti, Basti, Neti, Trāṭaka, Nauli and Kapālabhāti. These are called the six acts(Ṣaṭkarmāṇi).

karmaṣaṭkam idaṁ gopyaṁ ghaṭaśodhanakārakam /
vicitraguṇasandhāyi pūjyate yogipuṅgavaiḥ // 23 //

These six kinds of acts which cleanse the body should be kept secret. They produce extraordinary attributes and are performed with earnestness by the best of Yogīs.

Dhauti

tatra dhautiḥ :
caturaṅgulavistāraṁ hastapañcadaśāyutam /
gurūpadiṣṭamārgeṇa siktaṁ vastraṁ śanair graset /
punaḥ pratyāharec caitad uditaṁ dhautikarma tat // 24 //

A strip of cloth, about four fingers wide and 15 cubits long, is pushed in (swallowed), when moist with warm water, through the passage shown by the Guru, and is taken out again. This is called Dhauti Karma.

N.B. The strip should be moistened with a little warm water, and the end should be held with the teeth. It is swallowed slowly, little by little; thus, first day 1 cubit, 2nd day 2 cubits, 3rd day 3 cubits, and so on. After swallowing it the stomach should be given a good, round motion from left to right, and then it should be taken out slowly and gently.

kāsaśvāsaplīhakuṣṭhaṁ kapharogāś ca viṁśatiḥ /
dhautikarmaprabhāvena prayāntyeva na saṁśayaḥ // 25 //

There is no doubt that cough, asthma, enlargement of spleen, leprosy, and 20 kinds of diseases born of phlegm, disappear by the practice of Dhauti Karma.

Basti

nābhidaghnajale pāyau nyastanālotkaṭāsanaḥ /
ādhārākuñcanaṁ kuryāt kṣālanaṁ bastikarma tat // 26 //

Squatting in navel-deep water, and introducing a six inches long, smooth piece of 1/2 an inch diameter pipe, open at both ends, half inside the anus, it (anus) should be drawn up (contracted) and then expelled. This washing is called Basti Karma.

gulmaplīhodaraṁ cāpi vātapittakaphodbhavāḥ /
bastikarmaprabhāvena kṣīyante sakalāmayāḥ // 27 //

By practising this Basti Karma colic, enlarged spleen, and dropsy, arising from the disorders of Vāta (air); Pitta (bile) and Kapha (phlegm), are all cured.

dhātvindriyāntaḥkaraṇaprasādaṁ /
dadyāc ca kāntiṁ dahanapradīptim //
aśeṣadoṣopacayaṁ nihanyād /
abhyasyamānaṁ jalabastikarma // 28 //

By practising Basti with water, Dhātus, Indriyas and mind become calm. It gives glow and tone to the body and increases appetite. All the disorders disappear.

Neti

atha netiḥ :
sūtraṁ vitasti susnigdhaṁ nāsānāle praveśayet /
mukhān nirgamayec caiṣā netiḥ siddhair nigadyate // 29 //

A cord made of threads and about six inches long, should be passed through the passage of the nose and the end taken out in the mouth. This is called by adepts Neti Karma.

kapālaśodhinī caiva divyadṛṣṭipradāyinī //
jatrūrdhvajātarogaughaṁ netir āśu nihanti ca // 30 //

Neti is the cleaner of the brain and giver of divine sight. It soon destroys all the diseases of the cervical and scapular regions.

Trāṭaka

atha trāṭakam :
nirīkṣen niścaladṛśā sūkṣmalakṣyaṁ samāhitaḥ /
aśrusaṁpātaparyantaṁ ācāryais trāṭakaṁ smṛtam // 31 //

Being calm, one should gaze steadily at a small mark, till eyes are filled with tears. This is called Trāṭaka by Ācaryas.

mocanaṁ netrarogāṇāṁ tandrādīnāṁ kapāṭakam /
yatnatas trāṭakam gopyaṁ yathā hāṭakapeṭakam // 32 //

Trāṭaka destroys eye diseases and removes sloth, etc. It should be kept secret very carefully, like a box of jewellery.

Nauli

atha nauliḥ :
amandāvartavegena tundaṁ savyāpasavyataḥ /
natāṁso bhrāmayed eṣā nauliḥ siddhaiḥ pracakṣyate // 33 //

Sitting on the toes with heels raised above the ground, and the palms resting on the ground, in this bent posture the belly is moved forcibly from left to right just as in vomiting. This is called by adepts Nauli Karma.

mandāgnisandīpanapācanādi sandhāyikānandakarī sadaiva /
aśeṣadoṣāmayaśoṣaṇī ca haṭhakriyāmaulir iyaṁ ca mauliḥ // 34 //

It removes dyspepsia, increases appetite and digestion, and is like the goddess of creation, and causes happiness. It dries up all the disorders. This Nauli is an excellent exercise in Haṭha Yoga.

Kapālabhāti

atha kapālabhātiḥ :
bhastrāvallohakārasya recapūrau sasaṁbhramau /
kapālabhātir vikhyātā kaphadoṣaviśoṣaṇī // 35 //

When inhalation and exhalation are performed very quickly, like a pair of bellows of a blacksmith, it dries up all the disorders caused by excess of phlegm, and is known as Kapālabhāti.

ṣaṭkarmanirgatasthaulyakaphadoṣamalādikaḥ /
prāṇāyāmaṁ tataḥ kuryād anāyāsena siddhyati // 36 //

When Prāṇāyāma is performed after getting rid of obesity born of the defects of phlegm by performance of the six acts, it easily brings success.

prāṇāyāmair eva sarve praśuṣyanti malā iti /
ācāryāṇāṁ tu keṣāñcid anyatkarma na saṁmatam // 37 //

Some Ācāryas (teachers) do not advocate any other practice, being of opinion that all the impurities are dried up by the practice of Prāṇāyāma.

Gajakaraṇi

atha gajakaraṇi :
udaragatapadārthaṁ udvamanti pavanam apānam udīrya kaṇṭhanāle //
kramaparicayavaśyanāḍicakrā gajakaraṇīti nigadyate haṭhajñaiḥ//38 //

By carrying the Apāna Vāyu up to the throat, the food, etc., in the stomach are vomited. By degrees, the system of Nāḍis (Śaṅkhinī) becomes known. This is called Gajakaraṇi in Haṭha.

brahmādayo'pi tridaśāḥ pavanābhyāsatatparāḥ /
abhūvannantakabhayāt tasmāt pavanam abhyaset // 39 //

Brahmā and other Devas were always engaged in the exercise of Prāṇāyāma, and, by means of it, got rid of the fear of Death. Therefore, one should practise Prāṇāyāma regularly.

yāvad baddho marud dehe yāvac cittaṁ nirākulam /
yāvad dṛṣṭir bhruvor madhye tāvat kālabhayaṁ kutaḥ // 40 //

So long as the breath is retained in the body, so long as the mind is undisturbed, and so long as the gaze is fixed between the eyebrows, there is no fear of Death.

vidhivat prāṇasaṁyāmair nāḍīcakre viśodhite /
suṣumṇāvadanaṁ bhitvā sukhād viśati mārutaḥ // 41 //

When the system of Nāḍis becomes clear of the impurities by properly controlling Prāṇa, then the air, piercing the entrance of Suṣumṇā, enters it easily.

Manonmanī

atha manonmanī :
mārute madhyasañcāre manaḥsthairyaṁ prajāyate /
yo manaḥsusthirībhāvaḥ saivāvasthā manonmanī // 42 //

Steadiness of mind comes when the air moves freely in the middle. That is Manonmanī condition, which is attained when the mind becomes calm.

tatsiddhaye vidhānajñāś citrān kurvanti kumbhakān /
vicitrakumbhakābhyāsād vicitrāṁ siddhim āpnuyāt // 43 //

To accomplish it, various Kumbhakas are performed by those who are expert in the methods; for, by the practice of different Kumbhakas wonderful success is attained.

Different Kinds of Kumbhaka

atha kumbhakabhedāḥ :
sūryabhedanam ujjāyī sītkārī śītalī tathā /
bhastrikā bhrāmarī mūrcchā plāvinītyaṣṭakumbhakāḥ // 44 //

Kumbhakas are of eight kinds, viz., Sūryabhedana, Ujjāyī, Sītkāri, Śītalī, Bhastrikā, Bhrāmarī, Mūrcchā, and Plāvinī.

pūrakānte tu kartavyo bandho jālandharābhidhaḥ /
kumbhakānte recakādau kartavyastūḍḍiyānakaḥ // 45 //

At the end of Pūraka, Jālandhara Bandha should be performed, and at the end of Kumbhaka, and at the beginning of Recaka, Uḍḍīyāna Bandha should be performed.

adhastāt kuñcanenāśu kaṇṭhasaṅkocane kṛte /
madhye paścimatānena syāt prāṇo brahmanāḍigaḥ // 46 //

By drawing up from below (Mūla Bandha) and contracting the throat(Jālandhara Bandha) and by pulling back the middle of the front portion of the body (i.e., belly), Prāṇa goes to Brahma, Nāḍī (Suṣumṇā).

The middle hole, through the vertebral column, through which the spinal cord passes, is called Suṣumṇā Nāḍī by Yogīs. The two other sympathetic cords, one on each side of the spinal cord, are called Iḍā and Piṅgalā Nāḍīs. These will be described later on.

apānam ūrdhvam utthāpya prāṇam kaṇṭhād adho nayet /
yogī jarāvimuktaḥ san ṣoḍaśābdavayo bhavet // 47 //

By pulling up the Apāna Vāyu and by forcing the Prāṇa Vāyu down the throat, the Yogī, liberated from old age, becomes young, as it were 16 years old.

hṛdi prāṇo gude'pānaḥ samāno nābhimaṇḍale /
udānaḥ kaṇṭhadeśastho vyānaḥ sarvaśarīragaḥ //
(Śivasaṁhitā III. 7)

Note: The seat of Prāṇa is heart; of Apāna anus; of Samāna the region about navel; of Udāna throat; while Vyāna moves throughout the body.

Sūryabhedana

atha sūryabhedanam :
āsane sukhade yogī badhvā caivāsanaṁ tataḥ /
dakṣanāḍyā samākṛṣya bahiḥsthaṁ pavanaṁ śanaiḥ // 48 //

Taking any comfortable posture and performing the Āsana, the Yogī should draw in the air slowly through the right nostril.

ākeśād ānakhāgrāc ca nirodhāvadhi kumbhayet /
tataḥ śanaiḥ savyanāḍyā recayet pavanaṁ śanaiḥ // 49 //

Then it should be retained within, so that it fills from the nails to the tips of the hair, and then let it out through the left nostril slowly.

Note: This is to be done alternately with both the nostrils, drawing in through the one, expelling through the other, and vice versa.

kapālaśodhanaṁ vātadoṣaghnaṁ kṛmidoṣahṛt /
punaḥ punar idaṁ kāryaṁ sūryabhedanam uttamam // 50 //

This excellent Sūryabhedana cleanses the forehead (frontal sinuses), destroys the disorders of Vāta, and removes worms, and, therefore, it should be performed again and again.

Ujjāyī

athojjāyī :
mukhaṁ saṁyamya nāḍībhyām ākṛṣya pavanaṁ śanaiḥ /
yathā lagati kaṇṭhāt tu hṛdayāvadhi sasvanam // 51 //

Having closed the opening of the Nāḍi (Larynx), the air should be drawn in slowly in such a way that it goes touching from the throat to the chest, and making noise while passing.

pūrvavat kumbhayet prāṇaṁ recayed iḍayā tataḥ /
śleṣmadoṣaharaṁ kaṇṭhe dehānalavivardhanam // 52 //

It should be retained, as before, and then let out through Iḍā (left nostril). This removes Śleṣmā (phlegm) in the throat and increases appetite.

nāḍījalodarādhātugatadoṣavināśanam /
gacchatā tiṣṭhatā kāryam ujjāyyākhyaṁ tu kumbhakam // 53 //

It destroys the defects of the Nāḍīs, dropsy and disorders of Dhātu(humours). Ujjāyī should be performed in all conditions of life, even while walking or sitting.

Sītkārī

atha sītkārī :
sītkāṁ kuryāt tathā vaktre ghrāṇenaiva vijṛmbhikām /
evam abhyāsayogena kāmadevo dvitīyakaḥ // 54 //

Sītkārī is performed by drawing in the air through the mouth, keeping the tongue between the lips. The air thus drawn in should not be expelled through the mouth. By practising in this way, one becomes next to the God of Love in beauty.

yoginīcakrasaṁmānyaḥ sṛṣṭisaṁhārakārakaḥ /
na kṣudhā na tṛṣā nidrā naivālasyaṁ prajāyate // 55 //

He is regarded adorable by Yoginīs and becomes the destroyer of the cycle of creation. He is not afflicted with hunger, thirst, sleep or lassitude.

bhavet sattvaṁ ca dehasya sarvopadravavarjitaḥ /
anena vidhinā satyaṁ yogīndro bhūmimaṇḍale // 56 //

The Sattva of his body becomes free from all disturbances. In truth, he becomes the lord of Yogīs in this world.

Śītalī

atha śītalī :
jihvayā vāyum ākṛṣya pūrvavat kuṁbhasādhanam /
śanakair ghrāṇarandhrābhyāṁ recayet pavanaṁ sudhīḥ// 57 //

As in the above (Sītkārī), the tongue is to be protruded a little out of the lips, when the air is drawn in. It is retained, as before, and then expelled slowly through the nostrils.

gulmaplīhādikān rogān jvaraṁ pittaṁ kṣudhāṁ tṛṣām /
viṣāṇi śītalīnāma kumbhikeyaṁ nihanti hi // 58 //

This Śītalī Kumbhikā cures colic, (enlarged) spleen, fever, disorders of bile, hunger, thirst, and counteracts poisons.

Bhastrikā

atha bhastrikā :
ūrvorupari saṁsthāpya śubhe pādatale ubhe /
padmāsanaṁ bhaved etat sarvapāpapraṇāśanam // 59 //

Padma Āsana consists in crossing the feet and placing them on both the thighs; it is the destroyer of all sins.

samyak padmāsanaṁ badhvā samagrīvodaraṁ sudhīḥ /
mukhaṁ saṁyamya yatnena prāṇam ghrāṇena recayet // 60//

Assuming Padma-Āsana properly and keeping the body straight, closing the mouth carefully, let the air be expelled through the nose.

yathā lagati hṛtkaṇṭhe kapālāvadhi sasvanam /
vegena pūrayec cāpi hṛtpadmāvadhi mārutam // 61 //

It should be filled up to the lotus of the heart, by drawing it in with force, making noise and touching the throat, chest and head.

punar virecayet tadvat pūrayec ca punaḥ punaḥ /
yathaiva lohakāreṇa bhastrā vegena cālyate // 62 //

It should be expelled again and filled again and again as before, just as a pair of bellows of the blacksmith is worked.

tathaiva svaśarīrasthaṁ cālayet pavanaṁ dhiyā /
yadā śramo bhaved dehe tadā sūryeṇa pūrayet // 63 //

In the same way, the air of the body should be moved intelligently, filling it through Sūrya (right nostril), when fatigue is experienced.

yathodaraṁ bhavet pūrṇam anilena tathā laghu /
dhārayen nāsikāṁ madhyatarjanībhyāṁ vinā dṛḍham // 64 //

The air should be drawn in through the right nostril by pressing the thumb against the left side of the nose, so as to close the left nostril; and when filled to the full, it should be closed with the fourth finger (the one next to the little finger) and kept retained.

vidhivat kumbhakaṁ kṛtvā recayed iḍayānilam /
vātapittaśleṣmaharaṁ śarīrāgnivivardhanam // 65 //

Having retained it properly, it should be expelled through Iḍā (left nostril). This destroys Vāta, Pitta (bile) and Kapha (phlegm) and increases digestive power (gastric fire).

kuṇḍalībodhakaṁ kṣipraṁ pavanaṁ sukhadaṁ hitaṃ /
brahmanāḍīmukhesaṁsthakaphādyargalanāśanam // 66 //

It quickly awakens Kuṇḍalinī, purifies the system, gives pleasure, and is beneficial. It destroys phlegm and the impurities accumulated at the entrance of the Brahma Nāḍī (Suṣumṇā).

samyagagātrasamudbhūtagranthitrayavibhedakam /
viśeṣeṇaiva kartavyaṁ bhastrākhyaṁ kumbhakaṁ tvidam // 67 //

This Bhastrikā should be performed with special attention, for it breaks the three knots: Brahmagranthi (in the chest), Viṣṇugranthi (in the throat), and Rudragranthi (between the eyebrows) of the body.

Bhrāmarī

atha bhrāmarī :
vegād ghoṣaṁ pūrakaṁ bhṛṅganādaṁ
bhṛṅgīnādaṁ recakaṁ mandamandam /
yogīndrāṇām evam abhyāsayogāc
citte jātā kācid ānandalīlā // 68 //

By filling the air with force, making noise like Bhṛṅgī (wasp), and expelling it slowly, making noise in the same way, this practice causes a sort of ecstasy in the minds of Yogīndras.

Mūrcchā

atha mūrcchā :
pūrakānte gāḍhataraṁ badhvā jālandharaṁ śanaiḥ /
recayen mūrcchanākhyeyaṁ manomūrcchā sukhapradā // 69 //

Closing the passages with Jālandhara Bandha firmly at the end of Pūraka, and expelling the air slowly, is called Mūrcchā, from its causing the mind to swoon and giving comfort.

Plāvinī

atha plāvinī :
antaḥpravartitodāramārutāpūritodaraḥ /
payasyagādhe'pi sukhāt plavate padmapatravat // 70 //

When the belly is filled with air and the inside of the body is filled to its utmost with air, the body floats on the deepest water, like the leaf of a lotus.

* * *

prāṇāyāmas tridhā prokto recakapūrakakumbhakaiḥ /
sahitaḥ kevalaś ceti kumbhako dvividho mataḥ // 71 //

Considering Pūraka (filling), Recaka (expelling) and Kumbhaka (retaining), Prāṇāyāma is of three kinds, but considering it as accompanied by Pūraka and Recaka, and as without these, it is of two kinds only, i.e., Sahita (with) and Kevala (alone).

yāvat kevalasiddhiḥ syāt sahitaṁ tāvad abhyaset /
recakaṁ pūrakaṁ muktvā sukhaṁ yad vāyudhāraṇam // 72 //

Exercise in Sahita should be continued till success in Kevala is gained. This latter is simply retaining the air with ease, without Recaka and Pūraka.

prāṇāyāmo' yam ityuktaḥ sa vai kevalakumbhakaḥ /
kumbhake kevale siddhe recakapūrakavarjite // 73 //

In the practice of Prāṇāyāma when it can be performed successfully without Recaka and Pūraka, then it is called Kevala-Kumbhaka.

na tasya durlabhaṁ kiñcit triṣu lokeṣu vidyate /
śaktaḥ kevalakumbhena yatheṣṭaṁ vāyudhāraṇāt // 74 //

There is nothing in the three worlds which is difficult to obtain for him who is able to retain the air, as and when he wishes, by means of Kevala-Kumbhaka.

rājayogapadaṁ cāpi labhate nātra saṁśayaḥ /
kumbhakāt kuṇḍalībodhaḥ kuṇḍalībodhato bhavet // 75 //

He obtains the position of Rāja Yoga undoubtedly. Kuṇḍalinī awakens by Kumbhaka, and by its awakening, Suṣumṇā becomes free from impurities.

anargalā suṣumṇā ca haṭhasiddhiś ca jāyate /
haṭhaṁ vinā rājayogo rājayogaṁ vinā haṭhaḥ /
na sidhyati tato yugmam āniṣpatteḥ samabhyaset // 76 //

No success in Rāja Yoga is without Haṭha Yoga; and no success in Haṭha Yoga is without Rāja Yoga. One should, therefore, practise both of these well, till complete success is gained.

kumbhakaprāṇarodhānte kuryāc cittaṁ nirāśrayam /
evam abhyāsayogena rājayogapadaṁ vrajet // 77 //

On the completion of Kumbhaka, the mind should be given rest. By practising in this way one is raised to the position of (i.e. succeeds in getting) Rāja Yoga.

Indications of success in the practice of Haṭha Yoga

vapuḥ kṛśatvaṁ vadane prasannatā nādasphuṭatvaṁ nayane sunirmale /
arogatā bindujayo' gnidīpanaṁ nāḍīviśuddhir haṭhayogalakṣaṇam// 78 //

When the body becomes lean, the face glows with delight, Anāhatanāda manifests, and eyes are clear, body is healthy and Bindu under control, and appetite increases, then one should know that the Nāḍīs are purified and success in Haṭha Yoga is attained.

iti haṭhapradīpikāyāṁ dvitīyopadeśaḥ // 2 //

End of Chapter 2, On Prāṇāyāma.

CHAPTER 3

On Mudrās

Tritīyopadeśaḥ

saśailavanadhātrīṇāṁ yathādhāro'hināyakaḥ /
sarveṣāṁ yogatantrāṇāṁ tathādhāro hi kuṇḍalī // 1 //

As the Chief of Snakes is the support of the earth with all the mountains and forests on it, so all the Tantras (Yoga practices) rest on Kuṇḍalinī.

suptā guruprasādena yadā jāgarti kuṇḍalī /
tadā sarvāṇi padmāni bhidyante granthayo'pi ca // 2 //

When the sleeping Kuṇḍalinī awakens with the favour of a Guru, then all the lotuses (in the six Cakras or centres) and all the knots are pierced through.

prāṇasya śūnyapadavī tathā rājapathāyate /
tadā cittaṁ nirālambaṁ tadā kālasya vañcanam // 3 //

Suṣumṇā (Śūnyapadavī) becomes the main road for the passage of Prāṇa, and the mind then becomes free from all connections (with its objects of enjoyment) and Death is then evaded.

suṣumṇā śūnyapadavī brahmarandhraṁ mahāpathaḥ /
śmaśānaṁ śāṁbhavī madhyamārgaś cetyekavācakāḥ//4 //

Suṣumṇā, Śūnyapadavī, Brahma Randhra, Mahā Patha, Śmaṣāna, Śāmbhavī, Madhya Mārga are names of one and the same thing.

tasmāt sarvaprayatnena prabodhayitum īśvarīm /
brahmadvāramukhe suptāṁ mudrābhyāsaṁ samācaret // 5 //

In order, therefore, to awaken this goddess, who is sleeping at the entrance of Brahma Dvāra (the great door), Mudrās should be practised well.

The Mudrās

atha mudrābhedāḥ :
mahāmudrā mahābandho mahāvedhaś ca khecarī /
uḍḍiyānaṁ mūlabandhaś ca bandho jālandharābhidhaḥ // 6 //

Mahāmudrā, Mahābandha, Mahāvedha, Khecarī, Uḍḍīyāna Bandha, Mūla Bandha, Jālandhara Bandha,

karaṇī viparītākhyā vajrolī śakticālanam /
idaṁ hi mudrādaśakaṁ jarāmaraṇanāśanam // 7 //

Viparītakaraṇī, Vajrolī, and Śakticālana—these are the ten Mudrās which annihilate old age and death.

ādināthoditaṁ divyam aṣṭaiśvaryapradāyakam /
vallabhaṁ sarvasiddhānāṁ durlabhaṁ marutām api // 8 //

They have been explained by Ādinātha (Śiva) and give eight kinds of divine wealth. They are loved by all the Siddhas and are hard to attain even by Marut.

Note: The eight Aiśvaryas are: Aṇimā (becoming small, like an atom); Mahimā (becoming great, like Ākāsa, by drawing in atoms of Prakṛti); Garimā (light things, like cotton becoming very heavy like mountains); Prāpti (coming within easy reach of everything; as touching the moon with the little finger, while standing on the earth); Prākāmya (non-resistance to desires, as entering the earth like water); Īśatā (mastery over matter and objects made of it); Vaśitva (controlling the animate and inanimate objects).

gopanīyaṁ prayatnena yathā ratnakaraṇḍakam /
kasyacin naiva vaktavyaṁ kulastrīsurataṁ yathā // 9 //

These Mudrās should be kept secret by every means, as one keeps one's box of jewellery, and should, on no account be told to anyone, just as husband and wife keep their dealings secret.

Mahāmudrā

atha mahāmudrā :
pādamūlena vāmena yoniṁ saṁpīḍya dakṣiṇam /
prasāritaṁ padaṁ kṛtvā karābhyāṁ dhārayed dṛḍham // 10 //

Pressing the Yoni (perineum) with the heel of the left foot, and stretching forth the right foot, it should be grasped with the two hands.

kaṇṭhe bandhaṁ samāropya dhārayed vāyum ūrdhvataḥ /
yathā daṇḍahataḥ sarpo daṇḍākāraḥ prajāyate // 11 //
ṛjvībhūtā tathā śaktiḥ kuṇḍalī sahasā bhavet /
tadā sā maraṇāvasthā jāyate dvipuṭāśrayā // 12 //

By stopping the throat (by Jālandhara Bandha) the air is drawn in from the outside and carried down. Just as a snake struck with a stick becomes straight like a stick, in the same way, Śakti (Śuṣumṇā) becomes straight at once. Then the Kuṇḍalinī, becoming as it were dead, and, leaving both Iḍā and Piṅgalā, enters Suṣumṇā (the middle passage).

tataḥ śanaiḥ śanair eva recayen naiva vegataḥ /
mahāmudrāṁ ca tenaiva vadanti vibudhottamāḥ /
iyaṁ khalu mahāmudrā mahāsiddhaiḥ pradarśitā // 13 //
mahākleśādayo doṣāḥ kṣīyante maraṇādayaḥ /
mahāmudrāṁ ca tenaiva vadanti vibudhottamāḥ // 14 //

It should be expelled then slowly only and not violently. For this very reason, the best of the wise men call it Mahāmudrā. This Mahāmudrā has been propounded by great masters. Great evils and pains, like death, are destroyed by it, and for this reason wise men call it Mahāmudrā.

candrāṅge tu samabhyasya sūryāṅge punar abhyaset /
yāvat tulyā bhavet saṁkhyā tato mudrāṁ visarjayet // 15 //

Having practised with the left nostril, it should be practised with the right one; and, when the number on both sides becomes equal, then the Mudrā should be discontinued.

nahi pathyam apathyaṁ vā rasāḥ sarve'pi nīrasāḥ /
api bhuktaṁ viṣaṁ ghoraṁ pīyūṣam api jīryati // 16 //

There is nothing wholesome or injurious; for the practice of this Mudrā destroys the injurious effects of all the Rasas (chemicals). Even the deadliest of poisons, if taken, acts like nectar.

kṣayakuṣṭhagudāvartagulmājīrṇapurogamāḥ /
tasya doṣāḥ kṣayaṁ yānti mahāmudrāṁ tu yo'bhyaset // 17 //

Consumption, leprosy, prolapsus anii, colic, and the diseases caused by indigestion—all these evils are removed by the practice of this Mahāṃudrā.

kathiteyaṁ mahāmudrā mahāsiddhikarā nṛṇām /
gopanīyā prayatnena na deyā yasyakasyacit // 18 //

This Mahāmudrā has been described as the giver of great success (Siddhi) to men. It should be kept secret by every effort, and not revealed to any and everyone.

Mahābandha

atha mahābandhaḥ :
pārṣṇiṁ vāmasya pādasya yonisthāne niyojayet /
vāmorūpari saṁsthāpya dakṣiṇaṁ caraṇaṁ tathā // 19 //

Place the left heel at the perineum and the right foot on the left thigh.

pūrayitvā tato vāyuṁ hṛdaye cibukaṁ dṛḍham /
niṣpīḍya vāyum ākuñcya mano madhye niyojayet // 20 //

Fill in the air, keeping the chin firm against the chest, and, having pressed the air, the mind should be fixed on the middle of the eyebrows or in the Suṣumṇā.

dhārayitvā yathāśakti recayed anilaṁ śanaiḥ /
savyāṅge tu samabhyasya dakṣāṅge punar abhyaset // 21 //

Having kept it confined so long as possible, it should be expelled slowly. Having practised on the left side, it should be practised on the right side.

matam atra tu keṣāñcit kaṇṭhabandhaṁ vivarjayet /
rājadantasthajihvāyā bandhaḥ śasto bhaved iti // 22 //

Some are of opinion that the closing of throat is not necessary here, for keeping the tongue pressed against the roots of the upper teeth makes a good Bandha (stop).

ayaṁ tu sarvanāḍīnām ūrdhvagatinirodhakaḥ /
ayaṁ khalu mahābandho mahāsiddhipradāyakaḥ // 23 //

This stops the upward motion of all the Nāḍīs. Verily this Mahābandha is the giver of great Siddhis.

kālapāśamahābandhavimocanavicakṣaṇaḥ /
triveṇīsaṅgamaṁ dhatte kedāraṁ prāpayen manaḥ // 24 //

This Mahābandha is the most skilful means for cutting away the snares of Death. It brings about the conjunction of the Triveṇī (Iḍā, Piṅgalā and Suṣumṇā) and carries the mind to Kedāra (the space between the eyebrows, which is the seat of Śiva).

rūpalāvaṇyasampannā yathā strī puruṣaṁ vinā /
mahāmudrāmahābandhau niṣphalau vedhavarjitau // 25 //

Just as beauty and loveliness are of no use to a woman without husband, so Mahāmudrā and the Mahābandha are useless without Mahāvedha.

Mahāvedha

atha mahāvedhaḥ :
mahābandhasthito yogī kṛtvā pūrakam ekadhīḥ /
vāyūnāṁ gatim āvṛtya nibhṛtaṁ kaṇṭhamudrayā // 26 //

Sitting with Mahābandha, the Yogi should fill in the air and keep his mind collected. The movements of the Vāyus (Prāṇa and Apāṇa) should be stopped by closing the throat.

samahastayugo bhūmau sphicau santāḍayec chanaiḥ /
puṭadvayam atikramya vāyuḥ sphurati madhyagaḥ // 27 //

Resting both the hands equally on the ground, he should raise himself a little and strike his buttocks against the ground gently. The air, leaving both the passages (Iḍā and Piṅgalā), starts into the middle one.

somasūryāgnisambandho jāyate cāmṛtāya vai /
mṛtāvasthā samutpannā tato vāyuṁ virecayet // 28 //

The union of Iḍā and Piṅgalā is effected, in order to bring about immortality. When the air becomes as it were dead (by leaving its course through Iḍā and Piṅgalā) (i.e., when it has been kept confined), then it should be expelled.

mahāvedho'yam abhyāsān mahāsiddhipradāyakaḥ /
valīpalitavepaghnaḥ sevyate sādhakottamaiḥ // 29 //

The practice of this Mahāvedha, the giver of great Siddhis, destroys old age, grey hair, and shaking of the body, and therefore it is practised by the best masters.

etat trayaṁ mahāguhyaṁ jarāmṛtyuvināśanam /
vahnivṛddhikaraṁ caiva hyaṇimādiguṇapradam // 30 //

These three are the great secrets. They are destroyers of old age and death; increase appetite; confer the accomplishments of Aṇimā,etc.

aṣṭadhā kriyate caiva yāme yāme dine dine /
puṇyasaṁbhārasandhāyi pāpaughabhiduraṁ sadā /
samyakśikṣāvatām evaṁ svalpaṁ prathamasādhanam // 31 //

They should be practised in eight ways, daily and hourly. They increase collection of good actions and lessen the evil ones. People, instructed well, should begin their practice, little by little, first.

Khecarī

atha khecarī :
kapālakuhare jihvā praviṣṭā viparītagā /
bhruvor antargatā dṛṣṭir mudrā bhavati khecarī // 32 //

Khecarī Mudrā is accomplished by thrusting the tongue into the gullet, by turning it over itself, and keeping the eyesight in the middle of the eyebrows.

chedanacālanadohaiḥ kalāṁ krameṇa vardhayet tāvat /
sā yāvad bhrūmadhyaṁ spṛśati tadā khecarīsiddhiḥ // 33 //

To accomplish this, the tongue is lengthened by cutting the fraenum linguae, moving, and pulling it. When it can touch the space between the eyebrows, then Khecarī can be accomplished.

snuhīpatranibhaṁ śastraṁ sutīkṣṇaṁ snigdhanirmalam /
samādāya tatas tena romamātraṁ samucchinet // 34 //

Taking a sharp, smooth, and clean instrument, of the shape of a cactus leaf, the fraenum of the tongue should be cut a little (as much as a hair's thickness) at a time.

tataḥ saindhavapathyābhyāṁ cūrṇitābhyāṁ pragharṣayet /
punaḥ saptadine prāpte romamātraṁ samucchinet // 35 //

Then rock salt and yellow myrobalan (both powdered)should be rubbed in. On the 7th day, it should again be cut a hair's breadth.

evaṁ krameṇa ṣaṇmāsaṁ nityayuktaḥ samācaret /
ṣaṇmāsād rasanāmūlaśirābandhaḥ praṇaśyati // 36 //

One should go on doing thus regularly for six months. At the end of six months, the fraenum of the tongue will be completely cut.

kalāṁ parāṅmukhīṁ kṛtvā tripathe pariyojayet /
sā bhavet khecarī mudrā vyomacakraṁ tad ucyate // 37 //

Reversing the tongue, it is inserted into nasopharyngeal cavity. Thus, it makes the Khecarī Mudrā, and is called Vyoma Cakra.

rasanām ūrdhvagāṁ kṛtvā kṣaṇārdham api tiṣṭhati /
viṣair vimucyate yogī vyādhimṛtyujarādibhiḥ // 38 //

The Yogī who sits for a minute turning his tongue upwards, is saved from poisons, diseases, death, old age, etc.

na rogo maraṇaṁ tandrā na nidrā na kṣudhā tṛṣā /
na ca mūrcchā bhavet tasya yo mudrāṁ vetti khecarīm // 39 //

He who knows the Khecarī Mudrā is not afflicted with disease, death, sloth, sleep, hunger, thirst, and swooning.

pīḍyate na sa rogeṇa lipyate na ca karmaṇā /
bādhyate na sa kālena yo mudrāṁ vetti khecarīm // 40 //

He who knows the Khecarī Mudrā, is not troubled by diseases, is not bound by karmas, and is not snared by time.

cittaṁ carati khe yasmāj jihvā carati khe gatā /
tenaiṣā khecarī nāma mudrā siddhair nirūpitā // 41 //

Siddhas have devised this Khecarī Mudrā from the fact that the mind and the tongue reach Ākāśa by its practice.

khecaryā mudritaṁ yena vivaraṁ lambikordhvataḥ /
na tasya kṣarate binduḥ kāminyāśleṣitasya ca // 42 //

If the hole behind the palate be stopped with Khecarī by turning the tongue upwards, then Bindu cannot leave its place (is not discharged) even if a woman were embraced.

ūrdhvajihvaḥ sthiro bhūtvā somapānaṁ karoti yaḥ /
māsārdhena na sandeho mṛtyuṁ jayati yogavit // 43 //

If a Yogī drinks Somarasa (juice) by sitting with the tongue turned backwards and mind concentrated, there is no doubt, he conquers death within 15 days.

nityaṁ somakalāpūrṇaṁ śarīre yasya yoginaḥ /
takṣakeṇāpi daṣṭasya viṣaṁ tasya na sarpati // 44 //

If a Yogī, whose body is full of Somarasa (juice), were bitten even by Takṣaka (snake), its poison cannot permeate his body.

indhanāni yathā vahnis tailavartiṁ ca dīpakaḥ /
tathā somakalāpūrṇaṁ dehī dehaṁ na muñcati // 45 //

As fire is inseparably connected with wood and light is connected with wick and oil, so does the soul not leave the body full of nectar exuding from the Soma.

Note: Soma (Candra) is described later on as located in the thousand-petalled lotus in the human brain, and is the same as is seen on Śiva's head in pictures, and from which a sort of juice exudes. It is the retaining of this exudation which makes one immortal.

gomāṁsaṁ bhakṣayen nityaṁ pibed amaravāruṇīm /
kulīnaṁ tam ahaṁ manye itare kulaghātakāḥ // 46 //

One who eats the flesh of cow and drinks the immortal liquor daily, is regarded by me a man of noble family. Others are but a disgrace to their families.

Note: *kṛtārthau pitarau tena dhanyo deśaḥ kulaṁ ca tat /*
jāyate yogavān yatra dattam akṣayyatāṁ vrajet /
dṛṣṭaḥ sambhāṣitaḥ spṛṣṭaḥ pumprakṛtyā vivekavān /
bhavakoṭi śatāpātam punāti vṛjinaṁ nṛṇām //
(Brahmavaivarta)

Translation: Fortunate are the parents and blessed is the country and the family where a Yogī is born. Anything given to such a Yogī, becomes immortal. One, who discriminates between Puruṣa and Prakṛti, purges the sins of a million incarnations, by seeing, speaking, and touching such men (i.e., Yogī).

gṛhasthānāṁ sahasreṇa vānaprasthaśatena ca /
brahmacārisahasreṇa yogābhyāsī viśiṣyate //
(Brahmāṇḍa)

A Yogī far exceeds a thousand householders, a hundred Vānaprasthas, and a thousand Brahmacārīs.

rājayogasya māhātmyaṁ ko vijānāti tattvataḥ /
tajjñānī vasate yatra sa deśo puṇyabhājanam //
darśanād arcanād asya trisaptakulasaṁyutāḥ /
ajñā muktipadaṁ yānti kiṁ punas tatparāyaṇāḥ //
antaryogaṁ bahiryogaṁ yo jānāti viśeṣataḥ /
tvayā mayāpyasau vandyaḥ śeṣair vandyas tu kā punaḥ//
(Rājayoga, Rūrmapurāṇa)
ekakālaṁ dvikālaṁ vā trikālaṁ nityam eva vā /
ye yuñjate mahāyogaṁ vijñeyās te maheśvarāḥ //

Who can know the reality of Rāja Yoga? That country is very sacred where resides a man who knows it. By seeing and honouring him, generations of ignorant men get Mokṣa, what to speak of those who are actually engaged in it. He who knows internal and external Yoga, deserves adoration from you and me, what if he is adored by the rest of mankind !
Those who engage in the Great Yoga, once, twice or thrice daily, are to be known as masters of great wealth (Maheśvaras) or Lords.

gośabdenoditā jihvā tatpraveśo hi tāluni /
gomāṁsabhakṣaṇaṁ tat tu mahāpātakanāśanam // 47 //

The word '*go*' means tongue; eating it is thrusting it into the gullet which destroys great sins.

jihvāpraveśasambhūtavahninotpāditaḥ khalu /
candrāt sravati yaḥ sāraḥ sa syād amaravāruṇī // 48 //

Immortal liquor is the nectar exuding from the moon (Candra situated on the left side of the space between the eyebrows). It is produced by the fire which is generated by inserting the tongue into the nasopharyngeal cavity.

cuṁbantī yadi lambikāgram aniśam jihvārasaspandanī /
sakṣārā kaṭukāmladugdhasadṛśī madhvājyatulyā tathā //
vyādhīnāṁ haraṇaṁ jarāntakaraṇaṁ śastrāgamodīraṇam /
tasya syād amaratvam aṣṭaguṇitaṁ siddhāṅganākarṣaṇam // 49 //

If the tongue can touch with its end the hole from which falls the Rasa(juice) which is saltish, bitter, sour, milky and similar to ghee and honey, one can drive away disease, destroy old age, can evade an attack of arms, become immortal in eight ways and can attract fairies.

mūrdhnaḥ ṣoḍaśapatrapadmagalitaṁ prāṇād avāptaṁ haṭhād /
ūrdhvāsyo rasanāṁ niyamya vivare śaktiṁ parāṁ cintayan //
utkallolakalājalaṁ ca vimalaṁ dhārāmayaṁ yaḥ piben /
nirvyādhiḥ sa mṛṇālakomalavapur yogī ciraṁ jīvati // 50 //

He who drinks the clear stream of liquor of the moon (soma) falling from the brain to the sixteen-petalled lotus (in the heart), obtained by means of Prāṇa, by applying the tongue to the hole of the pendant in the palate, and by meditating on the great power (Kuṇḍalinī), becomes free from disease and tender in body, like the stalk of a lotus, and the Yogī lives a very long life.

yatprāleyaṁ prahitasuṣiraṁ merumūrdhāntarasthaṁ /
tasmiṁstattvaṁ pravadati sudhīs tanmukhaṁ nimnagānām //
candrāt sāraḥ sravati vapuṣas tena mṛtyur narāṇām /
tad badhnīyāt sukaraṇam atho nānyathā kāryasiddhiḥ // 51 //

On the top of the Meru (vertebral column), concealed in a hole, is the Somarasa (nectar of Candra); the wise, whose intellect is not overpowered by Rajas and Tamas Guṇas, but in whom Sattva Guṇa is predominant, say there is the (universal spirit) Ātman in it. It is the source of the down-going Iḍā, Piṅgalā and Suṣumṇā Nāḍīs, which are Gaṅgā, Yamunā and Sarasvatī. From that Candra is shed the essence of the body which causes death of men. It should, therefore, be stopped from shedding. This (Khecarī Mudrā) is a very good instrument for this purpose. There is no other means of achieving this end.

suṣiraṁ jñānajanakaṁ pañcasrotaḥ samanvitam /
tiṣṭhate khecarī mudrā tasmin śūnye nirañjane // 52 //

This hole is the generator of knowledge and is the source of the five streams (Iḍā, Piṅgalā, &c.). In that colorless vacuum, Khecarī Mudrā should be established.

ekaṁ sṛṣṭimayaṁ bījam ekā mudrā ca khecarī /
eko devo nirālamba ekāvasthā manonmanī // 53 //

There is only one seed germinating the whole universe from it; and there is only one Mudrā, called Khecarī. There is only one deva (god) without anyone's support, and there is one condition called Manonmanī.

Uḍḍīyāna Bandha

athoḍḍīyānabandhaḥ :
baddho yena suṣumṇāyāṁ prāṇas tūḍḍīyate yataḥ /
tasmād uḍḍīyanākhyo'yaṁ yogibhiḥ samudāhṛtaḥ // 54 //

Uḍḍīyāna is so called by the Yogīs, because by its practice the Prāṇa (Vāyu) flies (flows) in Suṣumṇā.

uḍḍīnaṁ kurute yasmād aviśrāntaṁ mahākhagaḥ /
uḍḍīyānaṁ tadeva syāt tatra bandho'bhidhīyate // 55 //

Uḍḍīyāna is so called, because the great bird, Prāṇa, tied to it, flies without being fatigued.
It is explained below :

udare paścimaṁ tānaṁ nābher ūrdhvaṁ ca kārayet /
uḍḍīyāno hyasau bandho mṛtyumātaṅgakesarī // 56 //

The belly above the navel is pressed backwards towards the spine. This Uḍḍīyāna Bandha is like a lion for the elephant of death.

uḍḍiyānaṁ tu sahajaṁ guruṇā kathitaṁ sadā /
abhyaset satataṁ yastu vṛddho'pi taruṇāyate // 57 //

Uḍḍīyāna is always very easy, when learnt from a Guru. The practitioner of this, if old, becomes young again.

nābher ūrdhvam adhaś cāpi tānaṁ kuryāt prayatnataḥ /
ṣaṇmāsam abhyasen mṛtyuṁ jayatyeva na saṁśayaḥ // 58 //

The portions above and below the navel, should be drawn backwards towards the spine. By practising this for six months one can undoubtedly conquer death.

sarveṣām api bandhānām uttamo hyuḍḍiyānakaḥ /
uḍḍiyāne dṛḍhe baddhe muktiḥ svābhāvikī bhavet // 59 //

Of all the Bandhas, Uḍḍīyāna is the best; for by binding it firmly liberation comes spontaneously.

Mūla Bandha

atha mūlabandhaḥ :
pārṣṇibhāgena saṁpīḍya yonim ākuñcayed gudam /
apānam ūrdhvam ākṛṣya mūlabandho'bhidhīyate // 60 //

Pressing Yoni (perineum)with the heel, contract up the anus. By drawing the Apāna thus, Mūla Bandha is made.

adhogatim apānaṁ vā ūrdhvagaṁ kurute balāt /
ākuñcanena taṁ prāhur mūlabandhaṁ hi yoginaḥ // 61 //

The Apāna, naturally going downward, is made to go up by force. This Mūla Bandha is spoken of by Yogīs as done by contracting the anus.

gudaṁ pārṣṇyā tu saṁpīḍya vāyum ākuñcayed balāt /
vāraṁ vāraṁ yathā cordhvaṁ samāyāti samīraṇaḥ // 62 //

Pressing the heel well against the anus, draw up the air by force, again and again till it (air) goes up.

prāṇāpānau nādabindū mūlabandhena caikatām /
gatvā yogasya saṁsiddhiṁ gaccato nātra saṁśayaḥ // 63 //

Prāṇa, Apāna, Nāda and Bindu uniting into one in this way, give success in Yoga, undoubtedly.

apānaprāṇayor aikyaṁ kṣayo mūtrapurīṣayoḥ /
yuvā bhavati vṛddho'pi satataṁ mūlabandhanāt // 64 //

By the purification of Prāṇa and Apāna, urine and excrements decrease. Even an old man becomes young by constantly practising Mūla Bandha.

apāne ūrdhvage jāte prayāte vahnimaṇḍalam /
tadānalaśikhā dīrghā jāyate vāyunā hatā // 65 //

Going up, Apāna enters the zone of fire, i.e., the stomach. The flame of fire struck by the air is thereby lengthened.

Note.: *dehamadhye śikhisthānaṁ taptajāmbūnadaprabham /*
trikoṇaṁ tu manuṣyāṇām caturasraṁ catuṣpadām //
maṇḍalaṁ tu pataṅgānāṁ satyam etat bravīmi te /
tanmadhye tu śikhā tanvī sadā tiṣṭhati pāvake //

(Yājñavalkya)

In the centre of the body is the seat of fire, like heated gold; in men it is triangular; in quadrupeds square; in birds circular. There is a long thin flame in this fire. It is gastric fire.

tato yāto vahnyapānau prāṇam uṣṇasvarūpakam /
tenātyantapradīptas tu jvalano dehajas tathā // 66 //

These, fire and Apāna, go to the naturally hot Prāṇa, which, becoming inflamed thereby, causes burning sensation in the body.

tena kuṇḍalinī suptā santaptā samprabudhyate /
daṇḍāhatā bhujaṅgīva niśvasya ṛjutāṁ vrajet // 67 //

Kuṇḍalinī, which has been sleeping all this time, becomes well heated by this means and awakens well. It becomes straight like a serpent struck dead with a stick.

bilaṁ praviṣṭeva tato brahmanāḍyantaraṁ vrajet /
tasmān nityaṁ mūlabandhaḥ kartavyo yogibhiḥ sadā // 68 //

It enters the Brahma Nāḍī, just as a serpent enters its hole. Therefore, the Yogī should always practise this Mūla Bandha.

Jālandhara Bandha

atha jālandharabandhaḥ :
kaṇṭham ākuñcya hṛdaye sthāpayec cibukaṁ dṛḍham /
bandho jālandharākhyo'yaṁ jarāmṛtyuvināśakaḥ // 69 //

Contract the throat and press the chin firmly against the chest. This is called Jālandhara Bandha, which destroys old age and death.

badhnāti hi śirājālam adhogāminabhojalam /
tato jālandharo bandhaḥ kaṇṭhaduḥkhaughanāśanaḥ // 70 //

It stops the opening (hole) of the group of Nāḍīs, through which the juice from the sky (from the Soma or Candra in the brain) falls down. It is, therefore, called Jālandhara Bandha, the destroyer of a host of diseases of the throat.

jālandhare kṛte bandhe kaṇṭhasaṅkocalakṣaṇe /
na pīyūṣaṁ patatyagnau na ca vāyuḥ prakupyati // 71 //

In Jālandhara Bandha, characterised by perfect contraction of throat, the nectar does not fall into the fire (Sūrya situated in the navel), and the air is not disturbed.

kaṇṭhasaṁkocanenaiva dve nāḍyau stambhayed dṛḍham /
madhyacakram idaṁ jñeyaṁ ṣoḍaśādhārabandhanam // 72 //

The two Nāḍīs should be stopped firmly by contracting the throat. This is called the middle circuit or centre (Maḍhya Cakra), and it stops the 16 Ādhāras (i.e., vital parts).

[Note: *aṅguṣṭha -gulpha-jānūru- sīvanī-liṅga -nābhayaḥ /*
hṛd-grīvā-kaṇṭhadeśaś ca lambikā nāsikā tathā //
bhrūmadhyaṁ ca lalāṭaṁ ca mūrdhā ca brahmarandhrakam /
ete hi ṣoḍaśādhārāḥ kathitā yogipuṅgavaiḥ //

The sixteen vital parts mentioned by renowned Yogīs are: (1)thumbs, (2) ankles, (3) knees, (4) thighs, (5) prepuce, (6) organs of generation, (7) navel, (8) heart, (9) neck, (10)throat, (11)palate, (12)nose, (13) middle of the eyebrows, (14) forehead, (15) head, and (16) Brahma-randhra.]

mūlasthānaṁ samākuñcya uḍḍīyānaṁ tu kārayet /
iḍāṁ ca piṅgalāṁ badhvā vāhayet paścime pathi // 73 //

By drawing up the Mūlasthāna (anus) Uḍḍīyāna Bandha should be performed. The flow of the air should be directed to Suṣumṇā, by closing Iḍā and Piṅgalā.

anenaiva vidhānena prayāti pavano layam /
tato na jāyate mṛtyur jarārogādikaṁ tathā // 74 //

Prāṇa becomes calm and latent by this means, and thus there is no death, old age, disease, etc.

bandhatrayam idaṁ śreṣṭhaṁ mahāsiddhaiś ca sevitam /
sarveṣāṁ haṭhatantrāṇāṁ sādhanaṁ yogino viduḥ // 75 //

These three Bandhas are the best of all and have been practised by the masters. Of all the means of success in Haṭha Yoga, they are known to the Yogīs as the chief ones.

yatkiñcit sravate candrād amṛtaṁ divyarūpiṇaḥ /
tat sarvaṁ grasate sūryas tena piṇḍo jarāyutaḥ // 76 //

The whole of the nectar, possessing divine qualities, which exudes from Soma (Candra) is devoured by Sūrya; and, owing to this, the body becomes old.

tatrāsti karaṇaṁ divyaṁ sūryasya mukhavañcanam /
gurūpadeśato jñeyaṁ na tu śāstrārthakoṭibhiḥ // 77 //

To remedy this, the opening of Sūrya is avoided by excellent means. It is to be learnt best from instructions by a Guru, but not from even a million discussions.

Viparītakaraṇī

atha viparītakaraṇī :
ūrdhvaṁ nābher adhas tālor ūrdhvaṁ bhānur adhaḥ śaśī /
karaṇī viparītākhyā guruvākyena labhyate // 78 //

Above the navel and below the palate respectively, are Sūrya and Candra. The exercise, called Viparītakaraṇī, is learnt from the Guru's instructions.

nityam abhyāsayuktasya jaṭharāgnivivardhinī /
āhāro bahulas tasya saṁpādyaḥ sādhakasya ca /
alpāhāro yadi bhaved agnir dahati tatkṣaṇāt // 79 //

This exercise increases appetite; and, therefore, one who practises it, should obtain a good supply of food. If the food be scanty, it will burn him at once.

adhaḥśirāś cordhvapādaḥ kṣaṇaṁ syāt prathame dine /
kṣaṇāc ca kiñcid adhikam abhyasec ca dine dine // 80 //

Place the head on the ground and the feet up into the sky, for a second only the first day, and increase this time daily.

valitaṁ palitaṁ caiva ṣaṇmāsordhvaṁ na dṛśyate /
yāmamātraṁ tu yo nityam abhyaset sa tu kālajit // 81 //

After six months, wrinkles and grey hair are not seen. He who practises it daily, even for two hours, conquers death.

Vajrolī

atha vajrolī :
svecchayā vartamāno'pi yogoktair niyamair vinā /
vajrolīṁ yo vijānāti sa yogī siddhibhājanam // 82 //

Even if one who lives a wayward life, without observing any rules of Yoga, but performs Vajrolī, deserves success and is a Yogī.

tatra vastudvayaṁ vakṣe durlabhaṁ yasyakasyacit /
kṣīraṁ caikaṁ dvitīyam tu nārī ca vaśavartinī // 83 //

Two things are necessary for this, and these are difficult to get for the ordinary people: (1) milk and (2) a woman behaving as desired.

mehanena śanaiḥ samyag ūrdhvākuñcanam abhyaset /
puruṣo'pyathavā nārī vajrolīsiddhim āpnuyāt // 84 //

By practising to draw in the *Bindu* discharged during cohabitation, whether one be a man or a woman, one obtains success in the practice of Vajrolī.

yatnataḥ śastanālena phūtkāraṁ vajrakandare /
śanaiḥ śanaiḥ prakurvīta vāyusañcārakāraṇāt // 85 //

By means of a pipe, one should blow air slowly into the passage in the male organ.

nārībhage patad bindum abhyāsenordhvam āharet /
calitaṁ ca nijaṁ bindum ūrdhvam ākṛṣya rakṣayet // 86 //

By practice, the discharged *Bindu* is drawn out. One can draw back and preserve one's own discharged *Bindu.*

evaṁ saṁrakṣayed binduṁ mṛtyuṁ jayati yogavit /
maraṇaṁ bindupātena jīvanaṁ bindudhāraṇāt // 87 //

The Yogī who can protect his *Bindu* thus, overcomes death; because death comes by discharging *Bindu,* and life is prolonged by its preservation.

sugandho yogino dehe jāyate bindudhāraṇāt /
yāvad binduḥ sthiro dehe tāvat kālabhayaṁ kutaḥ // 88 //

By preserving Bindu, the body of the Yogī emits a pleasing smell. There is no fear of death, so long as the Bindu is well-established in the body.

cittāyattaṁ nṛṇāṁ śukraṁ śukrāyattaṁ ca jīvitam /
tasmāc chukraṁ manaścaiva rakṣaṇīyaṁ prayatnataḥ // 89 //

Bindu of men is under the control of mind, and life is dependent on *Bindu.* Hence, mind and Bindu should be protected by all means.

Sahajolī

atha sahajolī :
sahajoli cāmarolir vajrolyā bheda ekataḥ /
jaleṣu bhasma nikṣipya dagdhagomayasaṁbhavam // 90 //

Sahajolī and Amarolī are only the different kinds of Vajrolī. Ashes from burnt up cowdung should be mixed with water.

vajrolī maithunād ūrdhvaṁ strīpuṁsoḥ svāṅgalepanam /
āsīnayoḥ sukhenaiva muktavyāpārayoḥ kṣaṇāt // 91 //

Being free from the exercise of Vajrolī, man and woman should both rub it on their bodies.

sahajolir iyaṁ proktā śraddheyā yogibhiḥ sadā /
ayaṁ śubhakaro yogo bhogayukto'pi muktidaḥ // 92 //

This is called Sahajolī, and should be relied on by Yogīs. It does good and gives Mokṣa.

ayaṁ yogaḥ puṇyavatāṁ dhīrāṇāṁ tattvadarśinām /
nirmatsarāṇāṁ sidhyeta na tu matsaraśālinām // 93 //

This Yoga is achieved by courageous wise men who are free from sloth, and cannot be accomplished by the slothful.

Amarolī

athāmarolī :
pittolvaṇatvāt prathamāmbudhārāṁ vihāya niḥsāratayāntyadhārā /
niṣevyate śītalamadhyadhārā kāpālike khaṇḍamate'marolī // 94 //

In the doctrine of the sect of Kāpālikas, Amarolī is the drinking of the mid stream; leaving the 1st, as it is a mixture of too much bile and the last, which is useless.

amarīṁ yaḥ piben nityaṁ nasyaṁ kurvan dine dine /
vajrolīm abhyaset samyag amarolīti kathyate // 95 //

He who drinks Amarī, snuffs it daily, and practises Vajrolī, is called one practising Amarolī.

abhyāsān niḥsṛtāṁ cāndrīṁ vibhūtyā saha miśrayet /
dhārayed uttamāṅgeṣu divyadṛṣṭiḥ prajāyate // 96 //

The Bindu discharged in the practice of Vajrolī should be mixed with ashes, and the rubbing of it on the best parts of the body gives divine sight.

Śakticālana

atha śakticālanam :
kuṭilāṅgī kuṇḍalinī bhujaṅgī śaktirīśvarī /
kuṇḍalyarundhatī caite śabdāḥ paryāyavācakāḥ // 97 //

Kuṭilāṅgī (crooked-bodied), Kuṇḍalinī, Bhujaṅgī (a she-serpent), Śakti, Īśvarī, Kuṇḍalī, Arundhatī—all these words are synonymous.

udghāṭayet kapāṭaṁ tu yathā kuñcikayā haṭhāt /
kuṇḍalinyā tathā yogī mokṣadvāraṁ vibhedayet // 98 //

As a door is opened with a key, so the Yogī opens the door of Mukti by opening Kuṇḍalinī by means of Haṭha Yoga.

yena mārgeṇa gantavyaṁ brahmasthānaṁ nirāmayam /
mukhenācchādya tad dvāraṁ prasuptā parameśvarī // 99 //

Parameśvarī (Kuṇḍalinī) sleeps, covering the hole of the passage by which one can go to the seat of Brahma which is free from pains.

kandordhvaṁ kuṇḍalīśaktiḥ suptā mokṣāya yoginām /
bandhanāya ca mūḍhānāṁ yas taṁ vetti sa yogavit // 100 //

Kuṇḍalī Śakti sleeps on the bulb for the purpose of giving Mokṣa to Yogīs and bondage to the ignorant. He who knows it, knows Yoga.

kuṇḍalī kuṭilākārā sarpavat parikīrtitā /
sā śaktis cālita yena sa mukto nātra saṁśayaḥ // 101 //

Kuṇḍalī is of a curved shape, and has been described to be like a serpent. He who has moved that Śakti is, no doubt, Mukta (released from bondage).

gaṅgāyamunayor madhye bālaraṇḍā tapasvinī /
balātkāreṇa gṛhṇīyāt tad viṣṇoḥ paramaṁ padam // 102 //

Young and a Tapasvinī (a female ascetic), lying between Gaṅgā and Yamunā (Iḍā and Piṅgalā) should be caught hold of by force, to get the highest position.

iḍā bhagavatī gaṅgā piṅgalā yamunā nadī /
iḍāpiṅgalayor madhye bālaraṇḍā ca kuṇḍalī // 103 //

Iḍā is called goddess Gaṅgā; Piṅgalā goddess Yamunā. In the middle of Iḍā and Piṅgalā is the young widow, Kuṇḍalī.

pucche pragṛhya bhujagīṁ suptām udbodhayec ca tām /
nidrāṁ vihāya sā śaktir ūrdhvam uttiṣṭhate haṭhāt // 104 //

This sleeping she-serpent should be awakened by catching hold of her tail. By the force of Haṭha, the Śakti leaves her sleep, and starts upwards.

avasthitā caiva phaṇāvatī sā prātaś ca sāyaṁ praharārdhamātram /
prapūrya sūryāt paridhānayuktyā pragṛhyā nityaṁ paricālanīyā//105 //

This she-serpent is situated in Mūlādhāra. She should be caught and moved daily, morning and evening, for ½ a Prahara (1 ½ hours), by filling with air through Piṅgalā by the Paridhāna method.

ūrdhvaṁ vitastimātraṁ tu vistāraṁ caturaṅgulam /
mṛdulaṁ dhavalaṁ proktaṁ veṣṭitāmbaralakṣaṇam // 106 //

The bulb is above the anus, a Vitasti (12 Aṅgulas) long, and measures 4 Aṅgulas (3 inches) in extent and is soft and white, and appears like a folded cloth.

sati vajrāsane pādau karābhyāṁ dhārayed dṛḍham /
gulphadeśasamīpe ca kandaṁ tatra prapīḍayet // 107 //

Keeping the feet in Vajrāsana (Padmāsana), hold them firmly with the hands. The position of the bulb then will be near the ankle joint, where it should be pressed.

vajrāsane sthito yogī cālayitvā ca kuṇḍalīm /
kuryād anantaraṁ bhastrāṁ kuṇḍalīm āśu bodhayet // 108 //

The Yogī, sitting in Vajrāsana and having moved Kuṇḍalī, should perform Bhastrikā to awaken Kuṇḍalī soon.

bhānor ākuñcanaṁ kuryāt kuṇḍalīm cālayet tataḥ /
mṛtyuvaktragatasyāpi tasya mṛtyubhayaṁ kutaḥ //109 //

Bhānu (Sūrya, near the navel)should be contracted (by contracting the navel) which will move the Kuṇḍalī. There is no fear to him who does so, even if he has entered the mouth of death.

muhūrtadvayaparyantaṁ nirbhayaṁ cālanād asau /
ūrdhvam ākṛṣyate kiñcit suṣumṇāyāṁ samudgatā // 110 //

By moving this, for two Muhūrtas, it is drawn up a little by entering Suṣumṇā (spinal column).

tena kuṇḍalinī tasyāḥ suṣumṇāyā mukhaṁ dhruvam /
jahāti tasmāt prāṇo'yaṁ suṣumṇāṁ vrajati svataḥ // 111//

By this Kuṇḍalinī leaves the entrance of Suṣumṇā at once, and Prāṇa enters it of itself.

tasmāt sañcālayen nityaṁ sukhasuptām arundhatīm /
tasyāḥ sañcālanenaiva yogī rogaiḥ pramucyate //112 //

Therefore, this comfortably sleeping Arundhatī should always be moved; for by so doing the Yogī gets rid of diseases.

yena sañcālitā śaktiḥ sa yogī siddhibhājanam /
kimatra bahunoktena kālaṁ jayati līlayā // 113 //

The Yogī, who has been able to move the Śakti deserves success. It is useless to say more; suffice it to say that he conquers death playfully.

brahmacaryaratasyaiva nityaṁ hitamitāśinaḥ /
maṇḍalād dṛśyate siddhiḥ kuṇḍalyabhyāsayoginaḥ // 114 //

The Yogī observing Brahmacarya (continence) and always eating sparingly, gets success within 40 days by practice with Kuṇḍalinī.

kuṇḍalīṁ cālayitvā tu bhastrāṁ kuryād viśeṣataḥ /
evam abhyāsato nityaṁ yamino yamabhīḥ kutaḥ // 115 //

After moving Kuṇḍalī, plenty of Bhastrā should be performed. By such practice, he has no fear of the god of death.

dvāsaptatisahasrāṇāṁ nāḍīnāṁ malaśodhane /
kutaḥ prakṣālanopāyaḥ kuṇḍalyabhyasanād ṛte // 116 //

There is no other way, but the practice of Kuṇḍalī, for washing away the impurities of 72,000 Nāḍīs.

iyaṁ tu madhyamā nāḍī dṛḍhābhyāsena yoginām /
āsanaprāṇasaṁyāmamudrābhiḥ saralā bhavet // 117 //

This middle Nāḍī becomes straight by steady practice of postures; Prāṇāyāma and Mudrās of Yogīs.

abhyāse tu vinidrāṇāṁ mano dhṛtvā samādhinā /
rudrāṇī vā parā mudrā bhadrāṁ siddhiṁ prayacchati // 118 //

Those whose sleep has decreased by practice and mind has

become calm by Samādhi, get beneficial accomplishments by Śāmbhavī and other Mudrās.

rājayogaṁ vinā pṛthvī rājayogaṁ vinā niśā /
rājayogaṁ vinā mudrā vicitrāpi na śobhate // 119 //

Without Rāja Yoga, this earth, the night, and the Mudrās, be they howsoever wonderful, do not appear beautiful.

Note: Rāja Yoga-āsana; Earth-steadiness, calmness; Night-Kumbhaka, cessations of the activity of Prāṇa, just as King's officials cease moving at night. Hence night means absence of motion, i.e., Kumbhaka.

mārutasya vidhiṁ sarvaṁ manoyuktaṁ samabhyaset /
itaratra na kartavyā manovṛttir manīṣiṇā // 120 //

All the practices relating to the air should be performed with a concentrated mind. A wise man should not allow his mind to wander away.

iti mudrā daśa proktā ādināthena śambhunā /
ekaikā tāsu yamināṁ mahāsiddhipradāyinī // 121 //

These are the Mudrās, as explained by Ādinātha (Śiva). Everyone of them is the giver of great accomplishments to the practitioner.

upadeśaṁ hi mudrāṇāṁ yo datte sāmpradāyikam /
sa eva śrīguruḥ svāmī sākṣād īśvara eva saḥ // 122 //

He is really the *Guru* and to be considered as Īśvara in human form who teaches the Mudrās as handed down from Guru to disciple.

tasya vākyaparo bhūtvā mudrābhyāse samāhitaḥ /
aṇimādiguṇaiḥ sārdhaṁ labhate kālavañcanam // 123 //

Engaging in practice, by putting faith in his words, one gets the Siddhis of Aṇimā, etc., and also evades death.

iti haṭhapradīpikāyāṁ tṛtīyopadeśaḥ // 3 //

End of chapter 3, On Mudrās.

CHAPTER 4

On Samādhi

Caturthopadeśaḥ

namaḥ śivāya gurave nādabindukalātmane /
nirañjanapadaṁ yāti nityaṁ yatra parāyaṇaḥ // 1 //

Salutation to Śiva, the Guru, who is of the nature of Nāda, Bindu and Kalā. One who is devoted to Him obtains the highest bliss.

athedānīṁ pravakṣyāmi samādhikramam uttamam //
mṛtyughnaṁ ca sukhopāyaṁ brahmānandakaraṁ param//2//

Now I will describe a regular method of attaining to Samādhi, which destroys death, is the means of obtaining happiness, and gives the bliss of Brahman.

rājayogaḥ samādhiś ca unmanī ca manonmanī /
amaratvaṁ layas tattvaṁ śūnyāśūnyaṁ paraṁ padam//3//
amanaskaṁ tathādvaitaṁ nirālambaṁ nirañjanam /
jīvanmuktiś ca sahajā turyā cetyekavācakāḥ // 4 //

Rāja Yoga, Samādhi, Unmanī, Manonmanī, Amaratva, Laya, Tattva, Śūnya, Aśūnya, Parama Pada, Amanaska, Advaita, Nirālamba, Nirañjana, Jīvanamukti, Sahajā, and Turyā are all synonymous.

salile saindhavaṁ yadvat sāmyaṁ bhajati yogataḥ /
tathātmamanasor aikyaṁ samādhir abhidhīyate// 5 //

As salt dissolved in water becomes one with it, so when Ātmā and mind become one, it is called Samādhi.

yadā saṁkṣīyate prāṇo mānasaṁ ca pralīyate/
tadā samarasatvaṁ ca samādhir abhidhīyate// 6 //

When Prāṇa becomes lean (vigourless) and the mind becomes absorbed, then their becoming equal is called Samādhi.

tatsamaṁ ca dvayor aikyaṁ jīvātmaparamātmanoḥ /
pranaṣṭasarvasaṅkalpaḥ samādhiḥ so'bhidhīyate // 7 //

This equality and oneness of the empirical self and the highest self, when all Saṁkalpas cease to exist, is called Samādhi.

rājayogasya māhātmyaṁ ko vā jānāti tattvataḥ /
jñānaṁ muktiḥ sthitiḥ siddhir guruvākyena labhyate //8 //

Or, who can know the true greatness of Rājayoga? Knowledge, Mukti, Sthiti, and Siddhi can be learnt from instructions by a Guru alone.

durlabho viṣayatyāgo durlabhaṁ tattvadarśanam /
durlabhā sahajāvasthā sadguroḥ karuṇāṁ vinā // 9 //

Indifference to worldly enjoyments is very difficult to obtain, and equally difficult is the knowledge of the Reality to obtain. It is very difficult to get the condition of Samādhi without the favour of a true Guru.

vividhair āsanaiḥ kumbhair vicitraiḥ karaṇair api /
prabuddhāyāṁ mahāśaktau prāṇaḥ śūnye pralīyate // 10 //

By means of various postures and different Kuṁbhakas, when the great power (Kuṇḍalī) awakens, then Prāṇa becomes absorbed in Śūnya (Samādhi).

utpannaśaktibodhasya tyaktaniḥśeṣakarmaṇaḥ /
yoginaḥ sahajāvasthā svayam eva prajāyate // 11 //

The Yogī whose Śakti has awakened, and who has renounced all actions, attains to the condition of Samādhi without any effort.

suṣumṇāvāhini prāṇe śūnye viśati mānase /
tadā sarvāṇi karmāṇi nirmūlayati yogavit // 12 //

When Prāṇa flows in Suṣumṇā, and the mind has entered Śūnya, then the Yogī is free from the effects of Karmas.

amarāya namas tubhyaṁ so'pi kālas tvayā jitaḥ /
patitaṁ vadane yasya jagad etac carācaram // 13 //

O Immortal one (that is, the yogī who has attained to the condition of Samādhi), I salute thee! Even death itself, into whose mouth the whole of this movable and immovable world has fallen, has been conquered by thee.

citte samatvam āpanne vāyau vrajati madhyame /
tadāmarolī vajrolī sahajolī prajāyate // 14 //

Amarolī, Vajrolī and Sahajolī are accomplished when the mind becomes calm and Prāṇa has entered the middle channel.

jñānaṁ kuto manasi sambhavatīha tāvat
prāṇo'pi jīvati mano mriyate na yāvat /
prāṇo mano dvayamidaṁ vilayam nayed yo
mokṣaṁ sa gacchati naro na kathaṁcid anyaḥ // 15 //

How can it be possible to get knowledge, so long as Prāṇa is living and mind has not died? No one else can get Mokṣa, except one who can make one's Prāṇa and mind latent.

jñātvā suṣumṇāsadbhedaṁ kṛtvā vāyuṁ ca madhyagam /
sthitvā sadaiva susthāne brahmarandhre nirodhayet // 16 //

Always living in a good locality and having known the secret of Suṣumṇā, which has a middle course, and making Vāyu move into it, (the Yogī) should restrain the Vāyu in the Brahmarandhra.

sūryācandramasau dhattaḥ kālaṁ rātrimdivātmakam /
bhoktrī suṣumṇā kālasya guhyam etad udāhṛtam //17 //

Time, in the form of night and day, is made by the Sun and the Moon. That Suṣumṇā devours this time (death) even, is a great secret.

dvāsaptatisahasrāṇi nāḍīdvārāṇi pañjare /
suṣumnā śāmbhavī śaktiḥ śeṣāstveva nirarthakāḥ // 18 //

In this body there are 72,000 openings of Nāḍīs; of these, Suṣumṇā, which has the Śāmbhavī Śakti in it, is the only important one; the rest are useless.

vāyuḥ paricito yasmād agninā saha kuṇḍalīm /
bodhayitvā suṣumṇāyāṁ praviśed anirodhataḥ // 19 //

Vāyu should be made to enter Suṣumṇā without restraint by him who has practised the control of breathing and has awakened Kuṇḍalī by the (gastric) fire.

suṣumṇā vāhinī prāṇe siddhyatyeva manonmanī /
anyathā tvitarābhyāsāḥ prayāsāyaiva yoginām // 20 //

Prāṇa, flowing through Suṣumṇā, brings about the condition of Manonmanī; other practices are simply futile for the Yogī.

pavano badhyate yena manas tenaiva badhyate /
manaś ca badhyate yena pavanas tena badhyate // 21 //

By one whose breathing has been controlled, the activities of the mind also have been controlled; and, conversely, by one whose mental activities have been controlled, breathing also has been controlled.

hetudvayaṁ tu cittasya vāsanā ca samīraṇaḥ /
tayor vinaṣṭa ekasmiṁs tau dvāvapi vinaśyataḥ // 22 //

There are two causes of the activities of mind: (1) Vāsanā (desires)and (2) respiration (Prāṇa). Of these, the destruction of one is the destruction of both.

mano yatra vilīyate pavanas tatra līyate /
pavano līyate yatra manas tatra vilīyate // 23 //

Breathing is lessened when the mind becomes absorbed, and the mind becomes absorbed when Prāṇa is restrained.

dugdhāmbuvat sammilitāvubhau
tau tulyakriyau mānasamārutau hi /
yato marut tatra manaḥpravṛttir
yato manas tatra marutpravṛttiḥ // 24 //

Both mind and breath are united together, like milk and water; and both of them are equal in their activities. Mind begins its activities where there is breath, and Prāṇa begins its activities where there is mind.

tatraikanāśād aparasya nāśa
ekapravṛtter aparapravṛttiḥ /
adhvas tayoś cendriyavargavṛttiḥ
pradhvastayor mokṣapadasya siddhiḥ // 25 //

By the suspension of one, therefore, comes the suspension of the other, and by the operations of one are brought about the operations of the other. When they are present, the Indriyas (the senses) remain engaged in their proper functions, and when they become latent then there is Mokṣa.

rasasya manasaś caiva cañcalatvaṁ svabhāvataḥ /
raso baddho mano baddhaṁ kinna sidhyati bhūtale // 26 //

By nature, mercury and mind are unsteady: there is nothing in the world which cannot be accomplished when these are made steady.

mūrcchito harate vyādhīn mṛto jīvayati svayam /
baddhaḥ khecaratāṁ dhatte raso vāyuś ca pārvati // 27 //

O Pārvati ! Mercury and breathing, when made steady, destroy diseases and the dead himself comes to life (by their means). By their (proper) control, moving in the air is accomplished.

manaḥsthairye sthiro vāyus tato binduḥ sthiro bhavet /
bindusthairyāt sadā sattvaṁ piṇḍasthairyaṁ prajāyate // 28 //

Breathing is calmed when mind becomes steady and calm; and hence the preservation of Bindu. The preservation of this latter makes Sattva established in the body.

indriyāṇāṁ mano nātho manonāthas tu mārutaḥ /
mārutasya layo nāthaḥ sa layo nādamāśritaḥ // 29 //

Mind is the master of senses, and breath is the master of mind. Breath in its turn is subordinate to Laya (absorption), and that Laya depends on Nāda.

so'yamevāstu mokṣākhyo māstu vāpi matāntare /
manaḥprāṇalaye kaścid ānandaḥ saṁpravartate // 30 //

This very Laya is what is called Mokṣa, or, as others say, you may not call it Mokṣa; but when the mind becomes absorbed, a sort of ecstasy is experienced.

pranaṣṭaśvāsaniśvāsaḥ pradhvastaviṣayagrahaḥ /
niśceṣṭo nirvikāraśca layo jayati yogināṁ // 31 //

By the suspension of respiration and the cessation of the activity of the senses, when the mind becomes devoid of all the activities and remains changeless, then the Yogī attains to the Laya stage.

ucchinnasarvasaṅkalpo niḥśeṣāśeṣaceṣṭitaḥ /
svāvagamyo layaḥ ko'pi jāyate vāgagocaraḥ // 32 //

When all the thoughts and activities cease, then the Laya Stage is produced, to describe which is beyond the power of speech, being known by self- experience alone.

layo laya iti prāhuḥ kīdṛśaṁ layalakṣaṇam /
apunarvāsanotthānāl layo viṣayavismṛtiḥ // 33 //

They often speak of Laya; but what is meant by it ? Laya is simply the forgetting of the objects of senses when the Vāsanās(desires)do not rise any more.

Śāmbhavī Mudrā

atha śāmbhavī mudrā :
vedaśāstrapurāṇāni sāmānyagaṇikā iva /
ekaiva śāṁbhavī mudrā guptā kulavadhūr iva // 34 //

Vedas, Śāstras and Purāṇas are like ordinary public women. Śāmbhavī Mudrā alone is like a wife of respectable family not exposed to everyone's gaze.

antarlakṣyaṁ bahirdṛṣṭir nimeṣonmeṣavarjitā /
eṣā sā śāmbhavī mudrā vedaśāstreṣu gopitā // 35 //

Aiming at Brahman inwardly, while keeping the sight directed to the external objects, without blinking the eyes, is called the Śāmbhavī Mudrā, preserved as a secret in the Vedas and Śāstras.

antarlakṣyavilīnacittapavano yogī yadā vartate /
dṛṣṭyā niścalatārayā bahir adhaḥ paśyannapaśyannapi /
mudreyaṁ khalu śāmbhavī bhavati sā labdhā prasādāt guroḥ /
śūnyāśunyavilakṣaṇam sphurati tat tattvaṁ paraṁ śāmbhavam// 36 //

When the Yogī remains inwardly attentive to Brahman, keeping the mind and Prāṇa absorbed, and the sight steady, as if seeing everything while in reality seeing nothing outside, below, or above, verily then it is called Śāmbhavī Mudrā, which is learnt by the favour of a Guru. Whatever, other than vacuum or not-vacuum is perceived, is to be regarded as the manifestation of that great Śambhu (Śiva).

śrīśāmbhavyāś ca khecaryā avasthādhāmabhedataḥ /
bhavec cittalayānandaḥ śūnye citsukharūpiṇi // 37 //

The two states, Śāmbhavī and Khecarī, are different because of their seats (being the heart and the space between the eyebrows respectively); but both cause happiness, for the mind becomes absorbed in the void which is of the nature of blissful existence.

Unmanī

athonmanī :
tāre jyotiṣi saṁyojya kiñcid unnamayed bhruvau /
pūrvayogaṁ mano yuñjannunmanīkārakaḥ kṣaṇāt // 38 //

Fix the gaze on the light (seen on the tip of the nose) and raise the eyebrows a little, with the mind contemplating as before (in the Śāmbhavī Mudrā, that is, inwardly thinking of Brahma, but apparently looking outside). This will create the Unmanī Avasthā at once.

Tāraka

kecid āgamajālena kecinnigamasaṅkulaiḥ /
kecit tarkeṇa muhyanti naiva jānanti tārakam // 39 //

Some are deluded by views expressed in the Vedas, some by those of Nigama, while others by those of their own reasoning, but none knows the value of this Mudrā, which enables one to cross the ocean of existence.

ardhonmīlitalocanaḥ sthiramanā nāsāgradattekṣaṇaḥ /
candrārkāvapi līnatām upanayan nispandabhāvena yaḥ //
jyotīrūpam aśeṣabījam akhilaṁ dedīpyamānaṁ paraṁ /
tattvaṁ tatpadam eti vastu paramaṁ vācyaṁ kim atrādhikam // 40 //

With steady, calm mind and half closed eyes fixed on the tip of the nose, stopping Iḍā and Piṅgalā without blinking, he who can see the light which is the all, the seed, the entire brilliant, great Tattva, approaches Him, who is the highest object. What is the use of more talk?

divā na pūjayel liṅgaṁ rātrau caiva na pūjayet /
sarvadā pūjayel liṅgaṁ divārātrinirodhataḥ // 41 //

One should not meditate on the Liṅga (i.e., Ātman) in the day (i.e., while Sūrya or Piṅgalā is working) or at night (when Iḍā is working), but should always contemplate after restraining both.

Khecarī

atha khecarī :
savyadakṣiṇanāḍistho madhye carati mārutaḥ /
tiṣṭhate khecarī mudrā tasmin sthāne na saṁśayaḥ // 42 //

When the air has ceased to move in the right and left nostrils, and has begun to flow in the middle path, then the Khecarī Mudrā can be accomplished there. There is no doubt of this.

iḍāpiṅgalayor madhye śūnyaṁ caivānilaṁ graset /
tiṣṭhate khecarī mudrā tatra satyaṁ punaḥ punaḥ // 43 //

If Prāṇa can be drawn into Śūnya (Suṣumṇā), which is between Iḍā and Piṅgalā, and made motionless there, then the Khecarī Mudrā can truly become steady there.

sūryācandramasor madhye nirālambāntare punaḥ /
saṁsthitā vyomacakre yā sā mudrā nāma khecarī // 44 //

That Mudrā is called Khecarī which is performed in the supportless space between Sūrya and Candra (Iḍā and Piṅgalā) and is called Vyomacakra.

somād yatroditā dhārā sākṣāt sā śivavallabhā /
pūrayed atulāṁ divyāṁ suṣumṇāṁ paścime mukhe // 45 //

Khecarī which causes the stream to flow from Candra (Soma) is the beloved of Śiva. The incomparable divine Suṣumṇā should be closed by the tongue drawn back.

purastāc caiva pūryeta niścitā khecarī bhavet /
abhyastā khecarī mudrāpyunmanī saṁprajāyate // 46 //

It can be closed from the front also (by stopping the movements of Prāṇa), and then surely it becomes Khecarī. By practice, this Khecarī leads to Unmanī.

bhruvor madhye śivasthānaṁ manas tatra vilīyate /
jñātavyaṁ tatpadaṁ turyaṁ tatra kālo na vidyate // 47 //

The seat of Śiva is between the eyebrows, and the mind becomes absorbed there. This condition (in which the mind is thus absorbed) is known as Turya, and death has no access there.

abhyaset khecarīṁ tāvad yāvat syād yoganidritaḥ /
saṁprāptayoganidrasya kālo nāsti kadācana // 48 //

Khecarī should be practised till there is Yoga-nidrā (Samādhi). One who has induced Yoga-nidrā, cannot fall a victim to death.

nirālambaṁ manaḥ kṛtvā na kiñcid api cintayet /
sabāhyābhyantare vyomni ghaṭavat tiṣṭhati dhruvam // 49 //

Freeing the mind from all thoughts and thinking of nothing, one should sit firmly like a pot in the space (surrounded and filled with ether).

bāhyavāyur yathā līnas tathā madhyo na saṁśayaḥ /
svasthāne sthiratām eti pavano manasā saha // 50 //

As the air, in and out of the body, remains unmoved, so the breath along with mind becomes steady in its place (i.e., in Brahmarandhra).

evam abhyasamānasya vāyumārge divāniśam /
abhyāsāj jīryate vāyur manas tatraiva līyate //51 //

By thus practising night and day, the breathing is brought under control, and, as the practice increases, the mind becomes calm and steady.

amṛtaiḥ plāvayed deham āpādatalamastakam /
siddhyatyeva mahākāyo mahābalaparākramaḥ // 52 //
iti khecarī /

By rubbing the body over with Amṛta (exuding from the Moon), from head to foot, one gets Mahākāya, i.e., great strength and energy.

End of Khecarī

***

śaktimadhye manaḥ kṛtvā śaktiṁ mānasamadhyagām /
manasā mana ālokya tad dhyāyet paramaṁ padam // 53 //

Placing the mind into Kuṇḍalinī, and getting the latter in mind, by looking upon mind with mind (reflexively), the Parama Pada (Brahma) should be obtained.

khamadhye kuru cātmānam ātmamadhye ca khaṁ kuru /
sarvaṁ ca khamayaṁ kṛtvā na kiñcid api cintayet // 54 //

Keep the ātmā inside Kha (Brahma) and place Brahma inside your Ātmā. Having made everything pervaded with Kha (Brahma), think of nothing else.

antaḥ śūnyo bahiḥ śūnyaḥ śūnyaḥ kumbha ivāmbare /
antaḥ pūrṇo bahiḥ pūrṇaḥ pūrṇaḥ kumbha ivārṇave // 55 //

One should become void in and void out, and void like a pot in the space and full in and full outside, like a jar in the ocean.

bāhyacintā na kartavyā tathaivāntaracintanam /
sarvacintāṁ parityajya na kiñcid api cintayet // 56 //

He should think neither of his inside nor of outside world; and, leaving all thoughts, he should think of nothing.

saṅkalpamātrakalanaiva jagat samagram /
saṅkalpamātrakalanaiva manovilāsaḥ /
saṅkalpamātramatim utsṛja nirvikalpam //
āśritya niścayam avāpnuhi rāma śāntim // 57 //

The whole of this world and all the schemes of the mind are but the creations of thought. Discarding these thoughts and taking leave of all conjectures, O Rāma, obtain peace.

karpūram anale yadvat saindhavaṁ salile yathā /
tathā sandhīyamānaṁ ca manastattve vilīyate // 58 //

As camphor disappears in fire, and salt in water, so the mind united with the Ātmā loses its identity.

jñeyaṁ sarvaṁ pratītaṁ ca jñānaṁ ca mana ucyate /
jñānaṁ jñeyaṁ samaṁ naṣṭaṁ nānyaḥ panthā dvitīyakaḥ // 59 //

When the knowable, and knowledge both are destroyed equally, then there is no second way (i.e., duality is destroyed).

manodṛśyam idaṁ sarvaṁ yatkiñcit sacarācaram /
manaso hyunmanībhāvād dvaitaṁ naivopalabhyate // 60 //

All this movable and immovable world is mind. When the mind has attained to the *Unmanī Avasthā*, there is no Dvaita (duality).

jñeyavastuparityāgād vilayaṁ yāti mānasam /
manaso vilaye jāte kaivalyam avaśiṣyate // 61 //

Mind disappears by removing the knowable, and, on its disappearance, Ātmā alone remains behind.

evaṁ nānāvidhopāyāḥ samyak svānubhavānvitāḥ /
samādhimārgāḥ kathitāḥ pūrvācāryair mahātmabhiḥ // 62 //

The high-souled Ācāryas (Teachers) of yore gained experience in the various methods of Samādhi themselves, and then they preached them to others.

suṣumṇāyai kuṇḍalinyai sudhāyai candrajanmane /
manonmanyai namastubhyaṁ mahāśaktyai cidātmane// 63 //

Salutions to Thee, O Suṣumṇā; to Thee, O Kuṇḍalinī; to Thee, O Sudhā, born of Candra; to Thee, O Manonmanī; to Thee, O great power, energy and the intelligent spirit.

aśakyatattvabodhānāṁ mūḍhānām api sammatam /
proktaṁ gorakṣanāthena nādopāsanam ucyate // 64 //

I will describe now the practice of Anāhata Nāda, as propounded by Gorakṣa Nātha, for the benefit of those who are unable to know the reality—a method which is liked by the ignorant also.

śrīādināthena sapādakoṭilayaprakārāḥ kathitā jayanti /
nādānusandhānakam ekam eva manyāmahe mukhyatamaṁ layānām//65//

Ādinātha propounded 1 1/4 crore methods of Laya (trance), and they are all extant. Of these, the hearing of the Anāhata Nāda is the only principal one, in my opinion.

muktāsane sthito yogī mudrāṁ sandhāya śāmbhavīm /
sṛṇuyād dakṣiṇe karṇe nādam antastham ekadhīḥ // 66 //

Sitting in Mukta Āsana and adopting the Śāmbhavī Mudrā, the Yogī should hear the sound inside his right ear, with collected mind.

śravaṇapuṭanayanayugalaghrāṇamukhānāṁ nirodhanaṁ kāryam /
śuddhasuṣumṇāsaraṇau sphuṭam amalaḥ śrūyate nādaḥ // 67 //

The ears, the eyes, the nose, and the mouth should be closed and then the clear sound is heard in the passage of Suṣumṇā which has been cleansed of all its impurities.

ārambhaś ca ghaṭaś caiva tathā paricayo' pi ca /
niṣpattiḥ sarvayogeṣu syād avasthācatuṣṭayam // 68 //

In all the Yogas there are four states : (1) Ārambha or the preliminary, (2) Ghaṭa or the state of a jar, (3) Paricaya (known) and (4) Niṣpatti (consummate).

Ārambhāvasthā

athārambhāvasthā :
brahmagranther bhaved bhedād ānandaḥ śūnyasaṁbhavaḥ /
vicitraḥ kvaṇako dehe'nāhataḥ śrūyate dhvaniḥ // 69 //

When the Brahma-granthi (in the heart) is pierced through by Prāṇāyāma, then a sort of joy is experienced in the vacuum of the heart, and the Anāhata sounds, like various tinkling sounds of ornaments, are heard inside the body.

divyadehaś ca tejasvī divyagandhas tvarogavān /
saṁpūrṇahṛdayaḥ śūnya ārambhe yogavān bhavet // 70 //

In the Ārambha state the Yogi's body becomes divine, glowing and healthy, and it emits a divine smell. The whole of his heart becomes void.

Ghaṭāvasthā

atha ghaṭāvasthā :
dvitīyāyāṁ ghaṭīkṛtya vāyur bhavati madhyagaḥ /
dṛḍhāsano bhaved yogī jñānī devasamas tadā // 71 //

In the second state, the airs are united into one and begin moving in the middle channel. The Yogī's posture becomes firm, and he becomes wise like a god.

viṣṇugranthes tato bhedāt paramānandasūcakaḥ /
atiśūnye vimardaś ca bherīśabdas tadā bhavet // 72 //

By this means the Viṣṇu knot (in the throat)is pierced, which is indicated by highest bliss experienced, and then the Bherī sound (like the beating of a kettle-drum) is heard in the vacuum in the throat.

Paricayāvasthā

atha paricayāvasthā :
tṛtīyāyāṁ tu vijñeyo vihāye mardaladhvaniḥ /
mahāśūnyaṁ tadā yāti sarvasiddhisamāśrayam // 73 //

In the third state, the sound of a drum is known to arise in the Śūnya between the eyebrows, and then the Vāyu goes to the Mahāśūnya, which is the abode of all the Siddhis.

cittānandaṁ tadā jitvā sahajānandasaṁbhavaḥ /
doṣaduḥkhajarāvyādhikṣudhānidrāvivarjitaḥ // 74 //

Conquering, then, the pleasures of the mind, ecstasy is spontaneously produced, which is devoid of evils, pains, old age, disease, hunger and sleep.

rudragranthiṁ yadā bhitvā śarvapīṭhagato'nilaḥ /
niṣpattau vaiṇavaḥ śabdaḥ kvaṇadvīṇākvaṇo bhavet // 75 //

When the Rudra-granthi is pierced and the air enters the seat of the Lord (the space between the eyebrows), then the perfect sound like that of a flute is produced.

ekībhūtaṁ tadā cittaṁ rājayogābhidhānakam /
sṛṣṭisaṁhārakartāsau yogīśvarasamo bhavet // 76 //

The union of the mind and the sound is called Rājayoga. The (real) Yogī becomes the creator and the destroyer of the universe, like God.

astu vā māstu vā muktir atraivākhaṇḍitaṁ sukham /
layodbhavam idaṁ saukhyaṁ rājayogād avāpyate // 77 //

Perpetual joy is achieved by this; the Yogī does not care if Mukti be attained or not. This joy, resulting from absorption (in Brahma), is obtained by means of Rājayoga.

rājayogam ajānantaḥ kevalaṁ haṭhakarmiṇaḥ /
etān abhyāsino manye prayāsaphalavarjitān // 78 //

Those who are ignorant of Rājayoga and practise only Haṭhayoga, will, in my opinion, waste their energy fruitlessly.

unmanyavāptaye śīghraṁ bhrūdhyānaṁ mama sammatam /
rājayogapadaṁ prāptaṁ sukhopāyo'lpacetasām //
sadya ānandasandhāyī jāyate nādajo layaḥ // 79 //

Contemplation on the space between the eyebrows is, in my opinion, best for accomplishing soon the Unmanī state. For people of small intellect, it is a very easy method for obtaining perfection in Rājayoga. The Laya produced by Nāda, at once gives experience (of spiritual powers).

nādānusandhānasamādhibhājāṁ yogīśvarāṇāṁ hṛdi vardhamānam /
ānandam ekaṁ vacasām agamyaṁ jānāti taṁ śrīgurunātha ekaḥ // 80 //

The joy which increases in the hearts of Yogīśvaras who have gained success in Samādhi by means of attention to Nāda, is beyond description, and is known to Śrī Guru Nātha alone.

karṇau pidhāya hastābhyāṁ yaṁ śṛṇoti dhvaniṁ muniḥ /
tatra cittaṁ sthirīkuryād yāvat sthirapadaṁ vrajet // 81 //

The sound which a Muni hears by closing his ears with his fingers, should be heard attentively, till the mind becomes steady in it.

abhyasyamāno nādo'yaṁ bāhyam āvṛṇute dhvanim /
pakṣād vīkṣepam akhilaṁ jitvā yogī sukhī bhavet // 82 //

By practising with this Nāda, all other external sounds are stopped. The Yogī becomes happy by overcoming all distractions within fifteen days.

śrūyate prathamābhyāse nādo nānāvidho mahān /
tato'bhyāse vardhamāne śrūyate sūkṣmasūkṣmakaḥ // 83 //

In the beginning, the sounds heard are of great variety and very loud; but, as the practice advances, they become more and more subtle.

ādau jaladhijīmūtabherījharjharasambhavāḥ /
madhye mardalaśaṅkhotthā ghaṇṭākāhalajās tathā // 84 //

In the first stage, the sounds are surging, thundering like the beating of kettle-drums and jingling ones. In the intermediate stage, they are like those produced by a conch, Mṛdaṅga, bells, &c.

ante tu kiṅkiṇīvaṁśavīṇābhramaranihsvanāḥ /
iti nānāvidhā nādāḥ śrūyante dehamadhyagāḥ // 85 //

In the last stage, the sounds resemble those produced by tinklets, flute, Vīṇā, bee, &c. These various kinds of sounds are heard as being produced in the body.

mahati śrūyamāṇe'pi meghabheryādike dhvanau /
tatra sūkṣmāt sūkṣmataraṁ nādam eva parāmṛśet // 86 //

Though hearing loud sounds like those of thunder, kettle-drums, etc., one should practise with the subtle sounds also.

ghanam utsṛjya vā sūkṣme sūkṣmam utsṛjya vā ghane /
ramamāṇaṁ api kṣiptam mano nānyatra cālayet // 87 //

Leaving the loudest, and taking up the subtle one, and leaving the subtle one and taking up the loudest: practising thus, the distracted mind does not wander elsewhere.

yatrakutrāpi vā nāde lagati prathamaṁ manaḥ /
tatraiva susthirībhūya tena sārdhaṁ vilīyate // 88 //

Wherever the mind attaches itself first, it becomes steady there; and then it becomes absorbed in it.

makarandaṁ piban bhṛṅgo gandhaṁ nāpekṣate yathā /
nādāsaktaṁ tathā cittaṁ viṣayān nahi kāṅkṣate // 89 //

Just as a bee, drinking sweet juice, does not care for the smell of the flower, so the mind, absorbed in the Nāda, does not wish for objects of enjoyment.

manomattagajendrasya viṣayodyānacāriṇaḥ /
niyamane samartho'yaṁ ninādaniśitāṅkuśaḥ // 90 //

The mind, like an elephant used to wander in the garden of enjoyments, is capable of being controlled by the sharp goad of Anāhata Nāda.

baddhaṁ tu nādabandhena manaḥ santyaktacāpalam /
prayāti sutarāṁ sthairyaṁ chinnapakṣaḥ khago yathā // 91 //

The mind, captivated in the snare of Nāda, gives up all its activity; and, like a bird with clipped wings, becomes calm at once.

sarvacintāṁ parityajya sāvadhānena cetasā /
nāda evānusandheyo yogasāmrājyam icchatā // 92 //

Those desirous of the kingdom of Yoga, should take to the practice of hearing the Anāhata Nāda, with mind collected and free from all cares.

nādo'ntaraṅgasāraṅgabandhane vāgurāyate /
antaraṅgakuraṅgasya vadhe vyādhāyate'pi ca // 93 //

Nāda is the snare for catching the mind; and, when it is caught like a deer, it can be killed also like it.

antaraṅgasya yamino vājinaḥ parighāyate /
nādopāstirato nityam avadhāryā hi yoginā // 94 //

Nāda is the bolt of the stable door for the horse (the minds of the Yogīs). A Yogī should determine to practise constantly the hearing of Nāda sounds.

baddhaṁ vimuktacāñcalyaṁ nādagandhakajāraṇāt /
manaḥ pāradam āpnoti nirālambākhyakhe'ṭanam // 95 //

The mind gets the properties of calcined mercury. When deprived of its unsteadiness it is calcined, combined with the sulphur of Nāda, and then it roams like it is in the supportless Ākāśa or Brahma.

nādaśravaṇataḥ kṣipram antaraṅgabhujaṅgamaḥ /
vismṛtya sarvam ekāgraḥ kutracin nahi dhāvati // 96 //

The mind is like a serpent, which forgetting all its unsteadiness by hearing the Nāda, does not run away anywhere.

kāṣṭhe pravartito vahniḥ kāṣṭhena saha śāmyati /
nāde pravartitaṁ cittaṁ nādena saha līyate // 97 //

The fire, catching firewood, is extinguished along with it (after burning it up); and so the mind also, fixed on the Nāda, becomes latent when it ceases.

ghaṇṭādiṇādasaktastabdhāntaḥkaraṇahariṇasya /
praharaṇam api sukaraṁ śarasandhānapravīṇaś cet // 98 //

The Antaḥkaraṇa (mind), like a deer, becomes absorbed and motionless on hearing the sounds of bells, etc., and then it is very easy for an expert archer to kill it.

anāhatasya śabdasya dhvanir ya upalabhyate /
dhvaner antargataṁ jñeyaṁ jñeyasyāntargataṁ manaḥ //
manas tatra layaṁ yāti tad viṣṇoḥ paramaṁ padam // 99 //

The knowable interpenetrates the Anāhata sound which is heard, and the mind interpenetrates the knowable. The mind becomes absorbed there, which is the seat of the all-pervading, almighty Lord.

tāvad ākāśasaṅkalpo yāvac chabdaḥ pravartate /
niḥśabdaṁ tat paraṁ brahma paramātmeti gīyate // 100 //

So long as the sounds continue, there is the idea of Ākāśa. When they disappear, then it is called Para Brahma, Paramātman.

yatkiñcin nādarūpeṇa śrūyate śaktireva sā /
yas tattvānto nirākāraḥ sa eva parameśvaraḥ // 101 //

Whatever is heard in the form of Nāda, is the Śakti (power). That which is formless, the final state of the Tattvas, is Parameśvara.

sarve haṭhalayopāyā rājayogasya siddhaye /
rājayogasamārūḍhaḥ puruṣaḥ kālavañcakaḥ // 102 //

All the methods of Haṭha are meant for gaining success in Rājayoga; for, the man, who is well-established in Rājayoga, overcomes death.

tattvaṁ bījaṁ haṭhaḥ kṣetram audāsīnyaṁ jalaṁ tribhiḥ /
unmanī kalpalatikā sadya eva pravartate // 103 //

Tattva is the seed, Haṭha the field, and indifference (Vairāgya) the water. By the action of these three, the creeper Unmanī thrives very rapidly.

sadā nādānusandhānāt kṣīyaṁte pāpasañcayāḥ /
nirañjane vilīyete niścitaṁ cittamārutau // 104 //

All the accumulations of sins are destroyed by always practising Nāda; and the mind and the airs do certainly become latent in the colourless (Paramātman).

śaṅkhadundubhinādaṁ ca na śṛṇoti kadācana /
kāṣṭhavaj jāyate deha unmanyavasthayā dhruvam // 105 //

Such a one does not hear the noise of conch and Dundubhi. Being in the Unmanī Avasthā, his body becomes like a piece of wood.

sarvāvasthāvinirmuktaḥ sarvacintāvivarjitaḥ /
mṛtavat tiṣṭhate yogī sa mukto nātra saṁśayaḥ // 106 //

There is no doubt that such a Yogī becomes free from all states, from all cares, and remains like one dead.

khādyate na ca kālena bādhyate na ca karmaṇā /
sādhyate na ca kenāpi yogī yuktaḥ samādhinā // 107 //

He is not devoured by death; is not bound by his actions. The Yogī who is engaged in Samādhi is overpowered by none.

na gandhaṁ na rasaṁ rūpaṁ na ca sparśaṁ na niḥsvanam /
nātmānaṁ na paraṁ vetti yogī yuktaḥ samādhinā // 108 //

The Yogī, absorbed in Samādhi, feels no smell, taste, colour, touch, or sound, nor is he conscious of his own self.

cittaṁ na suptaṁ no jāgrat smṛtivismṛtivarjitam /
na cāstam eti nodeti yasyāsau mukta eva saḥ // 109 //

He whose mind is neither sleeping, nor waking, neither remembering, nor forgetting, neither disappearing nor appearing, is liberated.

na vijānāti śītoṣṇaṁ na duḥkhaṁ na sukhaṁ tathā /
na mānaṁ nāpamānaṁ ca yogī yuktaḥ samādhinā // 110 //

He feels no heat, cold, pain, pleasure, respect or disrespect. Such a Yogī is absorbed in Samādhi.

svastho jāgradavasthāyāṁ suptavad yo'vatiṣṭhate /
niḥśvāsocchvāsahīnaś ca niścitaṁ mukta eva saḥ // 111 //

He who, though awake, appears like one sleeping, and is without inspiration and expiration, is certainly free.

avadhyaḥ sarvaśastrāṇām aśakyaḥ sarvadehinām /
agrāhyo mantrayantrāṇāṁ yogī yuktaḥ samādhinā // 112 //

The Yogī, absorbed in Samādhi, cannot be killed by any instrument, and is beyond the control of beings. He is beyond the reach of incantations and charms.

yāvan naiva praviśati caran māruto madhyamārge /
yāvad bindur na bhavati dṛḍhaprāṇavātaprabandhāt /

yāvad dhyāne sahajasadṛśaṁ jāyate naiva tattvam /
tāvaj jñānam vadati tad idaṁ dambhamithyāpralāpaḥ // 113 //

As long as the Prāṇa does not enter and flow into the middle channel and the Bindu does not become firm by the control of the movements of the Prāṇa, as long as the mind does not assume the form of Brahma without any effort in contemplation, so long all the talk of knowledge and wisdom is merely the nonsensical babbling of a mad man.

iti haṭhapradīpikāyāṁ samādhilakṣaṇaṁ nāma caturthopadeśaḥ //4//

End of Chapter 4, On Samādhi.

Section II

GHERAṆḌA-SAṀHITĀ

Chapter 1

On the Training of the Physical Body

Prathamopadeśaḥ

ādīśvarāya praṇamāmi tasmai yenopadiṣṭā haṭhayogavidyā/
virājate pronnatarājayogam āroḍhum icchor adhirohiṇīva //

Salutation

I bow to that Primeval Lord who taught in the beginning the science of Haṭha Yoga, a science that stands out as the first rung of the ladder that leads to the supreme heights of Rāja Yoga.

Note: The training of the body is the first step to the training of the mind. A healthy mind can exist only in a healthy body. Hence Haṭha Yoga or training of the body is the first step to the training of the mind or Rāja Yoga. Haṭha may be translated as "hard" or the training of or in Hardiness. Rāja in this connection may be translated as royal or softness, or training in royal graces or mental discipline.

Ghaṭasthayogakathanam

ekadā caṇḍakāpālir gatvā gheraṇḍakuṭṭiram /
praṇamya vinayād bhaktyā gheraṇḍaṁ paripṛcchati // 1//

Once Caṇḍakāpāli having gone to the cottage of Gheraṇḍa saluted him with reverence and devotion.

śrīcaṇḍakāpālir uvāca :

ghaṭasthayogaṁ yogeśa tattvajñānasya kāraṇam /
idānīṁ śrotum icchāmi yogeśvara vada prabho // 2//

Caṇḍakāpāli said :

O Master of Yoga ! I wish now to learn the Physical Discipline (Yoga), which leads to the knowledge of truth (Tattva-jñāna)

gheraṇḍa uvāca :

> *sādhu sādhu mahābāho yan māṁ tvaṁ paripṛcchasi /*
> *kathayāmi hi te vatsa sāvadhāno' vadhāraya // 3 //*

Gheraṇḍa replied :

Well asked, indeed, O mighty-armed one. I shall tell thee, O dear, what thou asked me. Attend to it carefully.

> *nāsti māyāsamaḥ pāśo nāsti yogāt paraṁ balam /*
> *nāsti jñānāt paro bandhur nāhaṅkārāt paro ripuḥ // 4 //*

There are no fetters like those of illusion (Māyā); no strength like that which comes from Yoga; there is no friend better than knowledge (Jñāna); and no enemy greater than Egoism (Ahaṅkāra).

> *abhyāsāt kādivarṇānāṁ yathā śāstrāṇi bodhayet /*
> *tathā yogaṁ samāsādya tattvajñānaṁ ca labhyate // 5//*

As by learning the alphabet one can master all the scriptures, so by thoroughly practising first the physical (Yoga), one acquires the Knowledge of Truth.

> *sukṛtair duṣkṛtaiḥ kāryair jāyate prāṇināṁ ghaṭaḥ /*
> *ghaṭād utpadyate karma ghaṭīyantraṁ yathā bhramet // 6//*

On account of good and bad deeds, the bodies of all animated beings are produced, and the bodies give rise to (Karma) (which leads to rebirth), and thus the circle is continued like that of a Persian Wheel.

> *ūrdhvādho bhramate yadvad ghaṭiyantraṁ gavāṁ vaśāt /*
> *tadvat karmavaśāj jīvo bhramate janmamṛtyubhiḥ // 7 //*

As the Persian Wheel in drawing water from a well goes up and down, moved by bullocks (filling and emptying the buckets again and again), so the soul passes through life and death moved by its deeds.

āmakumbha ivāmbhaḥstho jīryamāṇaḥ sadā ghaṭaḥ /
yogānalena saṁdahya ghaṭaśuddhiṁ samācaret // 8 //

Like an unbaked earthen pot thrown in water, the body is soon decayed (in this world). Bake it hard in the fire of Yoga in order to strengthen and purify the body.

The Seven Exercises

atha saptasādhanam :
śodhanaṁ dṛḍhatā caiva sthairyaṁ dhairyaṁ ca lāghavam /
pratyakṣaṁ ca nirliptaṁ ca ghaṭasya saptasādhanam // 9 //

The seven exercises which appertain to this training of the body are the following : Purification, strengthening, steadying, calming, and those leading to lightness, perception, and isolation.

atha saptasādhanalakṣaṇam :
ṣaṭkarmaṇā śodhanaṁ ca āsanena bhaved dṛḍham /
mudrayā sthiratā caiva pratyāhāreṇa dhīratā // 10//
prāṇāyāmāl lāghavaṁ ca dhyānāt pratyakṣam ātmanaḥ /
samādhinā nirliptaṁ ca muktir eva na saṁśayaḥ // 11 //

Purification is acquired by a regular performance of six acts (to be mentioned shortly); Āsana or posture gives Dṛḍhatā or strength; Mudrā gives Sthiratā or steadiness; Pratyāhāra gives Dhīratā or calmness; Prāṇāyāma gives lightness or Laghimā; Dhyāna gives perception (Pratyakṣa) of Self; and Samādhi gives isolation (Nirliptatā), which is verily the Freedom.

The Six Purificatory Acts

atha śodhanam :
dhautir vastis tathā netir laulikī trāṭakaṁ tathā /
kapālabhātiś caitāni ṣaṭkarmāṇi samācaret // 12 //

(1) Dhauti; (2) Vasti; (3) Neti; (4) Laulikī; (5) Trāṭaka; (6) Kapālabhāti are the Ṣaṭkarmas or six acts to be practised.

atha dhautiḥ :
antardhautir dantadhautir hṛddhautir mūlaśodhanam /
dhautiṁ caturvidhāṁ kṛtvā ghaṭaṁ kurvantu nirmalam // 13 //

Dhauti is of four kinds, which clear away the impurities of the body. They are : (i) Antardhauti (internal washing); (ii) Dantadhauti (cleaning the teeth); (iii) Hṛddhauti (cleaning the heart) and (iv) Mūlaśodhana (cleaning the rectum).

Antardhauti

atha antardhautiḥ :
vātasāraṁ vārisāraṁ vahnisāraṁ bahiṣkṛtam /
ghaṭasya nirmalārthāya hyantardhautiś caturvidhā // 14 //

Antardhauti is again sub-divided into four: Vātasāra (wind purification), Vārisāra (water purification), Vahnisāra (fire purification); and Bahiṣkṛta.

Vātasāra-dhauti

atha vātasāram :
kākacañcūvad āsyena pibed vāyuṁ śanaiḥ śanaiḥ /
cālayed udaraṁ paścādvartmanā recayec chanaiḥ // 15 //

Contract the mouth like the beak of a crow and draw the air in slowly, filling the stomach slowly with it; then move it therein, and slowly force it out through the lower passage.

vātasāraṁ paraṁ gopyaṁ dehanirmalakāraṇam /
sarvarogakṣayakaraṁ dehānalavivardhakam // 16 //

Vātasāra should be kept very secret; it causes purification of the body; it destroys all diseases and increases the gastric fire.

Vārisāra-dhauti

atha vārisāram :
ākaṇṭhaṁ pūrayed vāri vaktreṇa ca pibec chanaiḥ /
cālayed udareṇaiva codarād recayed adhaḥ // 17 //

Fill the mouth with water down to the throat, and then drink it slowly; then move it through the stomach, forcing it downwards and expelling it through the rectum.

vārisāraṁ paraṁ gopyaṁ dehanirmalakārakam /
sādhayet tat prayatnena devadehaṁ prapadyate // 18 //

This process should be kept very secret. It purifies the body. And by practising it with care, one gets a radiant body.

vārisāraṁ parāṁ dhautiṁ sādhayed yaḥ prayatnataḥ /
maladehaṁ śodhayitvā devadehaṁ prapadyate // 19 //

Vārisāra is the highest Dhauti. He who practises it carefully, purifies his filthy body and turns it into a radiant one.

Agnisāra-dhauti

atha agnisāram :
nābhigranthiṁ merupṛṣṭhe śatavāraṁ ca kārayet /
agnisāram iyaṁ dhautir yogināṁ yogasiddhidā /
udaryam āmayaṁ tyaktvā jāṭharāgniṁ vivardhayet // 20 //

Press in the navel knot or intestines towards the spine one hundred times. This is Agnisāra or fire process. It gives success in the practice of Yoga; it cures all the diseases of the stomach (gastric juice) and increases the internal fire.

eṣā dhautiḥ parā gopyā devānām api durlabhā /
kevalaṁ dhautimātreṇa devadeho bhaved dhruvam // 21 //

This form of Dhauti should be kept very secret, and it is hardly to be attained even by gods. By this Dhauti alone one certainly gets a radiant body.

Bahiṣkṛta-dhauti

atha bahiṣkṛtadhautiḥ :
kākīmudrāṁ sādhayitvā pūrayed udaraṁ marut /
dhārayed ardhayāmaṁ tu cālayed ardhavartmanā /
eṣā dhautiḥ parā gopyā na prakāśyā kadācana // 22 //

By *Kākacañcu* or crow-bill Mudrā fill the stomach with air, hold it there for one hour and a half, and then force it down towards the intestines. This Dhauti must be kept a great secret, and must not be revealed to anybody.

atha prakṣālanam :
nābhidaghne jale sthitvā śaktināḍīṁ visarjayet /
karābhyāṁ kṣālayen nāḍīṁ yāvan malavisarjanam /
tāvata prakṣālya nāḍīṁ ca udare veśayet punaḥ // 23 //

Then standing in navel-deep water, draw out the Śaktināḍī (long intestines), wash the Nāḍī with hand, and so long as its filth is not all washed away, wash it with care, and then draw it in again into the abdomen.

idaṁ prakṣālanaṁ gopyaṁ devānām api durlabham /
kevalaṁ dhautimātreṇa devadeho bhaved dhruvam // 24 //

This process should be kept secret. It is not easily to be attained even by the gods. Simply by this Dhauti one gets Deva-deha (godlike body).

atha bahiṣkṛtadhautiprayōgaḥ :
yāmārdhaṁ dhāraṇāṁ śaktiṁ yāvan na sādhayen naraḥ /
bahiṣkṛtā mahaddhautis tāvac caiva na jāyate // 25 //

As long as a person has not acquired the power of retaining the breath for an hour and a half (or retaining wind in the stomach for that period), so long he cannot achieve this grand Dhauti or purification, known as Bahiṣkṛtadhauti.

Danta-dhauti

atha dantadhautiḥ :
dantamūlaṁ jihvāmūlaṁ randhraṁ karṇayugasya ca /
kapālarandhraṁ pañcaite dantadhautiṁ pracakṣate // 26 //

Danta-Dhauti is of five kinds : purification of the teeth, of the root of the tongue, of the two holes of the ears, and of the frontal sinuses.

Danta-mūla-dhauti

atha dantamūladhautiḥ :
khādireṇa rasenātha mṛttikayā ca śuddhayā /
mārjayed dantamūlaṁ ca yāvat kilviṣam āharet // 27 //

Rub the teeth with catechu-powder or with pure earth, so long as dental impurities are not removed.

dantamūlaṁ parā dhautir yogināṁ yogasādhane /
nityaṁ kuryāt prabhāte ca dantarakṣāṁ ca yogavit /
dantamūlaṁ dhāvanādikāryeṣu yogināṁ matam // 28 //

This teeth-washing is a great Dhauti and an important process in the practice of Yoga for the Yogīs. It should be done daily in the morning by Yogīs in order to preserve the teeth. In purification this is approved by Yogīs.

Jihvā-Śodhana or Tongue-dhauti

atha jihvāśodhanaṁ :
athātaḥ saṁpravakṣyāmi jihvāśodhanakāraṇam /
jarāmaraṇarogādīn nāśayed dīrghalambikā // 29 //

I shall now tell you the method of cleansing the tongue. The elongation of the tongue destroys old age, death and disease.

atha jihvāmūladhautiprayogaḥ :
tarjanīmadhyamānāmākhyāṅgulitrayayogataḥ /
veśayed galamadhye tu mārjayel laṁbikāmalam /
śanaiḥ śanair mārjayitvā kaphadoṣaṁ nivārayet // 30 //

Join together the three fingers known as index, middle and ring finger, put them into the throat, and rub well and clean the root of the tongue, and by washing it again expel the phlegm.

mārjayen navanītena dohayec ca punaḥ punaḥ /
tadagraṁ lauhayantreṇa karṣayitvā śanaiḥ śanaiḥ // 31 //

Having thus washed it, rub it with butter, and squeeze it again and again, after holding the tip of the tongue with an iron instrument and pulling it out slowly.

nityaṁ kuryāt prayatnena raver udayake' stake /
evaṁ kṛte ca nityaṁ sā lambikā dīrghatāṁ vrajet // 32 //

Do this daily with diligence before the rising and setting of the sun. By so doing the tongue becomes elongated.

Karṇa-dhauti or Ear-cleaning

atha karṇadhautiprayogaḥ :
tarjanyanāmikāyogān mārjayet karṇarandhrayoḥ /
nityam abhyāsayogena nādāntaraṁ prakāśayet // 33 //

Clean the two holes of the ears by index and ring fingers. By practising it daily, the mystical sounds are heard.

Kapāla-randhra-dhauti

atha kapālarandhraprayogaḥ :
vṛddhāṅguṣṭhena dakṣeṇa mārjayed bhālarandhrakam /
evam abhyāsayogena kaphadoṣaṁ nivārayet // 34 //

Rub with the thumb of right hand the depression in the forehead near the bridge of nose. By the practice of this Yoga, diseases arising from derangements of phlegmatic humours are cured.

nāḍī nirmalatāṁ yāti divyadṛṣṭiḥ prajāyate /
nidrānte bhojanānte ca divānte ca dine dine // 35 //

The vessels become purified and clairvoyance is induced. This should be practised daily after awakening from sleep, after meals, and in the evening.

Hṛd-dhauti

atha hṛddhautiḥ :
hṛddhautiṁ trividhāṁ kuryād daṇḍavamanavāsasā // 36 //

Hṛd-dhauti, or purification of heart (or rather throat) is of three kinds, viz., by Daṇḍa (a stick), Vamana (vomiting), and by Vastra (cloth).

atha daṇḍadhautiḥ :
rambhādaṇḍaṁ hariddaṇḍaṁ vetradaṇḍam tathaiva ca /
hṛnmadhye cālayitvā tu punaḥ pratyāharec chanaiḥ // 37 //

Take either a plantain stalk or a stalk of turmeric (Haridrā) or one of cane, and thrust it slowly into the oesophagus and then draw it out slowly.

kaphaṁ pittaṁ tathā kledaṁ recayed ūrdhvavartmanā /
daṇḍadhautividhānena hṛdrogaṁ nāśayed dhruvam//38 //

By this process all the phlegm, bile and other impurities are expelled out of the mouth. By this Daṇḍa-dhauti every kind of heart-disease is surely cured.

Vamana-dhauti

atha vamanadhautiḥ :
bhojanānte pibed vāri cākaṇṭhapūritaṁ sudhīḥ /
ūrdhvāṁ dṛṣṭiṁ kṣaṇaṁ kṛtvā taj jalaṁ vamayet punaḥ /
nityam abhyāsayogena kaphapittaṁ nivārayet // 39 //

After meal, let the wise practitioner drink water full up to the throat; then looking for a short while upwards, let him vomit it out again. By daily practising this Yoga disorders of phlegm and bile are cured.

Vastra-dhauti

atha vāsodhautiḥ :
caturaṅgulavistāraṁ sūkṣmavastraṁ śanair graset /
punaḥ pratyāhared etat procyate dhautikarmakam // 40 //

Let him swallow slowly a thin cloth, four fingers wide; then let him draw it out again. This is called Vastra-dhauti.

gulmajvaraplīhākuṣṭhakaphapittaṁ vinaśyati /
ārogyaṁ balapuṣṭiś ca bhavet tasya dine dine // 41 //

This cures Gulma or abdominal diseases, fever, enlarged spleen, leprosy and other skin diseases and disorders of phlegm and bile, and day by day the practitioner gets health, strength, and cheerfulness.

Mūla-śodhana, or Purification of the Rectum

atha mūlaśodhanaṁ :
apānakrūratā tāvad yāvan mūlaṁ na śodhayet /
tasmāt sarvaprayatnena mūlaśodhanam ācaret // 42 //

The Apānavāyu does not flow freely so long as the rectum is not purified. Therefore with the greatest care let him practise this purification of the large intestine.

pittamūlasya daṇḍena madhyamāṅgulinā' pi vā /
yatnena kṣālayed guhyaṁ vāriṇā ca punaḥ punaḥ // 43 //

By a stalk of the root of Haridrā (turmeric) or the middle finger, the rectum should be carefully cleansed with water over and over again.

vārayet koṣṭhakāṭhinyam āmajīrṇam nivārayet /
kāraṇaṁ kāntipuṣṭyoś ca vahnimaṇḍaladīpanam // 44 //

This destroys constipation, indigestion, and dyspepsia, and increases the beauty and vigour of the body and kindles the gastric fire.

Vastis

atha vastiprakaraṇam :
jalavastiḥ śuṣkavastir vastiḥ syād dvividhā smṛtā /
jalavastiṁ jale kuryāc chuṣkavastiṁ sadā kṣitau // 45 //

Vasti is described of two kinds, viz. Jala Vasti (or water Vaṣti) and Śuṣka Vasti (or dry Vasti). Water vasti is done in water and dry Vasti always on land.

Jala-vasti

atha jalavastiḥ :
nābhimagnajale pāyuṁ nyastavān utkaṭāsanam /
ākuñcanaṁ prasārañ ca jalavastim samācaret // 46 //

Entering water up to the navel and assuming the posture called Utkaṭāsana, let him contract and dilate the sphincter-muscle of the anus. This is called Jala-vasti.

pramehañ ca udāvartaṁ krūravāyuṁ nivārayet /
bhavet svacchandadehaś ca kāmadevasamo bhavet // 47 //

This cures Prameha(urinary disorders), Udāvarta(disorders of digestion) and Krūravāyu (disorders of the wind). The body becomes free from all diseases and becomes as beautiful as that of Cupid.

Sthala-vasti

atha sthalavastiḥ :
vastiṁ paścimottānena cālayitvā śanair adhaḥ /
aśvinīmudrayā pāyum ākuñcayet prasārayet // 48 //

Assuming the posture called Paścimottāna, let him move the intestines slowly downwards, then contract and dilate the sphincter-muscle of the anus with Aśvinī-Mudrā.

evam abhyāsayogena koṣṭhadoṣo na vidyate /
vivardhayej jāṭharāgnim āmavātaṁ vināśayet // 49 //

By this practice of Yoga, constipation never occurs, and it increases gastric fire and cures flatulence.

Neti

atha netiyogaḥ :
vitastimānaṁ sūkṣmasūtraṁ nāsānāle praveśayet /
mukhān nirgamayet paścāt procyate netikarmakam // 50 //

Take a thin thread, measuring half a cubit, and insert it into the nostrils, and passing it through, pull it out by the mouth. This is called Neti-kriyā.

sādhanān netikāryasya khecarīsiddhim āpnuyāt /
kaphadoṣā vinaśyanti divyadṛṣṭiḥ prajāyate // 51 //

By practising the Neti-kriyā, one obtains Khecarī Siddhi. It destroys the disorders of phlegm and produces clairvoyance or clear sight.

Laulikī-yoga

atha laulikīyogaḥ :
amandavegena tundaṁ tu bhrāmayed ubhapārśvayoḥ /
sarvarogān nihantīh dehānalavivardhanam // 52 //

With great force move the stomach and intestines from one side to the other. This is called Laulikī-yoga. This destroys all diseases and increases the bodily fire.

Trāṭaka

atha trāṭakam :
nimeṣonmeṣakaṁ tyaktvā sūkṣmalakṣyam nirīkṣayet /
patanti yāvad aśrūṇi trāṭakaṁ procyate budhaiḥ // 53 //

Gaze steadily without winking at any small object, until tears begin to flow. This is called Trāṭaka by the wise.

evam abhyāsayogena śāmbhavī jāyate dhruvam /
netrarogā vinaśyanti divyadṛṣṭiḥ prajāyate // 54 //

By practising this Yoga, Śāmbhavī Siddhi is obtained; and certainly all diseases of the eye are destroyed and clairvoyance is induced.

Kapālabhāti

atha kapālabhātiḥ :
vāmakrameṇa vyutkrameṇa śītkrameṇa viśeṣataḥ /
bhālabhātiṁ tridhā kuryāt kaphadoṣaṁ nivārayet // 55 //

Kapālabhāti is of three kinds : Vāma-krama, Vyut-krama, and Śīt-krama. They destroy disorders of phlegm.

Vāma-krama

atha vāmakramakapālabhātiḥ :
iḍayā pūrayed vāyuṁ recayet piṅgalayā punaḥ /
piṅgalayā pūrayitvā punaś candreṇa recayet // 56 //

Draw the wind through the left nostril and expel it through the right, and draw it again through the right and expel it through the left.

pūrakaṁ recakaṁ kṛtvā vegena na tu cālayet /
evaṁ abhyāsayogena kaphadoṣaṁ nivārayet // 57 //

This inspiration and expiration must be done without any force. This practice destroys disorders of phlegm.

Vyut-krama

atha vyutkramakapālabhātiḥ :
nāsābhyāṁ jalam ākṛṣya punar vaktreṇa recayet /
pāyaṁ pāyaṁ vyutkrameṇa śleṣmadoṣaṁ nivārayet // 58 //

Draw water through the two nostrils and expel it through the mouth very slowly. This is called Vyut-krama which destroys disorders of phlegm.

Śīt-krama

atha śītkramakapālabhātiḥ :
śītkṛtya pītvā vaktreṇa nāsānālair virecayet /
evam abhyāsayogena kāmadevasamo bhavet // 59 //

Suck water noisily through the mouth and expel it through the nostrils. By this Yoga practice one becomes like Cupid.

na jāyate vārdhakaṁ ca jvaro naiva prajāyate /
bhavet svacchandadehaś ca kaphadoṣaṁ nivārayet // 60 //

Old age never comes to him and fever never touches him. The body becomes healthy and elastic, and disorders of phlegm are destroyed.

iti śrīgheraṇḍasaṁhitāyāṁ gheraṇḍacaṇḍasaṁvāde
ṣaṭkarmasādhanaṁ nāma prathamopadeśaḥ //1//

End of Chapter 1, On The Training of the Physical Body.

CHAPTER 2

The Āsanas or Postures

Dvitīyopadeśaḥ

gheraṇḍa uvāca :

āsanāni samastāni yāvanto jīvajantavaḥ /
caturaśītilakṣāṇi śivena kathitāni ca // 1 //

Gheraṇḍa Said :

There are eighty-four hundred thousand Āsanas described by Śiva. The postures are as many in number as there are species of living creatures in this universe.

teṣāṁ madhye viśiṣṭāni ṣoḍaśonaṁ śataṁ kṛtaṁ /
teṣāṁ madhye martyaloke dvātriṁśad āsanaṁ śubhaṁ // 2//

Among them eighty-four are the best; and among these eighty-four, thirty-two have been found useful for mankind in this world.

atha āsanānāṁ bhedāḥ:
siddhaṁ padmaṁ tathā bhadraṁ muktaṁ vajraṁ ca svastikam /
siṁhaṁ ca gomukhaṁ vīraṁ dhanurāsanameva ca // 3 //
mṛtaṁ guptaṁ tathā mātsyaṁ matsyendrāsanameva ca /
gorakṣaṁ paścimottānaṁ utkaṭaṁ saṅkaṭaṁ tathā // 4 //
mayūraṁ kukkuṭaṁ kūrmaṁ tathā cottānakūrmakam /
uttānamaṇḍūkaṁ vṛkṣaṁ maṇḍūkaṁ garuḍaṁ vṛṣam // 5 //
śalabhaṁ makaraṁ coṣṭraṁ bhujaṅgaṁ yogam āsanam /
dvātriṁśad āsanānāṁ tu martyaloke hi siddhidaṁ // 6 //

Different Kinds of Postures

The thirty-two Āsanas that give perfection in this mortal world are the following:

1. Siddha(Perfect posture)
2. Padma(Lotus posture)
3. Bhadra(Gentle posture)
4. Mukta(Free posture)
5. Vajra (Adamant posture)
6. Svastika(Prosperous posture)
7. Siṁha(Lion posture)
8. Gomukha (Cow-mouth posture)
9. Vīra(Heroic posture)
10. Dhanur (Bow posture)
11. Mṛta(Corpse posture)
12. Gupta(Hidden posture)
13. Matsya(Fish posture)
14. Matsendra
15. Gorakṣa
16. Paścimottāna
17. Utkaṭa (Hazardous posture)
18. Saṅkaṭa(Dangerous posture)
19. Mayūra (Peacock posture)
20. Kukkuṭa(Cock posture)
21. Kūrma(Tortoise posture)
22. Uttāna Maṇḍūka
23. Uttāna Kūrmaka
24. Vṛkṣa (Tree posture)
25. Maṇḍūka(Frog posture)
26. Garuḍa(Eagle posture)
27. Vṛṣa (Bull posture)
28. Śalabha(Locust posture)
29. Makara (Dolphin posture)
30. Uṣṭra (Camel posture)
31. Bhujaṅga (Snake posture)
32. Yoga

atha āsanānāṁ prayogāḥ :

Siddhāsana

atha siddhāsanaṁ :
yonisthānakam aṅghrimūlaghaṭitam saṁpīḍya gulphetaraṁ
meḍhroparyatha sannidhāya cibukaṁ kṛtvā hṛdi sthāpitam /
sthāṇuḥ saṁyamitendriyo'caladṛśā paśyan bhruvor antaraṁ
hyetan mokṣakavāṭabhedanakaraṁ siddhāsanaṁ procyate//7//

A practitioner who has subdued his passions, having placed one heel at the anal aperture, should keep the other heel on the root of the generative organ; afterwards he should affix his chin upon the chest, and being quiet and straight, gaze at the spot between the two eyebrows. This is called Siddhāsana which leads to emancipation.

Padmāsana

atha padmāsanam :
vāmorūpari dakṣiṇaṁ hi caraṇaṁ saṁsthāpya vāmaṁ tathā
dakṣorūpari paścimena vidhinā kṛtvā karābhyāṁ dṛḍham/
aṅguṣṭhau hṛdaye nidhāya cibukaṁ nāsāgram ālokayed
etad vyādhivināśanakaraṁ padmāsanaṁ procyate// 8 //

Place the right foot on the left thigh and similarly the left one on the right thigh; also cross the hands behind the back and firmly catch hold of the great toes of feet so crossed. Place the chin on the chest and fix the gaze on the tip of the nose. This posture is called Padmāsana (or Lotus posture). This posture destroys all diseases.

Bhadrāsana

atha bhadrāsanam :
gulphau ca vṛṣaṇasyādho vyutkrameṇa samāhitaḥ /
pādāṅguṣṭhau karābhyāṁ ca dhṛtvā ca pṛṣṭhadeśataḥ//9//
jālandharaṁ samāsādya nāsāgram avalokayet /
bhadrāsanaṁ bhaved etat sarvavyādhivināśakam// 10//

Place the heels crosswise under the testes attentively; cross the hands behind the back and take hold of the great toes of the feet. Fix the gaze on the tip of the nose, having first adopted the Mudrā called Jālandhara. This is Bhadrāsana (or gentle posture) which destroys all sorts of diseases.

Muktāsana

atha muktāsanam :
pāyumūle vāmagulphaṁ dakṣagulphaṁ tathopari /
samakāyaśirogrīvaṁ muktāsanaṁ tu siddhidam // 11 //

Place the left heel at the root of the organ of generation and the right heel above that; keep the head and the neck straight with the body. This posture is called Muktāsana. It gives Siddhi(perfection).

Vajrāsana

atha vajrāsanam :
jaṅghābhyāṁ vajravat kṛtvā gudapārśve padāvubhau /
vajrāsanaṁ bhaved etad yogināṁ siddhidāyakam // 12 //

Make the thighs tight like adamant and place the legs by the two sides of the anus. This is called Vajrāsana. It gives psychic powers to the Yogī.

Svastikāsana

atha svastikāsanam :
jānūrvor antare kṛtvā yogī pādatale ubhe /
ṛjukāyaḥ samāsīnaḥ svastikaṁ tat pracakṣate // 13//

Drawing the legs and thighs together and placing the feet underneath them while keeping the body in its easy condition and sitting straight, constitute the posture called Svastikāsana.

Siṁhāsana

atha siṁhāsanam :
gulphau ca vṛṣaṇasyādho vyutkrameṇordhvatāṁ gatau /
citimūlau bhūmisaṁsthau kṛtvā ca jānunopari // 14 //
vyāttavaktro jalandhreṇa nāsāgram avalokayet /
siṁhāsanaṁ bhaved etat sarvavyādhivināśakam // 15 //

The two heels to be placed under the scrotum contrariwise (i.e., left heel on the right side and right heel on left side of it) and turned upwards, the knees to be placed on the ground, (and the hands placed on the knees,) mouth to be kept open; practising the Jālandhara Mudrā one should fix his gaze on the tip of the nose. This is Siṁhāsana(Lion posture), the destroyer of all diseases.

Gomukhāsana

atha gomukhāsanam :
pādau ca bhūmau saṁsthāpya pṛṣṭhapārśve niveśayet /
sthirakāyaṁ samāsādya gomukhaṁ gomukhākṛti // 16 //

The two feet to be placed on the ground, and the heels to be placed contrariwise under the buttocks; the body to be kept steady and the mouth raised, and sitting equably: this is called Gomukhāsana resembling the mouth of a cow.

Vīrāsana

atha vīrāsanam :
ekaṁ pādam athaikasmin vinyased ūrusaṁsthitam /
itarasmiṁstathā paścād vīrāsanam itīritam // 17 //

One foot (the right foot) is to be placed on the other (left) thigh, and the other foot to be turned backwards : This is called Vīrāsana(Hero posture).

Dhanurāsana

atha dhanurāsanam :
prasārya pādau bhuvi daṇḍarūpau
karau ca pṛṣṭhe dhṛtapādayugmam /
kṛtvā dhanurvatparivartitāṅgaṁ
nigadyate vai dhanurāsanaṁ tat // 18 //

Spreading the legs on the ground, straight like a stick, and catching hold of (the great toes of) the feet with the hands, and making the body bent like a bow, is called by Yogīs Dhanurāsana or Bow posture.

Mṛtāsana

atha mṛtāsanam :
uttānaṁ śavavad bhūmau śayanaṁ tu śavāsanam /
śavāsanaṁ śramaharaṁ cittaviśrāntikāraṇam // 19 //

Lying flat on the ground like a corpse is called Mṛtāsana (Corpse posture). This posture destroys fatigue, and quietens the agitation of the mind.

Guptāsana

atha guptāsanam :
jānūrvor antare pādau kṛtvā pādau ca gopayet /
pādopari ca saṁsthāpya gudaṁ guptāsanaṁ viduḥ // 20 //

Hide the two feet under the two knees, and place the anus on the feet. This is known as Guptāsana.

Matsyāsana

atha matsyāsanam :
muktapadmāsanaṁ kṛtvā uttānaśayanaṁ caret /
kūrparābhyāṁ śiro veṣṭyaṁ rogaghnaṁ mātsyam āsanam // 21 //

Make the Padmāsana-posture (as stated in verse 8) without the crossing of the arms; lie on the back, holding the head by the two elbows. This is Matsyāsana (Fish posture), the destroyer of diseases.

Matsyendrāsana

atha matsyendrāsanam :
udaraṁ paścimābhāsaṁ kṛtvā tiṣṭhatyayatnataḥ /
namritaṁ vāmapādaṁ hi dakṣajānūpari nyaset // 22 //
tatra yāmyaṁ kūrparañ ca vaktraṁ yāmyakare' pi ca /
bhruvor madhye gatā dṛṣṭiḥ pīṭhaṁ mātsyendram ucyate // 23//

Keeping the abdominal region at ease like the back, bending the left leg, place it on the right thigh; then place on this the elbow of the right hand, and place the face on the palm of the right hand, and fix the gaze between the eyebrows. This is called Matsyendrāsana.

Paścimottāna Āsana

atha paścimottānāsanam :
prasārya pādau bhuvi daṇḍarūpau
saṁnyastabhālaṁ citiyugmamadhye /
yatnena pādau ca dhṛtau karābhyāṁ
tat paścimottānam ihāsanaṁ syāt // 24 //

Spread the two legs on the ground, stiff like a stick(the heels not touching), and place the forehead on the two knees, and catch with the hands the toes. This is called Paścimottāna Āsana.

Gorakṣāsana

atha gorakṣāsanam :
jānūrvor antare pādau uttānau vyaktasaṁsthitau /
gulphau cācchādya hastābhyām uttānābhyāṁ prayatnataḥ // 25//
kaṇṭhasaṁkocanaṁ kṛtvā nāsāgram avalokayet /
gorakṣāsanam ityāh yogināṁ siddhikāraṇam // 26 //

Between the knees and the thighs, place the two feet turned upward and in a hidden way, the heels being carefully covered by the two hands outstretched; the throat being contracted, let one fix the gaze on the tip of the nose. This is called Gorakṣāsana. It gives success to Yogīs.

Utkaṭāsana

atha utkaṭāsanam :
aṅguṣṭhābhyām avaṣṭabhya dharāṁ gulphau ca khe gatau /
tatropari gudaṁ nyasya vijñeyam utkaṭāsanam // 27 //

Let the toes touch the ground, and the heels be raised in the air; place the anus on the heels: this is known as Utkaṭāsana.

Saṅkaṭāsana

atha saṅkaṭāsanam :
vāmapādaṁ citer mūlaṁ saṁnyasya dharaṇītale /
pādadaṇḍena yāmyena veṣṭayed vāmapādakam /
jānuyugme karayugmam etat saṅkaṭam āsanam // 28 //

Placing the left foot on the ground, surround the left foot by the right leg; and place the two hands on the two knees. This is Saṅkaṭāsana.

Mayūrāsana

atha mayūrāsanam :
dharām avaṣṭabhya karayos talābhyāṁ
tat kūrpare sthāpitanābhipārśvam /
uccāsano daṇḍavadutthitaḥ khe
māyūram etat pravadanti pīṭham // 29 //
bahu kadaśanabhuktam bhasma kuryād aśeṣaṁ
janayati jaṭharāgniṁ jārayet kālakūṭam /
harati sakalarogān āśu gulmajvarādīn
bhavati vigatadoṣaṁ hyāsanaṁ śrīmayūram // 30 //

Place the palms of the two hands on the ground, place the umbilical region on the two elbows, and stand upon the hands, the legs being raised in the air and crossed like Padmāsana. This is called Mayūrāsana (Peacock posture). It destroys the effects of unwholesome food; it produces heat in the stomach; it destroys the effects of deadly poisons; it easily cures diseases like Gulma and fever. Such is this useful posture.

Kukkuṭāsana

atha kukkuṭāsanam :
padmāsanaṁ samāsādya jānūrvor antare karau /
kūrparābhyāṁ samāsīna uccasthaḥ kukkuṭāsanam // 31 //

Sitting on the ground, cross the legs as in Padmāsana posture; thrust down the hands between the thighs and knees; stand on the hands, supporting the body on the elbows. This is Kukkuṭāsana (Cock posture).

Kūrmāsana

atha kūrmāsanam :
gulphau ca vṛṣaṇasyādho vyutkrameṇa samāhitau /
ṛjukāyaśirogrīvaṁ kūrmāsanam itīritam // 32 //

Place the heels contrariwise under the scrotum with the head, neck and body kept straight. This is called Kūrmāsana (Tortoise posture).

Uttānakūrmāsana

atha uttānakūrmāsanam :
kukkuṭāsanabandhasthaṁ karābhyāṁ dhṛtakandharam /
pīṭhaṁ kūrmavad uttānam etad uttānakūrmakam // 33 //

Assume the Cock posture (as stated in verse 31), catch hold of the neck with both hands, and stand stretched like a tortoise. This is Uttānakūrmāsana.

Maṇḍūkāsana

atha maṇḍūkāsanam :
pṛṣṭhadeśe pādatalāvaṅguṣṭhau dvau ca saṁspṛśet /
jānuyugmaṁ puraskṛtya sādhayen maṇḍukāsanam // 34 //

Carry the feet towards the back, the toes touching each other, and place the knees forwards. This is called Frog posture.

Uttānamaṇḍūkāsana

atha uttānamaṇḍūkāsanam :
maṇḍūkāśanamadhyasthaṁ kūrparābhyāṁ dhṛtaṁ śiraḥ /
etat bhekavad uttānam etad uttānamaṇḍukam // 35 //

Assume the Frog posture (as in verse 34), hold the head by the elbows, and stand up like a frog. This is called Uttānamaṇḍūkāsana.

Vṛkṣāsana

atha vṛkṣāsanam :
vāmorumūladeśe ca yāmyaṁ pādaṁ nidhāya tu /
tiṣṭhet tu vṛkṣavad bhūmau vṛkṣāsanam idaṁ viduḥ // 36 //

Stand straight on one leg(the left), bending the right leg, and placing the right foot on the root of the left thigh; standing thus like a tree on the ground, is called Tree posture.

Garuḍāsana

atha garuḍāsanam :
jaṅghorubhyāṁ dharāṁ pīḍya sthirakāyo dvijānunā /
jānūpari karadvandvaṁ garuḍāsanam ucyate // 37//

Place the legs and the thighs on the ground pressing it; steady the body with the two knees; place the two hands on the knees: this is called Garuḍa posture.

Vṛṣāsana

atha vṛṣāsanam :
yāmyagulphe pāyumūlaṁ vāmabhāge padetaram /
viparītaṁ spṛśed bhūmiṁ vṛṣāsanam idaṁ bhavet // 38 //

Rest the anus on the right heel; on the left of it place the left leg, crossing it opposite way; and touch the ground. This is Bull posture.

Śalabhāsana

atha śalabhāsanam :
adhyāsya śete karayugmavakṣā
ālambya bhūmiṁ karayos talābhyām /
pādau ca śūnye ca vitasti cordhvaṁ
vadanti pīṭham śalabhaṁ munīndrāḥ // 39 //

Lie on the ground face downwards, the two hands being placed on the chest, touching the ground with the palms, and raise the legs in the air one cubit high. This is called Locust posture.

Makarāsana

atha makarāsanam :
adhyāsya śete hṛdayaṁ nidhāya
bhūmau ca pādau pravisāryamāṇau /
śiraśca dhṛtvā karadaṇḍayugme
dehāgnikāraṁ makarāsanaṁ tat // 40 //

Lie on the ground face downwards, the chest touching the earth, the two legs being stretched; then catch the head with the two arms. This is Makarāsana, the increaser of the bodily heat.

Uṣṭrāsana

atha uṣṭrāsanam :
adhyāsya śete padayugmavyastaṁ
pṛṣṭhe nidhāyāpi dhṛtaṁ karābhyām /
ākuñcya samyag udarāsyagāḍham
auṣṭraṁ ca pīṭhaṁ yatayo vadanti // 41 //

Lie on the ground face downwards; turn up the legs and place them towards the back; catch the legs with the hands; and contract forcibly the mouth and the abdomen. This is called Camel posture.

Bhujaṅgāsana

atha bhujaṅgāsanam :
aṅguṣṭhanābhiparyantam adhobhūmau vininyaset /
karatalābhyāṁ dharāṁ dhṛtvā ūrdhvaśīrṣaḥ phaṇīva hi // 42 //
dehāgnir vardhate nityaṁ sarvarogavināśanam /
jāgarti bhujagī devī bhujaṅgāsanasādhanāt // 43 //

Let the body, from the navel downwards to the toes, touch the ground; place the palms on the ground and raise the head (the upper portion of the body) like a serpent. This is called Serpent posture. This always increases the bodily heat; destroys all diseases; and by the practice of this posture the Serpent-Goddess (the Kuṇḍalinī force) wakes up.

Yogāsana

atha yogāsanam :
uttānau caraṇau kṛtvā saṁsthāpyopari jānunoḥ /
āsanopari saṁsthāpya cottānaṁ karayugmakam // 44 //
pūrakair vāyum ākṛṣya nāsāgram avalokayet /
yogāsanaṁ bhaved etad yogināṁ yogasādhane // 45 //

Turn the feet upwards; place them on the knees; then place the hands on the ground with the palms turned upwards; inspire, and fix the gaze on the tip of the nose. This is called Yoga posture, assumed by Yogīs when practising Yoga.

iti śrīgheraṇḍasaṁhitāyāṁ gheraṇḍacaṇḍasaṁvāde
āsanaprayogo nāma dvitīyopadeśaḥ //2//

End of Chapter 2, on Āsanas or Postures.

CHAPTER 3

On Mudrās

Tṛtīyopadeśaḥ

gheraṇḍa uvāca :

mahāmudrā nabhomudrā uḍḍīyānaṁ jalandharam /
mūlabandhaṁ mahābandhaṁ mahāvedhaś ca khecarī//1//
viparītakarī yonir vajrolī śakticālanī /
taḍāgī māṇḍukī mudrā śāmbhavī pañcadhāraṇā// 2//
aśvinī pāśanī kākī mātaṅgī ca bhujaṅginī /
pañcaviṁśati mudrāś ca siddhidā iha yoginām // 3//

Gheraṇḍa said :
There are twenty-five Mudrās, the practice of which gives success to Yogīs. They are:

(1) Mahāmudrā, (2) Nabhomudrā, (3) Uḍḍīyāna, (4) Jālandhara, (5) Mūlabandha, (6) Mahābandha, (7) Mahāvedha, (8)Khecarī, (9) Viparītakarī, (10) Yoni, (11)Vajrolī, (12)Śakticālanī, (13) Taḍāgī, (14)Māṇḍukī, (15)Śāmbhavī, (16) Pañcadhāraṇā (five dhāraṇās), (21)Aśvinī, (22)Pāśinī, (23)Kākī, (24)Mātaṅgī and (25) Bhujaṅginī.

The Advantages of Practising Mudrās

atha mudrāṇāṁ phalakathanam :
mudrāṇāṁ paṭalaṁ devi kathitaṁ tava sannidhau /
yena vijñātamātreṇa sarvasiddhiḥ prajāyate // 4//
gopanīyaṁ prayatnena na deyaṁ yasyakasyacit /
prītidaṁ yoginām caiva durlabhaṁ marutām api // 5//

Maheśvara, when addressing his consort, has praised advantages of Mudrās in these words: "O Devi ! I have told you all the Mūdras; their knowledge leads to adeptship. It should be kept secret with great care, and should not be revealed indiscriminately to everyone. This gives happiness to the Yogīs, and is not to be easily attained by the Maruts (gods of air) even."

Mahāmudrā

atha mahāmudrākathanam :
pāyumūlaṁ vāmagulphe saṁpīḍya dṛḍhayatnataḥ /
yāmyapādaṁ prasāryātha kare dhṛtapadāṅgulaḥ // 6 //
kaṇṭhasaṁkocanaṁ kṛtvā bhruvor madhyaṁ nirīkṣayet /
mahāmudrābhidhā mudrā kathyate caiva sūribhiḥ // 7 //

Pressing carefully the anus by the left heel, stretch the right leg, and take hold of the great toe by the hand; contract the throat (not expelling the breath), and fix the gaze between the eyebrows. This is called Mahāmudrā by the wise.

Its benefits :

atha mahāmudrāphalakathanam :
kṣayakāsagudāvartaplīhājīrṇajvaraṁ tathā /
nāśayet sarvarogāṁś ca mahāmudrā ca sādhanāt // 8//

The practice of Mahāmudrā cures consumption, obstruction of bowels, enlargement of spleen, indigestion and fever—in fact it cures all diseases.

Nabhomudrā

atha nabhomudrākathanam :
yatra yatra sthito yogī sarvakāryeṣu sarvadā /
ūrdhvajihvaḥ sthiro bhūtvā dhārayet pavanaṁ sadā /
nabhomudrā bhaved eṣā yogināṁ roganāśinī // 9//

In whatever business a Yogī may be engaged, wherever he may be, let him always keep his tongue turned upwards (towards the soft palate), and restrain the breath. This is called Nabhomudrā; it destroys all the diseases of the Yogī.

Uḍḍīyānabandha

atha uḍḍīyānabandhaḥ :
udare paścimaṁ tānaṁ nābher ūrdhvaṁ tu kārayet /
uḍḍīnaṁ kurute yasmād aviśrāntaṁ mahākhagaḥ /
uḍḍīyānaṁ tvasau bandho mṛtyumātaṅgakesarī // 10//

Contract the bowels equally above and below the navel towards the back, so that the abdominal viscera may touch the back. He who practises this Uḍḍīyāna (Flying-up), without ceasing, conquers death. The Great Bird(Breath), by this process, is instantly forced up into Suṣumṇā, and flies (moves) constantly therein only.

Its benefits:

atha uḍḍīyānabandhasya phalakathanam :
samagrād bandhanād hyetad uḍḍīyānaṁ viśiṣyate /
uḍḍīyāne samabhyaste muktiḥ svābhāvikī bhavet // 11 //

Of all Bandhanas, this is the best. The complete practice of this makes emancipation easy.

Jālandharabandha

atha jālandharabandhakathanam :
kaṇṭhasaṁkocanaṁ kṛtvā cibukaṁ hṛdaye nyaset /
jālandhare kṛte bandhe ṣoḍaśādhārabandhanam /
jālandharamahāmudrā mṛtyoś ca kṣayakāriṇī // 12 //

Contracting the throat; place the chin on the chest. This is called Jālandhara. By this Bandha the sixteen Ādhāras are closed. This Mahāmudrā destroys death.

Its benefits :

atha jālandharabandhasya phalakathanam :
siddhaṁ jālandharaṁ bandhaṁ yoginām siddhidāyakam /
ṣaṇmāsam abhyased yo hi sa siddho nātra saṁśayaḥ // 13//

Jālandhara is a success-giving and well-tried Bandha. He who practises it for six months, becomes an adept without doubt.

Mūlabandha

atha mūlabandhakathanam :
pārṣṇinā vāmapādasya yonim ākuñcayet tataḥ /
nābhigranthiṁ merudaṇḍe saṁpīḍya yatnataḥ sudhīḥ // 14 //
meḍhraṁ dakṣiṇagulphe tu dṛḍhabandhaṁ samācaret /
jarāvināśinī mudrā mūlabandho nigadyate // 15 //

Press with the heel of the left foot the region between the anus and the scrotum, and contract the rectum; carefully press the intestines near the navel on the spine, and put the right heel on the organ of generation. This is called Mūlabandha, the destroyer of decay.

Its benefits :

atha mūlabandhasya phalakathanam :
saṁsārasamudraṁ tartum abhilaṣati yaḥ pumān/
virale sugupto bhūtvā mudrām etāṁ samabhyaset // 16 //
abhyāsād bandhanasyāsya marutsiddhir bhaved dhruvam
sādhayed yatnato tarhi maunī tu vijitālasaḥ // 17 //

Let a person who desires to cross the ocean of birth and death, go to a secluded place, and practise in secrecy this Mudrā. By the practice of it, Vāyu (Prāṇa)is controlled undoubtedly. Let one silently practise this without laziness and with care.

Mahābandha

atha mahābandhakathanam :
vāmapādasya gulphena pāyumūlaṁ nīrodhayet /
dakṣapādena tadgulphaṁ sampīḍya yatnataḥ sudhīḥ // 18 //
śanaiḥ śanaiś cālayet pārṣṇiṁ yoniṁ ākuñcayec chanaīḥ /
jālandhare dhārayet prāṇaṁ mahābandho nigadyate // 19 //

Close the anal orifice with the heel of the left foot; press that heel with the right foot carefully; move slowly the musçles of the rectum; and slowly contract the muscles of the Yoni or perineum (space between anus and scrotum); restrain the breath by Jālandhara. This is called Mahābandha.

Its benefits :

atha mahābandhasya phalakathanam :
mahābandhaḥ paro bandho jarāmaraṇanāśanaḥ /
prasādād asya bandhasya sādhayet sarvavāñchitam //20 //

Mahābandha is the greatest Bandha; it destroys decay and death. By virtue of this Bandha a man accomplishes all his desires.

Mahāvedha

atha mahāvedhakathanam :
rūpayauvanalāvaṇyaṁ nārīṇāṁ puruṣaṁ vinā /
mūlabandhamahābandhau mahāvedhaṁ vinā tathā // 21//

mahābandhaṁ samāsādya uḍḍānakumbhakaṁ caret /
mahāvedhaḥ samākhyāto yogināṁ siddhidāyakaḥ // 22 //

As the beauty, youth and charms of women are in vain without men, so are Mūlabandha and Mahābandha without Mahāvedha. Sit first in Mahābandha posture; then restrain breath by Uḍḍāna Kumbhaka. This is called Mahāvedha—the giver of success to Yogīs.

Its benefits :

atha mahāvedhasya phalakathanam :
mahābandhamūlabandhau mahāvedhasamanvitau /
pratyahaṁ kurute yastu sa yogī yogavittamaḥ // 23//
na mṛtyuto bhayaṁ tasya na jarā tasya vidyate /
gopanīyaḥ prayatnena vedho' yaṁ yogipuṅgavaiḥ // 24 //

A Yogī who daily practises Mahābandha and Mūlabandha, accompanied with Mahāvedha, is the best of Yogīs. For him there is no fear of death, and decay does not approach him : this Vedha should be kept carefully secret by Yogīs.

Khecarīmudrā

atha khecarīmudrākathanam :
jihvādho nāḍīṁ saṁchinnāṁ rasanāṁ cālayet sadā /
dohayen navanītena lauhayantreṇa karṣayet // 25 //

Cut down the lower tendon of the tongue; and move the tongue constantly; rub it with fresh butter; and draw it out (to lengthen it)with an iron instrument.

N.B.: This is the preliminary to Khecarī Mudrā. Its object is so to lengthen the tongue, that when drawn out it may touch with its tip the space between the eyebrows. This can be done by cutting away the lower tendon. It takes about three years to cut away the whole tendon. I saw my Guru doing it in this wise. On every Monday he used to cut the tendon one-twelfth of an inch deep and sprinkle salt over it, so that the cut portions might not join together. Then rubbing the tongue with butter he used to pull it out. Peculiar iron instruments are employed for this purpose; the painful process is repeated every week till the tongue can be stretched out to the requisite length.

evaṁ nityaṁ samabhyāsāl lambikā dīrghatāṁ vrajet /
yāvad gacched bhruvor madhye tadā"gacchati khecarī // 26 //

By practising this always, the tongue becomes long, and when it reaches the space between the two eyebrows, then Khecarī is accomplished.

rasanāṁ tālumadhye tu śanaiḥ śanaiḥ praveśayet /
kapālakuhare jihvā praviṣṭā viparītagā /
bhruvor madhye gatā dṛṣṭir mudrā bhavati khecarī // 27 //

Then (the tongue being lengthened)practise turning it upwards and backwards so as to touch the palate, till at length it reaches the holes of the nostrils opening into the mouth. Close those holes with the tongue(thus stopping inspiration), and fix the gaze on the space between the two eyebrows. This is called Khecarī.

Its benefits :

atha khecarīmudrāyāḥ phalakathanam :
na ca mūrcchā kṣudhā tṛṣṇā naivālasyaṁ prajāyate /
na ca rogo jarā mṛtyur devadehaḥ sa jāyate // 28 //

By this practice there is neither fainting, nor hunger, nor thirst, nor laziness. There comes neither disease, nor decay, nor death. The body becomes divine.

nāgninā dahyate gātraṁ na śoṣayati mārutaḥ /
na dehaṁ kledayantyāpo daṁśayen na bhujaṅgamaḥ // 29 //

The body cannot be burned by fire, nor dried up by air, nor wetted by water, nor bitten by snakes.

lāvaṇyaṁ ca bhaved gātre samādhir jāyate dhruvam /
kapālavaktrasaṁyoge rasanā rasam āpnuyāt // 30 //

The body becomes beautiful; Samādhi is verily attained; and the tongue touching the holes obtains various juices(it drinks nectar).

nānārasasamudgatam ānandaṁ ca dine dine /
ādau tu lavaṇaṁ kṣāraṁ tatas tiktakaṣāyakam // 31 //
navanītaṁ ghṛtaṁ kṣīraṁ dadhitakramadhūni ca /
drākṣārasaṁ ca pīyūṣaṁ jāyate rasanodakam // 32 //

Various juices being produced, day by day the man experiences new sensations; first, he experiences a saltish taste, then alkaline, then bitter, then astringent, then he feels the taste of butter, then of ghee, then of milk, then of curd, then of whey, then of honey, then of palm juice, and, lastly, arises the taste of nectar.

Viparītakaraṇī

atha viparītakaraṇīmudrākathanam :
nābhimūle vaset sūryas tālumūle ca candramāḥ /
amṛtaṁ grasate sūryas tato mṛtyuvaśo naraḥ // 33 //
ūrdhve ca yojayet sūryaṁ candraṁ cāpyadha ānayet /
viparītakarī mudrā sarvatantreṣu gopitā // 34 //
bhūmau śiraś ca saṁsthāpya karayugmaṁ samāhitaḥ /
ūrdhvapādaḥ sthiro bhūtvā viparītakarī matā // 35 //

The Sun (the solar Nāḍī or plexus) dwells at the root of the navel, and the Moon at the root of the palate. The process by which the Sun is brought upward and the Moon carried downward is called Viparītakaraṇī. It is a secret Mudrā in all the Tantras. Place the head on the ground, with hands spread, raise the legs up, and thus remain steady. This is called Viparītakaraṇī.

Its benefits :

atha viparītakaraṇīmudrāyāḥ phalakathanam :
mudrāṁ ca sādhayen nityaṁ jarāṁ mṛtyuṁ ca nāśayet /
sa siddhaḥ sarvalokeṣu pralaye 'pi na sīdati // 36 //

By the constant practice of this Mudrā, decay and death are averted. He becomes an adept, and does not perish even at Pralaya.

Yonimudrā

atha yonimudrākathanam :
siddhāsanaṁ samāsādya karṇacakṣurnasāmukham /
aṅguṣṭhatarjanīmadhyānāmādibhiś ca sādhayet // 37 //
kākobhiḥ prāṇaṁ saṁkṛṣya apāne yojayet tataḥ /
ṣaṭcakrāṇi kramād dhyātvā huṁ haṁsamanunā sudhīḥ // 38 //
caitanyam ānayed devīṁ nidritā yā bhujaṅginī /
jīvena sahitāṁ śaktiṁ samutthāpya karāmbuje // 39 //
śaktimayaḥ svayaṁ bhūtvā paraṁ śivena saṅgamam /
nānāsukhaṁ vihāraṁ ca cintayet paramaṁ sukham // 40 //
śivaśaktisamāyogād ekāntaṁ bhuvi bhāvayet /
ānandamānaso bhūtvā ahaṁ brahmeti saṁbhavet // 41 //
yonimudrā parā gopyā devānām api durlabhā /
sakṛt tu labdhasaṁsiddhiḥ samādhisthaḥ sa eva hi // 42 //

Sitting in Siddhāsana, close the two ears with the two thumbs, the eyes with the index fingers, the nostrils with the middle fingers, the upper lip with the fore fingers, and the lower lip with the little fingers. Draw in the Prāṇa-Vāyu by Kākī-Mudrā, (as in verse 86) and join it with the Apāna-Vāyu. Contemplating the six Cakras in their order, let the wise one awaken the sleeping Serpent-Goddess Kuṇḍalinī, by repeating the Mantra Huṁ, and Haṁsa, and raising the Śakti (Kuṇḍalinī) with the Jīva, place them at the Thousand-Petalled Lotus. Being himself full of Śakti, being joined with the great Śiva, let him think of the various pleasures and enjoyments. Let him contemplate on the union of Śiva (Spirit) and Śakti (Force or Energy) in this world. Being himself all bliss, let him realise that he is Brahma. This Yoni-Mudrā is a great secret, difficult to be obtained even by Devas. By once obtaining perfection in its practice, one verily enters into Samādhi.

Its benefits :

atha yonimudrāphalakathanam :
brahmahā bhrūṇahā caiva surāpī gurutalpagaḥ /
etaiḥ pāpair na lipyeta yonimudrānibandhanāt // 43 //
yāni pāpāni ghorāṇi upapāpāni yāni ca /
tāni sarvāṇi naśyanti yonimudrānibandhanāt /
tasmād abhyasanaṁ kuryād yadi muktiṁ samicchati // 44 //

By the practice of this Mudrā, one is never polluted by the sins of killing a Brāhmaṇa, killing a foetus, drinking liquor, or polluting the bed of the preceptor. All the mortal sins and venial sins are completely destroyed by the practice of this Mudrā. Let him therefore practise it, if he wishes for emancipation.

Vajrolī Mudrā

atha vajrolīmudrākathanam :
āśritya bhūmiṁ karayos talābhyām
ūrdhvaṁ kṣipet pādayugaṁ śiraḥ khe /
śaktiprabuddhyai cirajīvanāya
vajrolimudrāṁ munayo vadanti // 45 //

Place the two palms on the ground; raise the legs in the air upward, the head not touching the earth. This awakens the Śakti, causes long life, and is called Vajrolī by the sages.

Its benefits :

atha vajrolīmudrāyāḥ phalakathanam :
ayaṁ yogo yogaśreṣṭho yogināṁ muktikāraṇam /
ayaṁ hitaprado yogo yogināṁ siddhidāyakaḥ // 46 //
etad yogaprasādena bindusiddhir bhaved dhruvam /
siddhe bindau mahāyatne kiṁ na siddhyati bhūtale // 47 //
bhogena mahatā yukto yadi mudrāṁ samācaret /
tathāpi sakalā siddhis tasya bhavati niścitam // 48 //

This practice is the best of all Yogas; it causes emancipation and this beneficial Yoga gives perfection to the Yogīs. By virtue of this Yoga, Bindu-Siddhi (retention of seed) is obtained, and when that Siddhi is obtained what else can he not attain in this world! Though immersed in manifold pleasures, if he practises this Mudrā, he attains verily all perfections.

Śakticālanī

atha śakticālanīmudrākathanam :
mūlādhāre ātmaśaktiḥ kuṇḍalī paradevatā /
śayitā bhujagākārā sārdhatrivalayānvitā // 49 //

The great goddess Kuṇḍalinī, the energy of Self, Ātma-Śakti (spiritual force), sleeps in Mūlādhāra (rectum); she has the form of a serpent having three coils and a half.

yāvat sā nidritā dehe tāvaj jīvaḥ paśur yathā /
jñānaṁ na jāyate tāvat koṭiyogaṁ samabhyaset // 50 //

So long as she is asleep in the body, the Jīva is a mere animal; and true knowledge does not arise, though he may practise ten millions of Yoga.

udghāṭayet kavāṭaṁ ca yathā kuñcikayā haṭhāt /
kuṇḍalinyāḥ prabodhena brahmadvāraṁ prabhedayet // 51 //

As by a key a door is opened, so by awakening Kuṇḍalinī by Haṭha Yoga, the door of Brahma is unlocked.

nābhiṁ saṁveṣṭya vastreṇa na ca nagno bahiḥsthitaḥ /
gopanīyagṛhe sthitvā śakticālanam abhyaset // 52 //

Covering the loins with a piece of cloth, seated in a secret room, not naked in an outer room, let him practise Śakticālana.

vitastipramitaṁ dīrghaṁ vistāre ċaturaṅgulam /
mṛdulaṁ dhavalaṁ sūkṣmaṁ veṣṭanāmbaralakṣaṇam /
evam ambarayuktaṁ ca kaṭisūtreṇa yojayet // 53 //

One cubit long and four fingers (3 inches) wide should be the covering cloth, soft, white and of fine texture. Join this cloth with the Kaṭi-Sūtra(a string worn round the loins).

bhasmanā gātraṁ saṁlipya siddhāsanaṁ samācaret /
nāsābhyāṁ prāṇam ākṛṣya apāne yojayet balāt // 54 //
tāvad ākuñcayed guhyam aśvinīmudrayā śanaiḥ /
yāvad gacchet suṣumṇāyāṁ vāyuḥ prakāśayed haṭhāt // 55 //

Rub the body with ashes; sit in Siddhāsana-posture; drawing the Prāṇa-Vāyu with the nostrils forcibly join it with the Apāna. Contract the rectum slowly by Aśvinī Mudrā, so long as the Vāyu does not enter Suṣumṇā, and manifests its presence.

tadā vāyuprabandhena kumbhikā ca bhujaṅginī /
baddhaśvāsas tato bhūtvā ūrdhvamārgaṁ prapadyate // 56 //

By restraining the breath by Kumbhaka in this way, the Serpent Kuṇḍalinī, feeling suffocated, awakes and rises upwards to the Brahmarandhra.

vinā śakticālanena yonimudrā na siddhyati /
ādau cālanam abhyasya yonimudrāṁ samabhyaset // 57 //

Without Śakticālana, Yoni-Mudrā is not complete or perfected. First Cālana should be practised, and then Yoni-Mudrā should be learnt.

iti te kathitaṁ caṇḍakapāle śakticālanam /
gopanīyaṁ prayatnena dine dine samabhyaset // 58 //

O Caṇḍakapāli ! Thus have I taught thee Śakticālana. Preserve it with care and practise it daily.

Its benefits :

atha śakticālanīmudrāyāḥ phalakathanam :
mudreyaṁ paramā gopyā jarāmaraṇanāśinī /
tasmād abhyasanaṁ kāryaṁ yogibhiḥ siddhikāṅkṣibhiḥ // 59 //

This Mudrā should be kept carefully concealed. It destroys decay and death. Therefore, a Yogī, desirous of perfection, should practise it.

nityaṁ yo' bhyasate yogī siddhis tasya kare sthitā /
tasya vigrahasiddhiḥ syād rogāṇāṁ saṁkṣayo bhavet // 60 //

A Yogī who practises this daily, acquires adeptship, attains Vigrahasiddhi and all his diseases are cured.

Taḍāgī Mudrā

atha taḍāgīmudrākathanam :
udaraṁ paścimottānaṁ taḍāgākṛti kārayet /
tāḍāgī sā parā mudrā jarāmṛtyuvināśinī // 61 //

Sitting in Paścimottāna posture, make the stomach like a tank (hollow). This is Taḍāgī (Tank) Mudrā, destroyer of old age and death.

Māṇḍukī Mudrā

atha māṇḍukīmudrākathanam :
mukhaṁ saṁmudritaṁ kṛtvā jihvāmūlaṁ pracālayet /
śanair graset tad amṛtaṁ māṇḍukīṁ mudrikāṁ viduḥ // 62 //

Closing the mouth, move the tip of the tongue towards the palate, and taste slowly the nectar (flowing from the Thousand-petalled Lotus). This is Frog Mudrā.

Its benefits :

atha māṇḍukīmudrāyāḥ phalakathanam :
valitaṁ palitaṁ naiva jāyate nityayauvanam /
na keśe jāyate pāko yaḥ kuryān nityamāṇḍukīm // 63 //

The body never sickens or becomes old, and it retains perpetual youth. The hair of him who practises this never grows white.

Śāmbhavī Mudrā

atha śāṃbhavīmudrākathanam :
netrāntaraṁ samālokya cātmārāmaṁ nirīkṣayet /
sā bhavec chāmbhavī mudrā sarvatantreṣu gopitā // 64 //

Fixing the gaze between the two eyebrows, behold the Self-existent. This is Śāmbhavī, secret in all the Tantras.

Its benefits :

atha śāṁbhavīmudrāyāḥ phalakathanam :
vedaśāstrapurāṇāni sāmānyagaṇikā iva /
iyaṁ tu śāmbhavī mudrā guptā kulavadhūriva // 65 //

The Vedas, the scriptures, the Purāṇas are like public women, but this Śāmbhavī should be guarded as if it were a lady of a respectable family.

sa eva hyādināthaś ca sa ca nārāyaṇaḥ svayam /
sa ca brahmā sṛṣṭikārī yo mudrāṁ vetti śāmbhavīm // 66 //

He, who knows this Śāmbhavī, is like Ādinātha; he is Nārāyaṇa; he is Brahmā the Creator.

satyaṁ satyaṁ punaḥ satyaṁ satyamāha maheśvaraḥ /
śāmbhavīṁ yo vijānīyāt sa ca brahma na cānyathā // 67 //

Maheśvara has said, "Truly, truly, and again truly, he who knows Śāmbhavī, is Brahman. There is no doubt in this."

The Five Dhāraṇā-Mudrās

atha pañcadhāraṇāmudrākathanam :
kathitā śāmbhavī mudrā śṛṇuṣva pañcadhāraṇām /
dhāraṇāni samāsādya kiṁ na siddhyati bhūtale // 68 //

Śāmbhavī has been explained; hear now the five Dhāraṇās. Learning these five Dhāraṇās, what cannot be accomplished in this world?

anena naradehena svargeṣu gamanāgamam/
manogatir bhavet tasya khecaratvaṁ na cānyathā // 69 //

With this human body one can visit and revisit Svarga-loka; he can go wherever he likes, as swiftly as mind; he acquires the faculty of walking in the sky. These five Dhāraṇās are : Pārthivī (Earthy), Āmbhasī (Watery), Vāyavī (Aerial), Āgneyī (Fiery), and Ākāśī (Ethereal).

Pārthivī

atha pārthivīdhāraṇākathanam :
yat tattvaṁ haritāladeśaracitaṁ bhaumaṁ lakārānvitam
vedāsraṁ kamalāsanena sahitaṁ kṛtvā hṛdi sthāyinam /
prāṇaṁ tatra vilīya pañcaghaṭikāś cittānvitaṁ dhārayed
eṣā stambhakarī sadā kṣitijayaṁ kuryād adhodhāraṇā // 70 //

The Pṛthivī-Tattva has the colour of orpiment (yellow); the letter (la) is its secret symbol or seed; its form is four-sided; and Brahmā, its presiding deity. Place this Tattva in the heart, and fix by Kumbhaki the Prāṇa-Vāyus and the Citta there for a period of five Ghaṭikās (2 hours). This is called Adhodhāraṇā. By this, one conquers the Earth, and no earthy elements can injure him; and it causes steadiness.

Its benefits :

atha pārthivīdhāraṇāmudrāyāḥ phalakathanam :
pārthivīdhāraṇāmudrāṁ yoḥ karoti ca nityaśaḥ /
mṛtyuñjayaḥ svayaṁ so ' pi sa siddho vicared bhuvi // 71 //

He who practises this dhāraṇā, becomes like the conqueror of Death; as an Adept he walks over this earth.

Āmbhasī

atha āmbhasīdhāraṇāmudrākathanam :
śaṅkhendupratimaṁ ca kundadhavalaṁ tattvaṁ kilālaṁ subhaṁ
tatpīyūṣavakārabījasahitaṁ yuktaṁ sadā viṣṇunā /
prāṇaṁ tatra vilīya pañcaghaṭikāś cittānvitaṁ dhārayed
eṣā duḥsahatāpapāpaharaṇī syād āmbhasī dhāraṇā // 72 //

The Water-Tattva is white like a Kunda flower or a conch or the moon; its form is circular like the moon; the letter 'va' is the seed of this ambrosial element; and Viṣṇu is its presiding deity. By Yoga, produce the water-Tattva in the heart, and fix there the Prāṇa with the Citta (Consciousness) for five Ghaṭikās, practising Kumbhaka. This is Watery Dhāraṇā. It is the destroyer of all sorrows. Water cannot injure him who practises this.

Its benefits :

atha āmbhasīmudrāyāḥ phalakathanam :
āmbhasīṁ paramāṁ mudrāṁ yo jānāti sa yogavit /
gabhīre ca jale ghore maraṇaṁ tasya no bhavet // 73 //
iyaṁ tu paramā mudrā gopanīyā prayatnataḥ /
prakāśāt siddhihāniḥ syāt satyaṁ vacmi ca tattvataḥ // 74 //

The Āmbhasī is a great Mudrā; a Yogī who knows it, never meets death even in deepest water. This should be kept carefully concealed. By revealing it success is lost. Verily I tell you the truth.

Āgneyī

atha āgneyīdhāraṇāmudrākathanam :
yan nābhisthitam indragopasadṛśaṁ bījaṁ trikoṇānvitam
tattvaṁ vahnimayaṁ pradīptam aruṇam rudreṇa yat siddhidam/
prāṇaṁ tatra vilīya pañcaghaṭikāś cittānvitaṁ dhārayed
eṣā kālagabhīrabhītiharaṇī vaiśvānarī dhāraṇā // 75 //

The Fire-Tattva is situated at the navel; its colour is red like an Indragopa insect; its form is triangular; its seed is 'ra'; its presiding deity is Rudra. It is refulgent like the sun, and the giver of success. Fix the Prāṇa along with the Citta in this Tattva for five Ghaṭikās. This is called Fire-Dhāraṇā, destroyer of the fear of dreadful death.

Its benefits :

atha āgneyīdhāraṇāmudrāyāḥ phalakathanam :
pradīpte jvalite vahnau yadi patati sādhakaḥ /
etan mudrāprasādena sa jīvati na mṛtyubhāk // 76 //

If the practitioner is thrown into burning fire, by virtue of this Mūdra he remains alive, without fear of death.

Vāyavi

atha vāyavīdhāraṇāmudrākathanam :
yadbhinnāñjanapuñjasannibham idaṁ dhūmrāvabhāsaṁ paraṁ
tattvaṁ sattvamayaṁ yakārasahitaṁ yatreśvaro devatā /
prāṇaṁ tatra vilīya pañcaghaṭikāś cittānvitam dhārayed
eṣā khe gamanaṁ karoti yamināṁ syād vāyavī dhāraṇā // 77 //

The Air-Tattva is black as unguent for the eyes (collyrium); the letter 'ya ' is its seed; and Īśvara its presiding deity. This Tattva is full of Sattva quality. Fix the Prāṇa and the Citta for five Ghaṭikās in this Tattva. This is Vāyavī-Dhāraṇā. By this, the practitioner walks in the air.

Its benefits :

atha vāyavīdhāraṇāmudrāyāḥ phalakathanam :
iyaṁ tu paramā mudrā jarāmṛtyuvināśinī /
vāyunā mriyate nāpi khe gateś ca pradāyinī // 78 //
śaṭhāya bhaktihīnāya na deyā yasyakasyacit /
datte ca siddhihāniḥ syāt satyaṁ vacmi ca caṇḍa te // 79 //

This great Mudrā destroys decay and death. Its practitioner is never killed by any aerial disturbances. By its virtue one walks in the air. This should not be taught to the wicked or to those devoid of faith. By so doing success is lost; O Caṇḍa, this is verily the truth.

Ākāśī Dhāraṇā

atha ākāśidhāraṇāmudrākathanam :
yat sindhau varaśuddhavārisadṛśam vyomaṁ paraṁ bhāsitam
tattvaṁ devasadāśivena sahitaṁ bījaṁ hakārānvitam /
prāṇaṁ tatra vilīya pañcaghaṭikāś cittānvitaṁ dhārayed
eṣā mokṣakavāṭabhedanakarī kuryān nabhodhāraṇām // 80 //

The Ether-Tattva has the colour of pure sea-water; 'ha' is its seed; its presiding deity is Sadāśiva. Fix the Prāṇa along with Citta for five Ghaṭikās in this Tattva. This is Ether-Dhāraṇā. It opens the gates of emancipation.

Its benefits :

atha ākāśīdhāraṇāmudrāyāḥ phalakathanam :
ākāśīdhāraṇāṁ mudrāṁ yo vetti sa ca yogavit /
na mṛtyur jāyate tasya pralaye nāvasīdati // 81 //

He who knows this Dhāraṇā is the real Yogī. Death does not approach him, nor does he perish during Pralaya.

Aśvinī Mudrā

atha aśvinīmudrākathanam :
ākuñcayed gudadvāraṁ prakāśayet punaḥ punaḥ /
sā bhaved aśvinīmudrā śaktiprabodhakāriṇī // 82 //

Contract and dilate the anal aperture again and again. This is called Aśvinī Mudrā. It awakens the Śakti (Kuṇḍalinī).

Its benefits :

atha aśvinīmudrāyāḥ phalakathanam :
aśvinī paramā mudrā guhyarogavināśinī /
balapuṣṭikarī caiva akālamaraṇaṁ haret // 83 //

This Aśvinī is a great Mudrā; it destroys all diseases of the rectum; it gives strength and vigour, and prevents premature death.

Pāśinī Mudrā

atha pāśinīmudrākathanam :
kaṇṭhapṛṣṭhe kṣipet pādau pāśavad dṛḍhabandhanam /
sā eva pāśinī mudrā śaktiprabodhakāriṇī // 84 //

Throw the two legs on the neck towards the back, holding them strongly together like a Pāśa (noose). This is called Pāśinī Mudrā; it awakens the Śakti (Kuṇḍalinī).

Its benefits :

atha pāśinīmudrāyāḥ phalakathanam :
pāśinī mahatī mudrā balapuṣṭividhāyinī /
sādhanīyā prayatnena sādhakaiḥ siddhikāṅkṣibhiḥ // 85 //

This grand Mudrā gives strength and nourishment. It should be practised with care by those who desire success.

Kākī Mudrā

atha kākīmudrākathanam :
kākacañcuvadāsyena pibed vāyuṁ śanaiḥ śanaiḥ /
kākīmudrā bhaved eṣā sarvarogavināśinī // 86 //

Contract the lips like the beak of a crow, and drink (draw in) the air slowly and slowly. This is Kākī (crow) Mudrā, destroyer of all diseases.

Its benefits :

atha kākīmudrāyāḥ phalakathanam :
kākīmudrā parā mudrā sarvatantreṣu gopitā /
asyāḥ prasādamātreṇa na rogī kākavad bhavet // 87 //

The Kākī Mudrā is a great Mudrā, kept secret in all Tantras. By virtue of this, one becomes free from disease like a crow.

Mātaṅginī Mudrā

atha mātaṅginīmudrākathanam :
kaṇṭhadaghne jale sthitvā nāsābhyāṁ jalam āharet /
mukhān nirgamayet paścāt punar vaktreṇa cāharet // 88 //
nāsābhyāṁ recayet paścāt kuryād evaṁ punaḥ punaḥ /
mātaṅginī parā mudrā jarāmṛtyuvināśinī // 89 //

Stand in neck-deep water; draw in the water through the nostrils, and throw it out by the mouth. Then draw in the water through the mouth and expel it through the nostrils. Let one repeat this again and again. This is called Elephant Mudrā, destroyer of decay and death.

Its benefits :

atha mātaṅginīmudrāyāḥ phalakathanam :
virale nirjane deśe sthitvā caikāgramānasaḥ /
kuryān mātaṅginīṁ mudrāṁ mātaṅga iva jāyate // 90 //
yatra yatra sthito yogī sukham atyantam aśnute /
tasmāt sarvaprayatnena sādhayen mudrikāṁ parām // 91 //

In a solitary place, free from human intrusion, one should practise with fixed attention this Elephant Mudrā; by so doing, he becomes strong like Elephant. Wherever he may be, by this process the Yogī enjoys great pleasure. Therefore, this Mudrā should be practised with great care.

Bhujaṅginī Mudrā

atha bhujaṅginīmudrākathanam :
vaktraṁ kiñcit suprasārya cānilaṁ galayā pibet /
sā bhaved bhujagī mudrā jarāmṛtyuvināśinī // 92 //

Extruding the mouth a little forward, let him drink (draw in) air through the gullet. This is called Serpent-Mudrā, destroyer of decay and death.

Its benefits:

atha bhujaṅginīmudrāyāḥ phalakathanam :
yāvantaś codare roga ajīrṇādi viśeṣataḥ /
tān sarvān nāśayed āśu yatra mudrā bhujaṅginī // 93 //

This Serpent-Mudrā quickly destroys all stomach diseases, especially indigestion, dyspepsia, etc.

The Benefits of Mudrās

atha mudrāṇāṁ phalakathanam :
idaṁ tu mudrāpaṭalaṁ kathitaṁ caṇḍa te śubham /
vallabhaṁ sarvasiddhānāṁ jarāmaraṇanāśanam // 94 //

O Caṇḍakāpālī, thus have I recited to thee the chapter on Mudrās. This is beloved of all adepts, and destroys decay and death.

śaṭhāya bhaktihīnāya na deyaṁ yasyakasyacit :
gopanīyaṁ prayatnena durlabhaṁ marutām api // 95 //

This should not be taught indiscriminately, not to a wicked person, not to one devoid of faith; this should be kept secret with great care; it is difficult to be attained even by Devas.

ṛjave śāntacittāya gurubhaktiparāya ca /
kulīnāya pradātavyaṁ bhogamuktipradāyakam // 96 //

These Mudrās which give happiness and emancipation should be taught to a guileless, calm and peace-minded person, who is devoted to his teacher and comes of good family.

mudrāṇāṁ paṭalaṁ hyetat sarvavyādhivināśanam /
nityam abhyāsaśīlasya jaṭharāgnivivardhanaṁ // 97 //

These Mudrās destroy all diseases. They increase the gastric fire of him who practises them daily.

na tasya jāyate mṛtyur nāsya jarādikaṁ tathā /
nāgnijalabhayaṁ tasya vāyorapi kuto bhayam // 98 //

To him death never comes, nor decay, etc.; there is no fear to him from fire and water, nor from air.

kāsaḥ śvāsaḥ plīhā kuṣṭhaṁ śleṣmarogāś ca viṁśatiḥ /
mudrāṇāṁ sādhanāc caiva vinaśyanti na saṁśayaḥ // 99 //

Cough, asthma, enlargement of spleen, leprosy, being diseases of twenty sorts, are verily destroyed by the practice of these Mudrās.

bahunā kim ihoktena sāraṁ vacmi ca caṇḍa te /
nāsti mudrāsamaṁ kiñcit siddhidaṁ kṣitimaṇḍale // 100 //

O Caṇḍa ! What more shall I tell thee ? In short, there is nothing in this world like the Mudrās for giving quick success.

iti śrīgheraṇḍasaṁhitāyāṁ gheraṇḍacaṇḍasaṁvāde
ghaṭasthayogaprakaraṇe mudrāprayogo nāma tṛtīyopadeśaḥ //2//

End of Chapter 3, On Mudrās.

CHAPTER 4

Pratyāhāra or Restraining the Mind

Caturthopadeśaḥ

gheraṇḍa uvāca:

athātaḥ sampravakṣyāmi pratyāhārakam uttamam /
yasya vijñānamātreṇa kāmādiripunāśanam // 1 //

Gheraṇḍa Said:

Now I shall tell thee Pratyāhāra-Yoga the best. By its knowledge all the passions like lust, etc., are destroyed.

yato yato niścarati manaś cañcalam asthiram /
tatas tato niyamyaitad ātmanyeva vaśaṁ nayet // 2 //

Let one bring the Citta(thinking principle) under one's control by withdrawing it, whenever it wanders away drawn by the various objects of sight.

puraskāraṁ tiraskāraṁ suśrāvyaṁ vā bhayānakam /
manas tasmān niyamyaitad ātmanyeva vaśaṁ nayet//3//

When there occur praise or censure, good speech or bad speech, let one withdraw one's mind from all these and bring the Citta under the control of the Self.

sugandhe vāpi durgandhe ghrāṇeṣu jāyate manaḥ /
tasmāt pratyāhared etad ātmanyeva vaśaṁ nayet // 4 //

From sweet smells or bad smells, from whatever odour distracts or attracts the mind, let one withdraw the mind and bring it under the control of the Self.

madhurāmlakatiktādirasaṁ gataṁ yadā manaḥ :
tasmāt pratyāhared etad ātmanyeva vaśaṁ nayet // 5 //

From sweet or acid tastes, from bitter or astringent tastes, from whatever taste attracts the mind, let one withdraw it from that, and bring it within the control of the Self.

iti śrīgheraṇḍasaṁhitāyāṁ gheraṇḍacaṇḍasaṁvāde
ghaṭasthayoge pratyāhāraprayogo nāma caturthopadeśaḥ //4//

End of Chapter 4, on Pratyāhāra.

Chapter 5

Prāṇāyāma

Pañcamopadeśaḥ

gheraṇḍa uvāca:

athātaḥ sampravakṣyāmi prāṇāyāmasya yadvidhim /
yasya sādhanamātreṇa devatulyo bhaven naraḥ // 1 //

Gheraṇḍa Said :

Now I shall tell thee the rules of Prāṇāyāma or regulation of breath. By its practice a man becomes like a god.

ādau sthānaṁ tathā kālaṁ mitāhāraṁ tathāparam /
nāḍīśuddhiṁ tataḥ paścāt prāṇāyāmaṁ ca sādhayet//2 //

Four things are necessary in practising Prāṇāyāma: (i) a good place; (ii) a suitable time; (iii) moderate food; and, (iv) purification of Nāḍīs (vessels of the body, i.e., alimentary canal, etc.).

Place

atha sthānanirṇayaḥ:
dūradeśe tathāraṇye rājadhānyāṁ janāntike /
yogārambhaṁ na kurvīta kṛtaś cet siddhihā bhavet // 3//

The practice of Yoga should not be attempted in a far-off country (from home), nor in a forest, nor in a capital city, nor in the midst of a crowd. If one does so, one fail to achieve success.

aviśvāsaṁ dūradeśe araṇye rakṣivarjitam /
lokāraṇye prakāśaś ca tasmāt trīṇi vivarjayet // 4 //

In a distant country, one loses faith (because of Yoga not being known there); in a forest, one is without protection; and in the midst of a thick population, there is danger of exposure (for then the curious will trouble him). Therefore, let one avoid these three.

sudeśe dhārmike rājye subhikṣe nirupadrave /
tatraikaṁ kuṭīraṁ kṛtvā prācīraiḥ pariveṣṭitam // 5 //

In a good country whose king is just, where food is easily and abundantly procurable, which is free from disturbances, let one erect a small hut, surrounded by a wall.

vāpīkūpataḍāgaṁ ca prācīramadhyavarti ca /
nātyuccaṁ nātinimnaṁ kuṭīraṁ kīṭavarjitam // 6 //

And in the centre of the enclosure, let him sink a well and dig a tank. Let the hut be neither too high nor too low. Let it be free from insects.

samyag gomayaliptaṁ ca kuṭīraṁ tatra nirmitam /
evaṁ sthāneṣu gupteṣu prāṇāyāmaṁ samabhyaset // 7//

It should be properly smeared with cowdung. In a hut thus built and situated in such a hidden place, let him practise Prāṇāyāma.

Time

atha kālanirṇayaḥ:
hemante śiśire grīṣme varṣāyāṁ ca ṛtau tathā /
yogārambhaṁ na kurvīta kṛte yogo hi rogadaḥ // 8 //

The practice of Yoga should not be commenced in these four seasons out of six : Hemanta (winter), Śiśira (cold), Grīṣma (hot), Varṣā (rainy). If one begins in these seasons, one will contract diseases.

vasante śaradi proktaṁ yogārambhaṁ samācaret /
tathā yogī bhavet siddho rogānmukto bhaved dhruvam // 9//

The practice of Yoga should be commenced by a beginner in spring (Vasanta)or autumn (Śarat). By so doing, he attains success; and verily he remains free from diseases.

caitrādiphālgunānte ca māghādiphālgunāntike /
dvau dvau māsau ṛtubhāgau anubhāvaś catuś catuḥ // 10 //

The six seasons occur in their order in the twelve months

beginning with Caitra and ending wth Phālguna, each being of two months duration. But each season is experienced for four months, beginning with Māgha and ending with Phālguna.

vasantaś caitra, vaiśākhau jyeṣṭhāṣāḍhānu ca grīṣmakou :
varṣā śrāvaṇabhādrābhyāṁ śarad āśvinakārttikau /
mārgapauṣau ca hemantaḥ śiśiro māghaphālgunau // 11 //

Six Seasons

11. The six seasons are as follows:

Season	*Months (Sanskrit)*	*English*
Vasanta or Spring	Caitra and Vaiśākha	March, April
Grīṣma or Summer	Jyeṣṭha and Āṣāḍha	May, June
Varṣā or Rainy	Śrāvaṇa and Bhādrapada	July, August
Śarat or Antumn	Āśvina and Kārttika	September, October
Hemanta or Winter	Agrahāyaṇa and Pauṣa	November, December
Śiśira or Cold	Māgha and Phālguna	January, February

anubhāvaṁ pravakṣyāmi ṛtūnāṁ ca yathoditam /
māghādimādhavānteṣu vasantānubhavaṁ viduḥ//12//
caitrādi cāṣāḍhāntaṁ ca nidāghānubhavaṁ viduḥ /
āṣāḍhādi cāśvināntaṁ prāvṛṣānubhavaṁ viduḥ // 13 //
bhādrādimārgaśīrṣāntaṁ śarado ' nubhavaṁ viduḥ /
kārttikādimāghamāsāntaṁ hemantānubhavaṁ viduḥ /
mārgādīṁścaturo māsān śiśirānubhavaṁ viduḥ // 14 //

The Experiencing of Seasons

Now I shall tell thee the experiencing of seasons. They are as follows:

Beginning from	*Ending*	*Season*	*English*
Māgha	Vaiśākha	Varṣhānubhava	January to April
Caitra	Āsāḍha	Grīṣmānubhava	March to June
Āṣāḍha	Āśvina	Varṣānubhava	June to September
Bhādrapada	Agrahāyaṇa	Sáradanubhava	August to November
Kārttika	Māgha	Hemantānubhava	October to January
Agrahāyaṇa	Phālguna	Śiśirānubhava	November to February

vasante vāpi śaradi yogārambhaṁ samācaret /
tadā yogo bhavet siddho vināyāsena kathyate // 15 //

The practice of Yoga should be commenced either in Vasanta

(spring) or Śarat (autumn). For in these seasons success is attained without much trouble.

Moderation in Diet

atha mitāhāraḥ:
mitāhāraṁ vinā yastu yogārambhaṁ tu kārayet /
nānārogo bhavet tasya kiñcid yogo na sidhyati // 16 //

He who practises Yoga without moderation in diet, incurs various diseases, and obtains no success.

śālyannaṁ yavapiṣṭaṁ vā godhūmapiṣṭakaṁ tathā /
mudgaṁ māṣacaṇakādi śubhraṁ ca tuṣavarjitam // 17 //

A Yogī should eat rice, barley(bread), or wheat bread. He may eat Mudga beans, Māṣa beans, gram, etc. These should be clean, white and free from chaff.

paṭolaṁ panasaṁ mānaṁ kakkolaṁ ca śukāśakam /
drāḍhikāṁ karkaṭīṁ rambhāṁ ḍumbarīṁ kaṇṭakaṇṭakam//18/
āmarambhāṁ bhālarambhāṁ rambhādaṇḍaṁ ca mūlakam /
vārtākīṁ mūlakaṁ ṛddhiṁ yogī bhakṣaṇaṁ ācaret // 19 //

A Yogī may eat Paṭola (a kind of cucumber), jack-fruit, Māna, Kakkola(a kind of berry), jujube, bonduc nut, cucumber, plantain, fig; unripe plantain, small plantain, plantain stem and roots, brinjal, radish and Ṛddhi (a kind of medicinal plant).

bālaśākaṁ kālaśākaṁ tathā paṭolapatrakam /
pañcaśākaṁ praśaṁsiyād vāstūkaṁ himalocikām // 20 //

He may eat green, fresh vegetables, black vegetables, leaves of paṭola, Vāstūka-śāka, and Himalocikā Śāka. These are the five Śākas(vegetable leaves)praised as food fit for Yogīs.

śuddhaṁ sumadhuraṁ snigdham udarārdhavivarjitam /
bhujyate surasaṁ prītyā mitāhāram imaṁ viduḥ // 21 //

Pure, sweet and soft food should be eaten to fill half the stomach: eating thus sweet juices with pleasure, and leaving the other half of the stomach empty is called moderation in diet.

annena pūrayed ardhaṁ toyena tu tṛtīyakam /
udarasya tṛtīyaṁśaṁ saṁrakṣed vāyucāraṇe // 22 //

Half the stomach should be filled with food, one quarter with water, and one quarter should be kept empty for free wind movement.

Prohibited Foods

kaṭvamlaṁ lavaṇaṁ tiktaṁ bhṛṣṭaṁ ca dadhi takrakam /
śākotkaṭaṁ tathā madyaṁ tālaṁ ca panasaṁ tathā // 23 //

In the beginning of Yoga-practice one should discard bitter, acid, salt, pungent and roasted things, curd, whey, heavy vegetables, wine, palmnuts, and over-ripe jack-fruit.

kulatthaṁ masūraṁ pāṇḍuṁ kūṣmāṇḍaṁ śākadaṇḍakam /
tumbī kolakapitthaṁ ca kaṇṭabilvaṁ palāśakam // 24 //

So also Kulattha and Masūra-beans, Pāṇḍu fruit, pumpkins and vegetable stems, gourds, berries, Kapittha, Kaṇṭa-bilva and Palāśa.

kadambaṁ jambīraṁ bimbaṁ lakacaṁ laśunaṁ viṣam /
kāmaraṅgaṁ piyalaṁ ca hiṅguśālmalikemukam // 25 //

So also Kadamba, Jambīra (citron), Bimba, Lukuca (a kind of bread-fruit), onions, lotus, Kāmaraṅga, Piyāla, Hiṅga (assafoetida), Śālmalī, Kemuka.

yogārambhe varjayec ca pathistrīvahnisevanam /
navanītaṁ ghṛtaṁ kṣīraṁ śarkarādyaikṣavaṁ guḍam // 26 //
pakvarambhāṁ nārikelaṁ dāḍimbamaśivāsavam /
drākṣāṅgulavanīṁ dhātrīṁ rasam amlavivarjitam // 27 //

A beginner should avoid much travelling, company of women, and warming himself by fire. So also he should avoid fresh butter, ghee, thickened milk, sugar, and date-sugar, etc., as well as ripe plantain, cocoanut, pomegranate, dates, Lavanī fruit, Āmalakī (myrobalan), and everything containing acid juices.

elājātilavaṅgaṁ ca pauru ṣaṁjambu jāmbalam /
harītakīṁ kharjūraṁ ca yogī bhakṣaṇam ācaret // 28 //

But cardamom, Jaiphal, cloves, aphrodisiacs or stimulants, rose-apple, Harītakī, and palm dates, a Yogī may eat while practising Yoga.

laghupākaṁ priyaṁ snigdhaṁ tathā dhātuprapoṣaṇam /
mano' bhilaṣitaṁ yogyaṁ yogī bhojanam ācaret // 29 //

Easily digestible, agreeable and soft foods which nourish the humours of body, a Yogī may eat according to his desire.

kāṭhinyaṁ duritaṁ pūtim uṣṇaṁ paryuṣitaṁ tathā /
atiśītaṁ cāticoṣṇaṁ bhakṣyaṁ yogī vivarjayet // 30 //

But a Yogī should avoid hard (not easily digestible), sinful food, putrid food, very hot, very stale food, as well as very cold food.

prātaḥsnānopavāsādi kāyakleśavidhiṁ tathā /
ekāhāraṁ nirāhāraṁ yāmānte ca na kārayet // 31 //

He should avoid early(morning before sunrise) baths, fasting, etc., or anything giving pain to the body; so also is prohibited to him eating only once a day, or not eating at all. But he may remain without food for 3 hours.

evaṁ vidhividhānena prāṇāyāmaṁ samācaret /
ārambhe prathame kuryāt kṣīrājyaṁ nityabhojanam /
madhyāhne caiva sāyāhne bhojanadvayam ācaret // 32 //

Regulating his life in this way, let him practise Prāṇāyāma. In the beginning before commencing it, he should take a little milk and ghee daily, and take his food twice daily, once at noon, and once in the evening.

Purification of Nāḍīs

atha nāḍīśuddhiḥ :
kuśāsane mṛgājine vyāghrājine ca kambale /
sthalāsane samāsīnaḥ prāṅmukho vāpyudaṅmukhaḥ /
nāḍīśuddhiṁ samāsādya prāṇāyāmaṁ samabhyaset // 33 //

He should sit on a seat of Kuśa-grass, or an antelope skin, or tiger skin, or a blanket, or on earth, calmly and quietly, facing east or north. Having purified the Nāḍīs, let him begin Prāṇāyāma.

caṇḍakāpāliruvāca:

nāḍīśuddhiṁ kathaṁ kuryān nāḍīśuddhis tu kīdṛśī /
tat sarvaṁ śrotum icchāmi tad vadasva dayānidhe // 34 //

Caṇḍakāpāli said :

O ocean of mercy! How are Nāḍīs purified: what is the purification of Nāḍīs? I want to learn all this; say this to me.

gheraṇḍa uvāca:

malākulāsu nāḍīṣu māruto naiva gacchati /
prāṇāyāmaḥ katham sidhyet tattvajñānaṁ kathaṁ bhavet /
tasmād ādau nāḍīśuddhiṁ prāṇāyāmaṁ tato ' bhyaset // 35 //

Gheraṇḍa said :

The Vāyu does not (cannot) enter the Nāḍīs so long as they are full of impurities(e.g., faeces, etc.). How then can Prāṇayāma be accomplished? How can there be knowledge of Tattvas? Therefore, first the Nāḍīs should be purified, and then Prāṇāyāma should be practised.

nāḍīśuddhir dvidhā proktā samanur nirmanus tathā /
bījena samanuṁ kuryān nirmanuṁ dhautikarmaṇā // 36 //

The purification of Nāḍīs is of two sorts : Samanu and Nirmanu. Samanu is done by a mental process with Bīja-mantra. Nirmanu is performed by physical cleanings.

dhautikarma purā proktaṁ ṣaṭkarmasādhane yathā /
śṛṇuṣva samanuṁ caṇḍa nāḍīśuddhir yathā bhavet // 37 //

The physical cleanings or Dhautis have already been taught. They consist of the six Sādhanas. Now, O Caṇḍa, listen to the Samanu process of purifying the vessels.

upaviśyāsane yogī padmāsanaṁ samācaret /
gurvādinyāsanaṁ kuryād yathaiva gurubhāṣitam /
nāḍīśuddhiṁ prakurvīta prāṇāyāmaviśuddhaye // 38 //

Sitting in the Padmāsana posture, and performing the adoration of the Guru, etc., as taught by the Teacher, let him perform purification of Nāḍīs for success in Prāṇāyāma.

vāyubījaṁ tato dhyātvā dhūmravarṇaṁ satejasam /
candreṇa pūrayed vāyuṁ bījaṁ ṣoḍaśakaiḥ sudhīḥ // 39 //
catuḥṣaṣṭyā mātrayā ca kumbhakenaiva dhārayet /
dvātriṃśan mātrayā vāyuṁ sūryanāḍyā ca recayet // 40 //

Contemplating on Vāyu-Bīja (i.e., yaṁ), full of energy and of smoke-colour, let him draw in breath by the left nostril, repeating the Bīja sixteen times. This is Pūraka. Let him restrain the breath for a period of sixty-four repetitions of the Mantra. This is

Kumbhaka. Then let him expel the air by the right nostril slowly during a period occupied by repeating the Mantra thirty-two times.

nābhimūlād vahnim utthāpya dhyāyet tejo ' vanīyutam /
vahnibījaṣoḍaśena sūryanāḍyā ca pūrayet // 41 //
catuḥṣaṣṭyā mātrayā ca kumbhakenaiva dhārayet /
dvātriṁśan mātrayā vāyuṃ śaśināḍyā ca recayet // 42 //

The root of the navel is the seat of Agni-Tattva. Raising the fire from that place, join the Pṛthivī-Tattva with it; then contemplate on this mixed light. Then repeating sixteen times the Agni-Bīja *(Raṁ)*, let him draw in breath by the right nostril, and retain it for the period of sixty-four repetitions of the Mantra, and then expel it by the left nostril for a period of thirty-two repetitions of the Mantra.

nāsāgre śaśadhṛgbimbaṁ dhyātvā jyotsnāsamanvitam /
ṭhaṁ bījaṣoḍaśenaiva iḍyā pūrayen marut // 43 //
catuḥṣaṣṭyā mātrayā ca vaṁ bījenaiva dhārayet /
amṛtaṁ plāvitaṁ dhyātvā nāḍīdhautiṁ vibhāvayet /
lakāreṇa dvātriṁśena dṛḍhaṁ bhāvyaṁ virecayet // 44 //

Then fixing the gaze on the tip of the nose and contemplating the luminous reflection of the Moon there, let him inhale through the left nostril, repeating the Bīja *Ṭhaṁ* sixteen times; let him retain it by repeating the Bīja sixty-four times; in the meanwhile imagine (or contemplate) that the nectar flowing from the Moon at the tip of the nose runs through all the vessels of the body, and purifies them. Thus contemplating, let him expel the air by repeating thirty-two times the Pṛthivī Bīja *Laṁ.*

evaṁvidhāṁ nāḍīśuddhiṁ kṛtvā nāḍīṁ viśodhayet /
dṛḍho bhūtvāsanaṁ kṛtvā prāṇāyāmaṁ samācaret // 45 //

By these three Prāṇāyāmas the Nāḍīs are purified. Then sitting firmly in a posture, let him begin regular Prāṇāyāma.

Kinds of Kumbhaka

sahitaḥ sūryabhedaś ca ujjāyī śītalī tathā /
bhastrikā bhrāmarī mūrchā kevalī cāṣṭakumbhikāḥ // 46 //

Kumbhaka or retention of breath is of eight kinds: Sahita, Sūryabheda, Ujjāyī, Śītalī, Bhastrikā, Bhrāmarī, Mūrcchā and Kevalī.

Sahita

sahito dvividhaḥ proktaḥ sagarbhaś ca nigarbhakaḥ /
sagarbho bījam uccārya nigarbho bījavarjitaḥ // 47 //

Sahita Kumbhaka is of two kind: Sagarbha and Nigarbha. Kumbhaka performed by the repetition of Bīja Mantra is Sagarbha; that done without such repetition is Nigarbha.

prāṇāyāmaṁ sagarbhaṁ ca prathamaṁ kathayāmi te /
sukhāsane copaviśya prāṅmukho vāpyudaṅmukhaḥ /
dhyāyed vidhiṁ rajoguṇaṁ raktavarṇam avarṇakam // 48 //

First I shall tell thee the Sagarbha Prāṇāyāma. Sitting in Sukhāsana posture, facing east or north, let him contemplate on Brahmā full of Rajas quality, of a blood-red colour, in the form of the letter *A* (अ).

iḍayā pūrayed vāyuṁ mātrayā ṣoḍaśaiḥ sudhīḥ /
pūrakānte kumbhakādye kartavyas tūḍḍīyānakaḥ // 49 //

Let the wise practitioner inhale by the left nostril, repeating *Aṁ* (अं) sixteen times. Then before he begins retention (but at the end of inhalation), let him perform Uḍḍīyāna Bandha.

sattvamayaṁ hariṁ dhyātvā ukāraṁ kṛṣṇavarṇakam /
catuḥṣaṣṭyā ca mātrayā kumbhakenaiva dhārayet // 50 //

Then let him retain breath by repeating U (उ) sixty-four times, contemplating on Hari, of a black colour and of Sattva quality.

tamomayaṁ śivaṁ dhyātvā makāraṁ śuklavarṇakam /
dvātriṁśanmātrayā caiva recayed vidhinā punaḥ // 51 //

Then let him exhale the breath through the right nostril by repeating *Maṁ* (मं) thirty-two times, contemplating Śiva of a white colour and of Tamas quality.

punaḥ piṅgalayāpūrya kumbhakenaiva dhārayet /
iḍayā recayet paścāt tadbījena krameṇa tu // 52 //

Then again inhale through Piṅgalā (right nostril), retain by Kumbhaka, and exhale by Iḍā (left), in the method taught above, changing the nostrils alternately.

anulomavilomena vāraṁvāraṁ ca sādhayet /
pūrakānte kumbhakāntaṁ dhṛtanāsāpuṭadvayam /
kaniṣṭhānāmikāṅguṣṭhais tarjanīmadhyame vinā // 53 //

Let him practise, thus alternating the nostrils again and again. When inhalation is completed, close both nostrils, the right one by the thumb and the left one by the ring-finger and little-finger, never using the index and middle-fingers. The nostrils are to be closed so long as Kumbhaka lasts.

prāṇāyāmo nigarbhas tu vinā bījena jāyate /
vāmajānūparinyastavāmapāṇitalaṁ bhramet /
ekādiśataparyantaṁ pūrakumbhakorecanam // 54 //

The Nirgarbha (or simple or Mantra-less) Prāṇāyāma is performed without the repetition of Bīja Mantra; and the period of Pūraka (inhalation or inspiration), Kumbhaka (retention), and Recaka (expiration), may be extended from one to one hundred Mātrās.

uttamā viṁśatirmātrā ṣoḍaśī mātrā madhyamā /
adhamā dvādaśī mātrā prāṇāyāmās tridhā smṛtāḥ // 55 //

The best is twenty Mātrās: i.e., Pūraka 20 seconds, Kumbhaka 80, and Recaka 40 seconds. The middling is sixteen Mātrās, i.e., 16, 64 and 32. The lowest is twelve Mātrās, i.e., 12, 48, 24. Thus Prāṇāyāma is of three sorts.

adhamāj jāyate gharmo merukampaśca madhyamāt /
uttamāc ca bhūmityagas trividhaṁ siddhilakṣaṇam // 56 //

By practising the lowest Prāṇāyāma for some time, the body begins to perspire copiously; by practising the middling, the body begins to quiver (especially, there is a feeling of quivering along the spinal cord). By the highest Prāṇāyāma, one leaves the ground, i.e., there is levitation. These signs attend the success of these three sorts of Prāṇāyāma.

prāṇāyāmāt khecaratvam prāṇāyāmād roganāśanam /
prāṇāyāmād bodhayec chaktiṁ prāṇāyāmād manonmanī /
ānando jāyate citte prāṇāyāmī sukhī bhavet // 57 //

By Prāṇāyāma is attained the power of levitation (Khecarī Śakti); by Prāṇāyāma diseases are cured; by Prāṇāyāma the Śakti (spiritual energy)is awakened; by Prāṇāyāma is obtained the calmness of mind and exaltation of mental powers (clairvoyance, etc.); by this mind becomes full of bliss; verily the practitioner of Prāṇāyāma is happy.

Sūryabheda Kumbhaka

atha sūryabhedakumbhakaḥ :

gheraṇḍa uvāca :

kathitaṁ sahitaṁ kumbhaṁ sūryabhedanakaṁ śṛṇu /
pūrayet sūryanāḍyā ca yathāśakti bahirmarut // 58 //
dhārayed bahuyatnena kumbhakena jalandharaiḥ /
yāvat svedaṁ nakhakeśābhyāṁ tāvat kurvantu kumbhakam//59//

Gheraṇḍa said:

I have told thee Sahita Kumbhaka; now hear Sūryabheda. Inspire with all your strength the external air through the Sun-tube (right nostril): retain this air with the greatest care, while performing the Jālandhara Mudrā. Let Kumbhaka be kept up so long as the perspiration does not burst out from the tips of the nails and the roots of the hair.

The Vāyus

prāṇo'pānaḥ samānaścodānavyānau tathaiva ca /
nāgaḥ kūrmaśca kṛkaro devadatto dhanañjayaḥ // 60 //

The Vāyus are ten, namely Prāṇa, Apāna, Samāna, Udāna and Vyāna; Nāga, Kūrma, Kṛkara, Devadatta and Dhanañjaya.

Their Seats

hṛdi prāṇo vahen nityaṁ apāno gudamaṇḍale /
samāno nābhideśe tu udānaḥ kaṇṭhamadhyagaḥ // 61 //
vyāno vyāpya śarīre tu pradhānāḥ pañca vāyavoḥ /
prāṇādyāḥ pañca vikhyātā nāgādyāḥ pañca vāyavaḥ // 62 //

Prāṇa moves always in the heart; Apāna in the region of anus; Samāna in the navel region; Udāna in the throat; and Vyāna pervades the whole body. These are the five principal Vāyus, known as Prāṇādi. They belong to the inner body. Nāgādi five Vāyus belong to the outer body.

teṣām api ca pañcānāṁ sthānāni ca vadāmyaham /
udgāre nāga ākhyātaḥ kūrmas tūnmīlane smṛtaḥ // 63 //
kṛkaraḥ kṣutkṛte jñeyo devadatto vijṛmbhaṇe /
na jahāti mṛtaṁ vāpi sarvavyāpī dhanañjayaḥ // 64 //

I now tell thee the seats of these five external Vāyus. Nāga-Vāyu performs the function of belching; Kūrma opens the eyelids; Kṛkara causes sneezing; Devadatta does yawning; Dhanañjaya pervades the whole gross body and does not leave it even after death.

nāgo gṛhṇāti caitanyaṁ kūrmaś caiva nimeṣaṇam /
kṣuttṛṣaṁ kṛkaraś caiva caturthena tu jṛmbhaṇam /
bhaved dhanañjayāc chabdaḥ kṣaṇamātraṁ na niḥsaret // 65 //

Nāga-Vāyu gives rise to consciousness; Kūrma causes vision; Kṛkara, hunger and thirst; Devadatta produces yawning and by Dhanañjaya sound is produced; this does not ever leave the body.

sarve te sūryasaṁbhinnā nābhimūlāt samuddharet /
iḍayā recayet paścād dhairyeṇākhaṇḍavegataḥ // 66 //
punaḥ sūryeṇa cākṛṣya kumbhayitvā yathāvidhi /
recayitvā sādhayet tu krameṇa ca punaḥ punaḥ // 67 //

All these Vāyus, separated by Sūrya-nāḍī, let him raise up from the root of the navel; then let him expire by the Iḍā-nāḍī, slowly and with unbroken, continuous force. Let him again draw the air through the right nostril, retaining it, as taught above, and exhale it again. Let him do this again and again. In this process, the air is always inspired through the Sūrya-nāḍī.

Its benefits :

kumbhakaḥ sūryabhedas tu jarāmṛtyuvināśakaḥ /
bodhayet kuṇḍalīṁ śaktiṁ dehānalaṁ vivardhayet /
iti te kathitaṁ caṇḍa sūryabhedanam uttamam // 68 //

Sūryabheda Kumbhaka destroys decay and death; awakens the Kuṇḍalī śakti; increases the bodily fire. O Caṇḍa, thus have I taught thee Sūryabhedana Kumbhaka.

N.B.: The description of this process, as given in Haṭha-Yoga Pradīpikā, is somewhat different. Soon after Pūraka (inspiration), one should perform Jālandhara and at the end of Kumbhaka but before Recaka perform Uḍḍīyānabandha. Then quickly contract the anal orifice by Mūlabandha, contract the throat, pull in the stomach towards the back; by this process the air is forced into Brahma-nāḍī (Suṣumṇā). Raise Apāna up, lower Prāṇa, below Kaṇṭha; a Yogī becomes free from decay. The air should be drawn through the right nostril and expelled through the left.

Ujjāyī

atha ujjāyī kumbhakaḥ :
nāsābhyāṁ vāyum ākṛṣya mukhamadhye ca dhārayet /
hṛdgalābhyām samākṛṣya vāyuṁ vaktre ca dhārayet // 69 //

Close the mouth, draw in the external air by both the nostrils, and pull up the internal air from the lungs and throat; retain them in the mouth.

mukhaṁ prakṣālya saṁvandya kuryāj jālandharaṁ tataḥ /
āśakti kumbhakaṁ kṛtvā dhārayed avirodhataḥ // 70 //

Then having washed the mouth (i.e., expelled air through mouth) perform Jālandhara. Let him perform Kumbhaka with all his might and retain the air unhindered.

ujjāyīkumbhakaṁ kṛtvā sarvakāryāṇi sādhayet /
na bhavet kapharogaś ca krūravāyur ajīrṇakam // 71 //
āmavātaḥ kṣayo kāso jvaraplīhā na vidyate /
jarāmṛtyuvināśāya cojjāyīṁ sādhayen naraḥ // 72 //

All works are accomplished by Ujjāyī Kumbhaka. He is never attacked by phlegmatic diseases, and nervous diseases, indigestion, dysentery, consumption, cough, fever and (enlarged) spleen. Let a man perform Ujjāyī to conquer old age and death.

N.B.: See Haṭha-Yoga-Pradīpikā, II 51, 53 for a different description of this.

Śītalī

atha śītalīkumbhakaḥ :
jihvayā vāyum akṛṣya udare pūrayec chanaiḥ /
kṣaṇaṁ ca kumbhakaṁ kṛtvā nāsābhyāṁ recayet punaḥ // 73 //

Draw in the air through the mouth (with the lips contracted and tongue thrown out), and fill the stomach slowly. Retain it there for a short time. Then exhale it through both the nostrils.

sarvadā sādhayed yogī śītalīkumbhakaṁ śubham /
ajīrṇaṁ kaphapittaṁ ca naiva tasya prajāyate // 74 //

Let the Yogī always practise this Śītalī Kumbhaka, giver of bliss; by so doing, he will be free from indigestion, phlegmatic and bilious disorders.

Bhastrikā (Bellow)

atha bhastrikākumbhakaḥ :
bhastrikā lohakārāṇāṁ yathā krameṇa saṁbhramet /
tathā vāyuṁ ca nāsābhyām ubhābhyāṁ cālayec chanaiḥ // 75 //

As the bellows of an ironsmith constantly dilate and contract, similarly let him slowly draw in the air by both the nostrils and expand the stomach; then throw it out quickly (the wind making sound like bellows).

evaṁ viṁśativāraṁ ca kṛtvā kuryāc ca kumbhakam /
tadante cālayed vāyuṁ pūrvoktaṁ ca yathavidhi // 76 //
trivāraṁ sādhayed evaṁ bhastrikākumbhakaṁ sudhīḥ /
na ca rogo na ca kleśa ārogyaṁ ca dine dine // 77 //

Having thus inspired and expired quickly twenty times, let him perform Kumbhaka; then let him expel it by the previous method. Let the wise one perform this Bhastrikā (bellows-like) Kumbhaka thrice. He will never suffer from any disease and will be always healthy.

Bhrāmarī or Beetle-droning Kumbhaka

atha bhrāmarīkumbhakaḥ :
ardharātre gate yogī jantūnāṁ śabdavarjite /
karṇau pidhāya hastābhyāṁ kuryāt pūrakakumbhakam // 78 //

At past midnight, in a place where there are no sounds of any animals, etc., to be heard, let the Yogī practise Pūraka and Kumbhaka, closing the ears by the hands.

śṛṇuyād dakṣiṇe karṇe nādam antargataṁ śubham /
prathamaṁ jhillikānādaṁ vaṁśīnādaṁ tataḥ param // 79 //
meghajharjharabhramarī ghaṇṭā kāṁsyaṁ tataḥ param /
turībherīmṛdaṁgādininādānakadundubhiḥ // 80 //

He will hear then various internal sounds in his right ear. The first sound will be like that of crickets, then that of a lute, then that of a thunder, then that of a drum, then that of a beetle, then that of bells, then those of gongs of bell-metal, trumpets, kettle-drums, Mṛdaṅga, military drums, and Dundubhi, etc.

evaṁ nānāvidho nādo jāyate nityam abhyasāt /
anāhatasya śabdasya tasya śabdasya yo dhvaniḥ // 81 //
dhvaner antargataṁ jyotir jyotirantargataṁ manaḥ /
tanmano vilayaṁ yāti tadviṣṇo paramaṁ padam /
evaṁ bhrāmarīsaṁsiddhiḥ samādhisiddhim āpnuyāt // 82 //

Thus various sounds are cognised by daily practice of this Kumbhaka. Last of all is heard the Anāhata sound rising from the heart; of this sound there is a resonance; in that resonance there is a light. In that light the mind should be immersed. When the mind is absorbed, then it reaches the highest seat of Viṣṇu (Parama-pada). By success in this Bhrāmarī Kumbhaka one gets success in Samādhi.

Mūrcchā

atha mūrcchākumbhakaḥ :
sukhena kumbhakaṁ kṛtvā manaś ca bhruvor antaram /
santyajya viṣayān sarvān manomūrcchā sukhapradā /
ātmani manāso yogād ānando jāyate dhruvam // 83 //

Having performed Kumbhaka with comfort, let him withdraw the mind from all objects and fix it in the space between the two eyebrows. This causes fainting of the mind, and gives happiness. For, by thus joining the Manas with the Ātmā, bliss is certainly obtained.

Kevalī

atha kevalīkumbhakaḥ :
haṅkāreṇa bahir yāti saḥkāreṇa viśet punaḥ /
ṣaṭśatāni divārātrau sahasrāṇyekaviṁśatiḥ /
ajapāṁ nāma gāyatrīṁ jīvo japati sarvadā // 84 //

The breath of every person in entering makes the sound of "saḥ" and in coming out, that of "haṁ". These two sounds make "so', ham" "I am That" or haṁsa "The Great Swan". Throughout a day and a night there are twenty-one thousand six hundred such respirations(that is, 15 respirations per minute). Every living being

(Jīva) performs this Japa unconsciously, but constantly. This is called Ajapā Gāyatrī.

mūlādhāre yathā haṁsas tathā hi hṛdi paṅkaje /
tathā nāsāpuṭadvandve tribhirhaṁsasamāgamaḥ // 85 //

This Ajapā-japa is performed in three places, viz, Mūlādhāra, Anāhata lotus (heart) and Ājñā lotus (the space where the two eyebrows join).

ṣaṇnavatyaṅgulīmānaṁ śarīraṁ karmarūpakam /
dehād bahirgato vāyuḥ svabhāvād dvādaśāṅguliḥ // 86 //
gāyane ṣoḍaśāṅgulyo bhojane viṁśatis tathā /
caturviṁśāṅguliḥ panthe nidrāyāṁ triṁśadaṅguliḥ /
maithune ṣaṭtriṁśad uktaṁ vyāyāme ca tatodhikam // 87 //

This body of Vāyu is ninety-six digits length (i.e., six feet) as a standard. The ordinary length of the air-current when expired is twelve digits (nine inches); in singing, its length becomes sixteen digits (one foot); in eating, it is twenty digits (15 inches); in walking, it is twenty-four digits (18 inches); in sleep, it is thirty digits (27 1/2 inches); in copulation, it is thirty-six digits (27 inches); and in taking physical exercise, it is more than that.

svabhāve ' sya gater nyūne paramāyuḥ pravardhate /
āyuḥkṣayo ' dhike prokto mārute cāntarādgate // 88 //

By decreasing the natural length of the expired current from nine inches to less and less, there takes place increase of life; and by increasing the current, there is decrease of life.

tasmāt prāṇe sthite dehe maraṇaṁ naiva jāyate /
vāyunā ghaṭasambandhe bhavet kevalakumbhakam // 89 //

So long as breath remains in the body there is no death. When the full length of the wind is all confined in the body, nothing being allowed to go out, it is Kevala Kumbhaka.

yāvajjīvaṁ japen mantraṁ ajapāsaṅkhyakevalam /
adyāvadhi dhṛtaṁ saṁkhyāvibhramaṁ kevalīkṛte // 90 //
ata eva hi kartavyaḥ kevalīkumbhako naraiḥ /
kevalī cājapāsaṅkhyā dviguṇā ca manonmanī // 91 //

All Jīvas are constantly and unconsciously reciting this Ajapā

Mantra, only for a fixed number of times everyday. But a Yogī should recite this consciously and counting the numbers. By doubling the number of Ajapā (i.e., by 30 respirations per minute), the state of Manonmanī (fixedness of mind) is attained. There are no regular Recaka and Pūraka in this process. It is only (Kevala) Kumbhaka.

nāsābhyāṁ vāyum akṛṣya kevalaṁ kumbhakaṁ caret /
ekādikacatuḥṣaṣṭiṁ dhārayet prathame dine // 92 //

By inspiring air by both nostrils, let him perform Kevala Kumbhaka. On the first day, let him retain breath from one to sixty-four times.

kevalīm aṣṭadhā kuryād yāme yāme dine dine /
athavā pañcadhā kuryād yatha tat kathayāmi te // 93 //
prātarmadhyāhnasāyāhne madhye rātricaturthake /
trisandhyam atha vā kuryāt samamāne dine dine // 94 //

This Kevalī should be performed eight times a day, once in every three hours; or one may do it five times a day, as I shall tell thee. First in the early morning, then at noon, then in the twilight, then at midnight, and then in the fourth quarter of the night. Or one may do it thrice a day, i.e., in the morning, noon and evening.

pañcavāraṁ dine vṛddhir vāraikaṁ ca dine tathā /
ajapāparimāṇaṁ ca yāvat siddhiḥ prajāyate // 95 //
prāṇāyāmaṁ kevalīṁ ca tadā vadati yogavit /
kevalīkumbhake siddhe kiṁ na siddhyati bhūtale // 96 //

So long as success is not obtained in Kevalī, he should increase the length of Ajapā-japa every day, one to five times. He who knows Prāṇāyāma and Kevalī is the real Yogī. What can he not accomplish in this world who has acquired success in Kevalī Kumbhaka?

iti śrīgheraṇḍasaṁhitāyāṁ gheraṇḍacaṇḍasaṁvāde
ghaṭasthayogaprakaraṇe prāṇāyāmaprayogo nāma pañcamopadeśaḥ //5//

End of Chapter 5. on Prāṇāyāma.

CHAPTER 6

Dhyāna Yoga

Ṣaṣṭhopadeśaḥ

atha dhyānayogaḥ :

gheraṇḍa uvāca:

sthūlaṁ jyotis tathā sūkṣmaṁ dhyānasya trividhaṁ viduḥ /
sthūlaṁ mūrtimayaṁ proktaṁ jyotis tejomayaṁ tathā/
sūkṣaṁ bindumayaṁ brahma kuṇḍalī paradevatā// 1 //

Gheraṇḍa said :

Dhyāna or contemplation is of three kinds: gross, luminous and subtle. When a particular figure, such as one's Guru or Deity, is contemplated, it is Sthūla or gross contemplation. When Brahma or Prakṛti is contemplated as a mass of light, it is called Jyotis contemplation. When Brahma as a Bindu (point) and Kuṇḍalī as a great deity are contemplated, it is sūkṣma or Subtle contemplation.

Sthūla Dhyāna

atha sthūladhyānam :
svakāyahṛdaye dhyāyet sudhāsāgaram uttamam /
tanmadhye ratnadīpaṁ tu suratnavālukāmayam // 2 //
caturdikṣu nīpataruṁ bahupuṣpasamanvitam /
nīpopavanasaṅkulair veṣṭitaṁ parikhā iva // 3 //
mālatīmallikājātikeśarais campakais tathā /
pārijātaiḥ sthalapadmair gandhāmoditadiṅmukhaiḥ// 4 //
tanmadhye saṁsmared yogī kalpavṛkṣaṁ manoharam /
catuḥśākhācaturvedaṁ nityapuṣpaphalānvitam // 5 //

bhramarāḥ kokilās tatra guñjanti nigadanti ca /
dhyāyet tatra sthiro bhūtvā mahāmāṇikyamaṇḍapam//6//
tanmadhye tu smared yogī paryaṅkaṁ sumanoharam /
tatreṣṭadevatāṁ dhyāyet yaddhyānaṁ gurubhāṣitam//7//
yasya devasya yad rūpaṁ yathā bhūṣaṇavāhanam /
tad rūpaṁ dhyāyate nityaṁ sthūladhyānam idaṁ viduḥ//8//

(Having closed the eyes) let him contemplate that there is a sea of nectar in his heart : that in the midst of that sea there is an island of precious stones, the very sand of which is pulverised diamonds and rubies; that on all sides of it, there are Kadamba trees, laden with sweet flowers; that, next to these trees, like a rampart, there is a row of flowering trees, such as Mālatī, Mallikā, Jāti, Keśara, Campaka, Pārijāta and Padma; and that the fragrance of these flowers is spread all round, in every quarter. In the middle of this garden, let the Yogī imagine that there stands a beautiful Kalpa tree, having four branches, representing the four Vedas, and that it is full of flowers and fruits; bees are humming there and cuckoos singing. Beneath that tree, let him imagine a rich platform of precious gems, and on that a costly throne inlaid with jewels; and that on that throne sits his particular Deity, as taught to him by his Guru. Let him contemplate on the appropriate form, ornaments and vehicle of that Deity. Constant contemplation of such a form is Sthūla Dhyāna.

Prakārāntaram

sahasrāre mahāpadme karṇikāyāṁ vicintayet /
vilagnasahitaṁ padmaṁ dvādaśair dalasaṁyutam // 9//
śuklavarṇaṁ mahātejo dvādaśair bījabhāṣitam /
hasakṣamalavarayuṁ hasakhaphreṁ yathākramam // 10 //
tanmadhye karṇikāyāṁ tu akathādi rekhātrayam /
halakṣakoṇasaṁyuktaṁ praṇavaṁ tatra vartate // 11 //

Another Method

Let the Yogī imagine that in the pericarp of the great thousand-petalled Lotus (Brain) there is a smaller lotus having twelve petals. Its colour is white. It is highly luminous, having twelve Bīja letters, named ha, sa, kṣa, ma, la, va, ra, yuṃ, ha, sa, kha, phreṃ. In the pericarp of this smaller lotus there are three lines forming a triangle: a, ka, tha : having three angles called ha, la, kṣa : and in the middle of this triangle, there is the Praṇava, Om.

nādabindumayaṁ pīṭhaṁ dhyāyet tatra manoharam /
tatropari haṁsayugmaṁ pādukā tatra vartate // 12 //

Then let him contemplate that in that there is a beautiful seat having Nāda and Bindu. On that seat there are two swans, and a pair of wooden sandals or shoes.

dhyāyet tatra guruṁ devaṁ dvibhujaṁ ca trilocanam /
śvetāmbaradharaṁ devaṁ śuklagandhānulepanam // 13 //
śuklapuṣpamayaṁ mālyaṁ raktaśaktisamanvitam /
evaṁvidhagurudhyānāt sthūladhyānaṁ prasidhyati // 14 //

There let him contemplate his Guru Deva, having two arms and three eyes, and dressed in pure white, anointed with white sandalpaste, wearing garlands of white flowers; to the left of whom stands Śakti of blood-red colour. By thus contemplating the Guru, Sthūla Dhyāna is attained.

Jyoti Dhyāna

atha jyotirdhyānaṁ :

gheraṇḍa uvāca:

kathitaṁ sthūladhyānaṁ tu tejodhyānaṁ śṛṇuṣva me /
yaddhyānena yogasiddhir ātma pratyakṣam eva ca // 15 //

Gheraṇḍa said :

I have told thee Sthūla Dhyāna; listen now to the contemplation of Light, by which a Yogī attains success and sees his Self.

mūlādhāre kuṇḍalinī bhujagākārarūpiṇī /
jīvātmā tiṣṭhati tatra pradīpakalikākṛtiḥ /
dhyāyet tejomayaṁ brahma tejodhyānaṁ parātparam // 16 //

In the Mūlādhāra is Kuṇḍalinī, having the form of a serpent. Jīvātmā is there like the flame of a lamp. Contemplate on this flame as the Luminous Brahma. This is Tejo Dhyāna or Jyoti Dhyāna.

Prakārāntaram

bhruvor madhye manaūrdhve yat tejaḥ praṇavātmakam /
dhyāyej jvālāvalīyuktaṁ tejodhyānaṁ tadeva hi // 17 //

Another Method

In the middle of the two eyebrows, above the Manas, there is a Light consisting of Om. Let him contemplate on this flame. This is another method of contemplation of Light.

Sūkṣma Dhyāna

atha sūkṣmadhyānam :

gheraṇḍa uvāca :

tejodhyānaṁ śrutaṁ caṇḍa sūkṣmadhyānaṁ śṛṇuṣva me /
bahubhāgyavaśād yasya kuṇḍalī jāgratī bhavet // 18 //
ātmanā saha yogena netrarandhrād vinirgatā /
vihared rājamārge ca cañcalatvān na dṛśyate // 19 //

Gheraṇḍa Said:

O Caṇḍa, thou hast heard Tejo Dhyāna; listen now to Sūkṣma Dhyāna. When by a great good fortune, Kuṇḍalī is awakened, it joins with the Ātmā and leaves the body through the portals of the two eyes and enjoys itself by walking on the royal road (Astral Light). It cannot be seen on account of its subtleness and great changeability.

śāmbhavīmudrayā yogī dhyānayogena sidhyati /
sūkṣmadhyānam idaṁ gopyaṁ devānām api durlabham // 20 //

The Yogī, however, attains this success by performing Śāmbhavī Mudrā, i.e., by gazing fixedly at space without winking. (Then he will see his Sūkṣma Śarīra.) This is called Sūkṣma Dhyāna, difficult to be attained even by Devas, as it is a great mystery.

sthūladhyānāc chataguṇaṁ tejodhyānaṁ pracakṣate /
tejodhyānāl lakṣaguṇam sūkṣmadhyānaṁ parātparam // 21 //

The contemplation of Light is a hundred times superior to contemplation of Form; and a hundred thousand times superior to Tejo Dhyāna is the contemplation of the Sūkṣma.

iti te kathitaṁ caṇḍa dhyānayogaṁ sudurlabham /
ātmā sākṣād bhaved yasmāt tasmād dhyānaṁ viśiṣyate // 22 //

O Caṇḍa, thus have I told thee the Dhyāna Yoga—a most precious knowledge; for, by it, there is direct perception of the Self. Hence Dhyāna has special importance.

iti śrīgheraṇḍasaṁhitāyāṁ gheraṇḍacaṇḍasaṁvāde ghaṭasthayoge saptamasādhane dhyānayogo nāma ṣaṣṭhopadeśaḥ //6//

End of Chapter 6 on Dhyāna Yoga.

CHAPTER 7

Samādhi Yoga

Saptamopadeśaḥ

atha samādhiyogaḥ :

gheraṇḍa uvāca :

samādhiś ca paro yogo bahubhāgyena labhyate /
guroḥ kṛpāprasādena prāpyate gurubhaktitaḥ // 1 //

gheraṇḍa said :

Samādhi is a great Yoga; it is acquired by great good fortune. It is obtained through the grace and kindness of a Guru, and by intense devotion to him.

vidyāpratītiḥ svagurupratītir ātmapratītir manasaḥ prabodhaḥ /
dine dine yasya bhavet sa yogī suśobhanābhyāsam upaiti sadyaḥ // 2 //

That Yogī quickly attains this most beautiful practice of Samādhi, who has confidence(or faith)in knowledge, faith in his own Guru, faith in his own Self, and whose mind (Manas)awakens to intelligence from day to day.

ghaṭād bhinnaṁ manaḥ kṛtvā aikyaṁ kuryāt parātmani/
samādhiṁ taṁ vijānīyān muktasañjño daśādibhiḥ// 3 //

Separate the Manas from the body, and unite it with Paramātmā. This is known as Samādhi or Mukti from all states of consciousness.

ahaṁ brahma na cānyo'smi brahmaivāhaṁ na śokabhāk /
saccidānandarūpo'haṁ nityamuktaḥ svabhāvavān// 4 //

I am Brahma; I am nothing else; Brahma is certainly I; I am not participator of sorrow; I am Existence, Intelligence and Bliss; always free; of one essence.

śāmbhavyā caiva khecaryā bhrāmaryā yonimudrayā /
dhyānaṁ nādaṁ rasānandaṁ layasiddhiś caturvidhā // 5 //
pañcadhā bhaktiyogena manomūrcchā ca ṣaḍvidhā /
ṣaḍvidho'yaṁ rājayogaḥ pratyekam avadhārayet // 6 //

Samādhi is fourfold, viz., Dhyāna-Samādhi, Nāda-Samādhi, Rasānanda-Samādhi, and Laya-Samādhi; respectively accomplished by Śāmbhavī Mudrā, Khecarī Mudrā, Bhrāmarī Mudrā and Yoni-Mudrā. Bhakti-Yoga Samādhi is fifth, and Rāja-Yoga Samādhi, attained through Mano-Mūrcchā Kumbhaka, is the sixth form of Samādhi.

Dhyāna-yoga Samādhi

atha dhyānayogasamādhiḥ :
śāmbhavīṁ mudrikāṁ kṛtvā ātmapratyakṣam ānayet /
bindubrahmamayaṁ dṛṣṭvā manas tatra niyojayet // 7 //

Performing the Śāmbhavī Mudrā perceive the Ātmā. Having seen once Brahma in a Bindu (point of light), fix the mind on that point.

khamadhye kuru cātmānam ātmamadhye ca khaṁ kuru /
ātmānaṁ khamayaṁ dṛṣṭvā na kiñcid api bādhate /
sadānandamayo bhūtvā samādhistho bhaven naraḥ // 8 //

Bring the Ātmā in Kha (Ether); bring the Kha (Ether or Space)in the Ātmā. Thus seeing the Ātmā full of Kha(Space or Brahma), nothing will obstruct him. Being full of perpetual bliss, the man enters Samādhi (Trance or Ecstasy).

Nāda-yoga Samādhi

atha nādayogasamādhiḥ :
sādhanāt khecarīmudrā rasanordhvagatā yadā /
tadā samādhisiddhiḥ syāddhitvā sādhāraṇakriyām // 9 //

Turn the tongue upwards, closing the wind-passage by performing Khecarī Mudrā; by so doing, Samādhi will be induced; there is no necessity of performing anything else.

Rasānanda-yoga Samādhi

atha rasānanandayogasamādhiḥ :
anilaṁ mandavegena bhrāmarīkumbhakaṁ caret /
mandaṁ mandaṁ recayed vāyuṁ bhṛṅganādaṁ tato bhavet// 10//
antaḥsthaṁ bhrāmarīnādaṁ śrutvā tatra mano nayet /
samādhir jāyate tatra ānandaḥ so ' ham ityataḥ // 11 //

Let him perform the Bhrāmarī Kumbhaka, drawing in the air slowly; expel the air slowly and slowly, with a buzzing sound like that of a beetle. Let him carry the Manas and place it in the centre of this sound of humming beetle. By so doing, there will be Samādhi and by this, knowledge of 'so' ham' (I am That) arises, and a great happiness takes place.

Laya-siddhi-yoga Samādhi

atha layasiddhiyogasamādhiḥ :
yonimudrāṁ samāsādya svayaṁ śaktimayo bhavet /
suśṛṅgārarasenaiva viharet paramātmani // 12 //
ānandamayaḥ saṁbhūtvā aikyaṁ brahmaṇi sambhavet /
ahaṁ brahmeti cādvaitaṁ samādhis tena jāyate // 13 //

Perform Yoni-Mudrā, and let him imagine that he is Śakti and Paramātmā is Puruṣa, and that both have been united in one. By this he becomes full of bliss, and realises *Ahaṁ Brahmāsmi,* 'I am Brahma.' This leads to Advaita Samādhi.

Bhakti-yoga Samādhi

atha bhaktiyogasamādhiḥ :
svakīyahṛdaye dhyāyed iṣṭadevasvarūpakam /
cintayed bhaktiyogena paramāhlādapūrvakam // 14 //
ānandāśrupulakena daśābhāvaḥ prajāyate /
samādhiḥ saṁbhavet tena saṁbhavec ca manonmanī // 15 //

Let him contemplate within his heart his special Deity; let him be full of ecstasy by such contemplation; let him shed tears of happiness; and by so doing he will become entranced. This leads to Samādhi and Manonmanī.

Rāja-yoga Samādhi

atha rājayogasamādhiḥ :
manomūrcchāṁ samāsādya mano ātmani yojayet /
paramātmanaḥ samāyogāt samādhiṁ samavāpnuyāt // 16 //

Performing Manomūrchhā Kumbhaka, unite the Manas with the Ātmā. By this union is obtained Rāja-yoga Samādhi.

Praise of Samādhi

atha samādhiyogamāhātmyam :
iti te kathitaś caṇḍa samādhir muktilakṣaṇam /
rājayogasamādhiḥ syād ekātmanyeva sādhanam /
unmanī sahajāvasthā sarve caikātmavācakāḥ // 17 //

O Caṇḍa, thus have I told thee about Samādhi which leads to emancipation. Rājayoga Samādhi, Unmanī, Sahajāvasthā are all synonyms, and mean the Union of Manas with Ātmā.

jale viṣṇuḥ sthale viṣṇur viṣṇuḥ parvatamastake /
jvālāmālākule viṣṇuḥ sarvaṁ viṣṇumayaṁ jagat // 18 //

Viṣṇu is in water; Viṣṇu is in earth; Viṣṇu is on the peak of the mountain; Viṣṇu is in the midst of volcanic fires and flames: the whole universe is full of Viṣṇu.

bhūcarāḥ khecarāś cāmī yāvanto jīvajantavaḥ /
vṛkṣagulmalatāvallītṛṇādyā vāriparvatāḥ /
sarvaṁ brahma vijānīyāt sarvaṁ paśyati cātmani // 19 //

All those that walk on land or move in the air, all living and animate creation, trees, shrubs, roots, creepers and grass, etc., oceans and mountains—all, know ye, to be Brahma. See them all in Ātmā.

ātmā ghaṭasthacaitanyam advaitaṁ śāśvataṁ param /
ghaṭād vibhinnato jñātvā vītarāgaṁ vivāsanam // 20 //

The Ātmā confined in the body is Caitanya or Consciousness; it is without a second, the Eternal, the Highest; knowing it separate from body, let him be free from desires and passions.

evaṁ mithaḥ samādhiḥ syāt sarvasaṁkalpavarjitaḥ /
svadehe putradārādibāndhaveṣu dhanādiṣu /
sarveṣu nirmamo bhūtvā samādhiṁ samavāpnuyāt // 21 //

Thus is Samādhi obtained, free from all desires. Free from attachment to his own body, to son, wife, friends, kinsmen, or riches, being free from all, let him fully obtain Samādhi.

tattvaṁ layāmṛtaṁ gopyaṁ śivoktaṁ vividhāni ca /
teṣāṁ saṅkṣepam ādāya kathitaṁ muktilakṣaṇam // 22 //

Śiva has revealed many Tattvas, such as Laya Amṛta, etc.; of them, I have told thee an abstract, leading to emancipation.

iti te kathitaś caṇḍa samādhir durlabhaḥ paraḥ /
yaṁ jñātvā na punarjanma jāyate bhūmimaṇḍale // 23 //

O Caṇḍa, thus have I told thee of Samādhi, difficult of attainment. By knowing this, there is no rebirth on this earth.

iti śrīgheraṇḍasaṁhitāyāṁ gheraṇḍacaṇḍasaṁvāde
ghaṭasthayogasādhane yogasya saptasāre samādhiyogo nāma
saptamopadeśaḥ samāptaḥ //7//

End of Chapter 7 on Samādhi Yoga.

Section III

ŚIVA-SAṀHITĀ

CHAPTER 1

The Path of Harmony

Prathamaḥ Paṭalaḥ

Existence One Only

ekaṁ jñānaṁ nityam ādyantaśūnyaṁ nānyat kiñcid vartate vastu satyam /
yadbhedo'sminnindriyopādhinā vai jñānasyāyaṁ bhāsate nānyathaiva // 1 //

Jñāna [Gnosis] alone is eternal; it is without beginning and end; there exists no other real thing. Diversities which we see in the world are results of sense-conditions; when the latter cease, then this Jñāna alone, and nothing else, remains.

atha bhaktānurakto hi vakti yogānuśāsanam /
īśvaraḥ sarvabhūtānām ātmamuktipradāyakaḥ // 2 //
tyaktvā vivādaśīlānāṁ mataṁ durjñānahetukam /
ātmajñānāya bhūtānām ananyagatícetasām // 3 //

The Lord, Īśvara, the lover of his devotees and giver of spiritual emancipation to all creatures, now expounds the science of Yoga. In it are discarded all those doctrines of disputants which lead to false knowledge. It is for the spiritual enlightenment of persons whose minds exclusively resort to Him.

Differences of Opinion

satyaṁ kecit praśaṁsanti tapaḥ śaucaṁ tathāpare /
kṣamāṁ kecit praśaṁsanti tathaiva samam ārjavam // 4 //

Some praise truth; others purification and asceticism; some praise forgiveness; others equality and sincerity.

kecid dānaṁ praśaṁsanti pitṛkarma tathāpare /
kecit karma praśaṁsanti kecid vairāgyam uttamam // 5 //

Some praise charity; others laud offerings made in honour of one's ancestors; some praise action *(Karma)*; others think non-attachment *(Vairāgya)* to be the best.

kecid gṛhasthakarmāṇi praśaṁsanti vicakṣaṇāḥ /
agnihotrādikaṁ karma tathā kecit paraṁ viduḥ // 6 //

Some wise persons praise performance of the duties of householders; other authorities hold fire-offerings etc. as the highest.

mantrayogaṁ praśaṁsanti kecit tīrthānusevanam /
evaṁ bahūn upāyāṁs tu pravadanti hi muktaye // 7 //

Some praise *Mantra Yoga;* others pilgrimage to sacred places. Thus, diverse are the ways which people declare as leading to emancipation.

evaṁ vyavasitā loke kṛtyākṛtyavido janāḥ /
vyāmoham eva gacchanti vimuktāḥ pāpakarmabhiḥ // 8 //

Being thus diversely engaged in this world, even those who still know what actions are good and what evil, though free from sin, become subject to bewilderment.

etanmatāvalambī yo labdhvā duritapuṇyake /
bhramatītyavaśaḥ so'tra janmamṛtyuparamparām // 9 //

Persons who follow these doctrines, having committed good and bad actions, constantly wander in the worlds, in the cycle of births and deaths, bound by dire necessity.

anyair matimatām śreṣṭhair guptālokanatatparaiḥ /
ātmāno bahavaḥ proktā nityāḥ sarvagatās tathā // 10 //

Others, wiser among the many, and eagerly devoted to the investigation of the occult, declare that the souls are many and eternal, and omnipresent.

yad yat pratyakṣaviṣayaṁ tad anyan nāsti cakṣate /
kutaḥ svargādayaḥ santītyanye niścitamānasāḥ // 11 //

Others say, "Only those things can be said to exist which are perceived through the senses and nothing besides them; where is heaven or hell ?" Such is their firm belief.

jñānapravāha ityanye śūnyaṁ kecit paraṁ viduḥ /
dvāveva tattvaṁ manyante' pare prakṛtipūruṣau // 12 //

Others believe the world to be a series of cognitions; some say the void as the ultimate. Still others believe in two ultimate reals viz., Matter *(Prakṛti)* and Spirit *(Puruṣa)*.

atyantabhinnamatayaḥ paramārthaparāṅmukhāḥ /
evam anye tu saṁcintya yathāmati yathāśrutam // 13 //
nirīśvaram idaṁ prāhuḥ seśvaraṁ ca tathāpare /
vadanti vividhair bhedaiḥ suyuktyā sthitikātarāḥ // 14 //

Thus believing in widely different doctrines, with faces turned away from the supreme goal, they think, according to their understanding and education, that this universe is without God; others say there is a God, basing their assertions on various good arguments, anxious to know the correct position.

ete cānye ca munayaḥ saṁjñābhedā pṛthagvidhāḥ /
śāstreṣu kathitā hyete lokavyāmohakārakāḥ // 15 //
etad vivādaśīlānāṁ mataṁ vaktuṁ na śakyate /
bhramantyasmin janāḥ sarve muktimārgabahiṣkṛtāḥ // 16 //

These and many other sages with various different denominations, have been declared in the Śāstras as creators of confusion in peoples' minds. It is not possible to describe fully the doctrines of these persons so fond of disputation. People thus wander in this universe, being driven away from the path of emancipation.

Yoga the Only True Method

ālokya sarvaśāstrāṇi vicārya ca punaḥ punaḥ /
idam ekaṁ suniṣpannaṁ yogaśāstraṁ paraṁ matam // 17 //

Having studied all the Śāstras and having pondered over them well, again and again, this Yoga Śāstra has been found to be the only true and firm doctrine.

yasmin jñāte sarvam idaṁ jñātaṁ bhavati niścitam /
tasmin pariśramaḥ kāryaḥ kim anyac chāstrabhāṣitam // 18 //

One should exert to know that which being known everything else becomes known as a certainty. Why then should one care to know what other texts say.

yogaśāstram idaṁ gopyam asmābhiḥ paribhāṣitam /
subhaktāya pradātavyaṁ trailokye ca mahātmane // 19 //

This Yoga Śāstra, now being declared by us, is a very secret doctrine, only to be revealed to a high-souled pious devotee throughout the three worlds.

Karmakāṇḍa

karmakāṇḍaṁ jñānakāṇḍam iti vedo dvidhā mataḥ /
bhavati dvividho bhedo jñānakāṇḍasya karmaṇaḥ // 20 //

There are two parts (of the Veda): *Karmakāṇḍa* (ritualism) and *Jñānakāṇḍa* (wisdom). *Jñānakāṇḍa* and *Karmakāṇḍa* are again each subdivided into two parts.

dvividhaḥ karmakāṇḍaḥ syān niṣedhavidhipūrvakaḥ // 21 //

Karmakāṇḍa is twofold: one consisting of injunctions and the other of prohibitions.

niṣiddhakarmakaraṇe pāpaṁ bhavati niścitam /
vidhinā karmakaraṇe puṇyaṁ bhavati niścitam // 22 //

Prohibited acts when done will certainly bring forth sin; from performance of enjoined acts there certainly results merit.

trividho vidhikūṭaḥ syān nityanaimittakāmyataḥ /
nitye'kṛte kilviṣaṁ syāt kāmye naimittike phalam // 23 //

Injunctions are of three kinds according as they prescribe *nitya* (regular), *naimittika* (occasional), and *kāmya* (optional) acts. By the non-performance of *nitya* or daily rites there accrues sin (but by their performance no merit is gained). On the other hand, occasional and optional acts, if done or left undone, result in merit or demerit as their fruit.

dvividhan tu phalaṁ jñeyaṁ svargo naraka eva ca /
svargo nānāvidhaś caiva narako' pi tathā bhavet // 24 //

Fruits of actions are of two kinds—heaven and hell. The heavens are of various kinds and so also hells are diverse.

puṇyakarmaṇi vai svargo narakaḥ pāpakarmaṇi /
karmabandhamayī sṛṣṭir nānyathā bhavati dhruvam // 25 //

Good actions lead verily to heaven, and sinful deeds verily lead to hell; creation is surely the natural outcome of *Karma* and not otherwise.

jantubhiś cānubhūyante svarge nānāsukhāni ca /
nānāvidhāni duḥkhāni narake duḥsahāni vai // 26 //

Creatures enjoy many pleasures of various kinds in heaven; many intolerable pains are suffered in hell.

pāpakarmavaśād duḥkhaṁ puṇyakarmavaśāt sukham /
tasmāt sukhārthī vividhaṁ puṇyaṁ prakurute dhruvam // 27 //

From sinful acts suffering; from good acts happiness results. For the sake of happiness, a man performs good actions.

pāpabhogāvasāne tu punarjanma bhavet khalu /
puṇyabhogāvasāne tu nānyathā bhavati dhruvam // 28 //

When the sufferings for evil actions are gone through, then there takes place re-birth certainly; when the fruits of good actions have been exhausted, then also, verily, the result is the same.

svarge'pi duḥkhasaṁbhogaḥ paraśrīdarśanādiṣu /
tato duḥkham idaṁ sarvaṁ bhaven nāstyatra saṁśayaḥ // 29 //

Even in heaven there is experiencing of pain by seeing the higher enjoyment of others; verily, there is no doubt that this whole universe is full of suffering.

tatkarmakalpakaiḥ proktaṁ puṇyaṁ pāpam iti dvidhā /
puṇyapāpamayo bandho dehināṁ bhavati kramāt // 30 //

Thinkers have divided Karma into two kinds viz., good and bad. Embodied souls have to undergo bondage of righteous and sinful type successively.

ihāmutra phaladveṣī saphalaṁ karma santyajet /
nityanaimittike saṅgaṁ tyaktvā yoge pravartate // 31 //

Those who are not desirous of enjoying the fruits of their actions in this or next world, should renounce all actions which are done with an eye to their fruits, and having similarly discarded the attachment for the regular and occasional acts, should engage themselves in the practice of Yoga.

Jñānakāṇḍa

karmakāṇḍasya māhātmyaṁ jñātvā yogī tyajet sudhīḥ /
puṇyapāpadvayaṁ tyaktvā jñānakāṇḍe pravartate // 32 //

A wise Yogī, having realised the truth of *Karmakāṇḍa* (works), should renounce them; and having renounced both merit and demerit, he must engage in *Jñānakāṇḍa* (knowledge).

ātmā vā're tu draṣṭavyaḥ śrotavyetyādi yacchrutiḥ /
sā sevyā tatprayatnena muktidā hetudāyinī // 33 //

The Vedic texts, " The ātman ought to be seen,", " About it one must hear," etc., are the real saviours and givers of true knowledge. They must be studied with great care.

duriteṣu ca puṇyeṣu yo dhīvṛttiṁ pracodayāt /
so'haṁ pravartate matto jagat sarvaṁ carācaram //
sarvaṁ ca dṛśyate mattaḥ sarvaṁ ca mayi līyate /
na tadbhinno'ham asmīh madbhinno na tu kiṁcana // 34 //

I am that Intelligence which prompts the mental functions into the paths of virtue or vice. All this universe, moveable and immoveable, is from me; all things are preserved by me; all are absorbed into me (at the time of *pralaya*); because there exists nothing but spirit and I am that spirit—There exists nothing else.

jalapūrṇeṣvasaṁkhyeṣu śarāveṣu yathā bhavet /
ekasya bhātyasaṅkhyatvaṁ tadbhedo'tra na dṛśyate //
upādhiṣu śarāveṣu yā saṅkhyā vartate parā /
sā saṅkhyā bhavati yathā ravau cātmani tat tathā // 35 //

As in innumerable cups full of water, many reflections of the sun are seen, but the substance is the same; similarly individuals, like cups, are innumerable, but the vivifying spirit, like the sun, is one.

yathaikaḥ kalpakaḥ svapne nānāvidhitayeṣyate /
jāgare'pi tathāpyekas tathaiva bahudhā jagat // 36 //

As in a dream the one soul creates many objects by mere willing, but on awaking everything vanishes but the one soul; so is this universe.

sarpabuddhir yathā rajjau śuktau vā rajatabhramaḥ /
tadvad evam idaṁ viśvaṁ vivṛtaṁ paramātmani // 37 //

As through illusion a rope·appears as snake, or pearl-shell as silver; similarly, all this universe is superimposed on Paramātmā (the Universal Spirit).

rajjujñānād yathā sarpo mithyārūpo nivartate /
ātmajñānāt tathā yāti mithyābhūtam idaṁ jagat // 38 //

As, when the knowledge of the rope is obtained, the erroneous notion of its being a snake ceases; so, by the arising of the knowledge of self, vanishes this universe based on illusion.

raupyabhrāntir iyaṁ yāti śuktijñānāt yathā khalu /
jagadbhrāntir iyaṁ yāti cātmajñānāt sadā tathā // 39 //

As, when the knowledge of the mother- of-pearl is obtained, the erroneous notion of its being silver disappears; so, through the knowledge of Ātman, the world illusion always goes away.

yathā vaṁśoragabhrāntir bhaved bhekavasāñjanāt /
tathā jagad idaṁ bhrāntir adhyāsakalpanāñjanāt // 40 //

As, when a man besmears his eyelids with the collyrium prepared from the fat of frog, a bamboo mistakenly appears as a serpent; so the world illusorily appears, owing to the pigment, in the form of superimposition (on Brahman).

ātmajñānād yathā nāsti rajjujñād bhujaṅgamaḥ /
yathā doṣavaśāc chuklaḥ pīto bhavati nānyathā /
ajñānadoṣād ātmā'pi jagad bhavati dustyajam // 41 //

As through knowledge of rope the illusory serpent disappears; similarly, through the knowledge of self, the world disappears. As through jaundiced eyes white appears yellow; similarly, through the disease of ignorance, the self becomes this world—an error very difficult to be removed.

doṣanāśe yathā śuklo gṛhyate rogiṇā svayam /
śuklajñānāt tathā 'jñānanāśād ātmā tathā kṛtaḥ // 42 //

As when jaundice is removed the patient sees the white colour as it is, so when ignorance is destroyed, the true nature of the spirit is made manifest.

kālatraye'pi na yathā rajjuḥ sarpo bhaved iti /
tathātmā na bhaved viśvaṁ guṇātīto nirañjanaḥ // 43 //

As a rope can never become a snake, in all the three times; so the spirit which is beyond all *guṇas* and which is pure, never becomes the universe.

āgamāpāyino' nityā nāśyatveneśvarādayaḥ /
ātmabodhena kenāpi śāstrād etat viniścitam // 44 //

Some wise men, well-versed in the scriptures, receiving the knowledge of spirit, have declared that even Devas like Indra, etc., are non-eternal, subject to birth and death, and liable to destruction.

yathā vātavaśāt sindhāvutpannāḥ phenabudbudāḥ /
tathātmani samudbhūtaṁ saṁsāraṁ kṣaṇabhaṅguram // 45 //

Like foam and bubbles in the sea arising through the agitation caused by the wind, this transitory world arises from the Spirit.

abhedo bhāsate nityaṁ vastubhedo na bhāsate /
dvidhātridhādibhedo ' yaṁ bhramatve paryavasyati // 46 //

The Unity exists always; the Diversity does not exist always. There comes a time when it ceases: distinctions as two, three, many etc. arise only through illusion.

yad bhūtaṁ yac ca bhāvyaṁ vai mūrtāmūrtaṁ tathaiva ca /
sarvam eva jagad idaṁ vivṛtaṁ paramātmani // 47 //

Whatever was, is or will be, either with form or without form, in short, all this universe is superimposed on the Supreme Spirit.

kalpakaiḥ kalpitāvidyā mithyā jātā mṛṣātmikā /
etanmūlaṁ jagad idaṁ kathaṁ satyaṁ bhaviṣyati // 48 //

Avidyā is a fabrication of those given to imagine things. It is born of untruth, and its very essence is unreal. How can this world with such antecedents (foundations) be true ?

The Spirit

caitanyāt sarvam utpannaṁ jagad etac carācaram /
tasmāt sarvaṁ parityajya caitanyaṁ taṁ samāśrayet // 49 //

All this universe, moveable or immoveable, has come out of Intelligence. Renouncing everything else, take shelter in it (Intelligence).

> *ghaṭasyābhyantare bāhye yathākāśaṁ pravartate /*
> *tathātmābhyantare bāhye kāryavargeṣu nityaśaḥ // 50 //*

As space pervades a jar both in and out, similarly within and beyond this ever- changing universe, there exists one Universal Spirit.

> *asaṁlagnaṁ yathākāśaṁ mithyābhūteṣu pañcasu /*
> *asaṁlagnas tathātmā tu kāryavargeṣu nānyathā // 51 //*

As the space pervading the five unreal states of matter does not mix with them, so the self does not mix with the groups of effects.

> *īśvarādijagat sarvaṁ ātmavyāpyaṁ samantataḥ /*
> *eko' sti saccidānandaḥ pūrṇo dvaitavivarjitaḥ // 52 //*

From God down to this universe all are pervaded by one Self. There is one *Saccidānanda* (Existence-Intelligence-Bliss), perfect and secondless.

> *yasmāt prakāśako nāsti svaprakāśo bhavet tataḥ /*
> *svaprakāśo yatas tasmād ātmā jyotiḥsvarūpakaḥ // 53 //*

Since it is not illumined by another, therefore it is self-luminous; and because of that self-luminosity, the very nature of Self is Light.

> *paricchedo yato nāsti deśakālasvarūpataḥ /*
> *ātmanaḥ sarvathā tasmād ātmā pūrṇo bhavet khalu // 54 //*

Since the Self in its nature is not limited by time or space, it is, therefore, infinite, all-pervading and entirety itself.

> *yasmān na vidyate nāśaḥ pañcabhūtair vṛthātmakaiḥ /*
> *tasmād ātmā bhaven nityas tannāśo na bhavet khalu // 55 //*

Since the Self does not undergo destruction due to the five elements that are false, therefore, it is eternal. It is never destroyed.

> *yasmāt tadanyo nāstīha tasmād eko ' sti sarvadā /*
> *yasmāt tadanyo mithyā syād ātmā satyo bhavet khalu // 56 //*

Since beyond it there is no other substance, therefore, it is one; without it everything else is false; therefore, it is True Existence.

avidyābhūtasaṁsāre duḥkhanāśe sukhaṁ yataḥ /
jñānād ādyantaśūnyaṁ syāt tasmād ātmā bhavet sukham // 57 //

Since in this world created by Nescience, the destruction of suffering means the gaining of happiness, and, through Gnosis, immunity from all suffering ensues, therefore, the Self is Bliss.

yasmān nāśitam ajñānaṁ jñānena viśvakāraṇam /
tasmād ātmā bhavej jñānaṁ jñānaṁ tasmāt sanātanam // 58 //

Since by Gnosis is destroyed the Ignorance, which is the cause of the universe, therefore, the Self is Gnosis; and this Gnosis is consequently eternal.

kālato vividhaṁ viśvaṁ yadā caiva bhaved idam /
tadeko'sti sa evātmā kalpanāpathavarjitaḥ // 59 //

Since in time this manifold universe takes its origin, therefore, there is One who is verily the Self, unchanging through all times, who is one, and unthinkable.

bāhyāni sarvabhūtāni vināśaṁ yānti kālataḥ /
yato vāco nivartante ātmā dvaitavivarjitaḥ // 60 //

All these external substances will perish in the course of time; (but) that Self which is indescribable by word (will exist) without a second.

na khaṁ vāyur na cāgniś ca na jalaṁ pṛthivī na ca /
naitat kāryaṁ neśvarādi pūrṇaikātmā bhavet khalu // 61 //

Neither ether, air, fire, water, earth, nor their products, nor God etc. are perfect; the Self alone is so.

Yoga and Māyā

ātmānam ātmano yogī paśyatyātmani niścitam /
sarvasaṁkalpasaṁnyāsī tyaktamithyābhavagrahaḥ // 62 //

Having renounced all desires and abandoned all false worldly attachments, the Yogī sees certainly in his own self, the Ātman.

ātmanātmani cātmānaṁ dṛṣṭvānantaṁ sukhātmakam /
vismṛtya viśvaṁ ramate samādhes tīvratas tathā // 63 //

Having seen the Spirit, that brings forth happiness, in his own spirit by the help of the self, he forgets this universe, and enjoys the ineffable bliss of *Samādhi* (profound meditation).

māyaiva viśvajananī nānyā tattvadhiyāparā /
yadā nāśaṁ samāyāti viśvaṁ nāsti tadā khalu // 64 //

Māyā (illusion) alone is the mother of the universe. Not from any other principle has the universe been created; when this *Māyā* is destroyed, the world certainly does not exist.

heyaṁ sarvam idaṁ yasya māyāvilasitaṁ yataḥ /
tato na prītiviṣayas tanuvittasukhātmakaḥ // 65 //

He, to whom this world is but the pleasure-ground of *Māyā*, and therfore, contemptible and worthless, cannot find any happiness in riches, body, etc., nor in pleasures.

arir mitram udāsīnas trividhaṁ syād idaṁ jagat /
vyavahāreṣu niyataṁ dṛśyate nānyathā punaḥ /
priyāpriyādibhedas tu vastuṣu niyataḥ sphuṭam // 66 //

This world appears in three different aspects to men—either friendly, inimical, or indifferent; such is always found in worldly dealings; there is distinction also in substances, as they are pleasant, unpleasant or indifferent.

ātmopādhivaśād evaṁ bhavet putrādi nānyathā /
māyāvilasitaṁ viśvaṁ jñātvaivaṁ śrutiyuktitaḥ /
adhyāropāpavādābhyāṁ layaṁ kurvanti yoginaḥ // 67 //

That one Self, through extraneous conditions, verily becomes a son, a father, etc. The sacred scriptures have demonstrated the universe to be the freak of *Māya* (illusion). The Yogī destroys this phenomenal universe by realising that it is but the result of *Adhyāropa* (superimposition) and by means of *Apavāda* (refutation of a wrong belief).

Definition of a Paramahaṁsa

nikhilopādhihīno vai yadā bhavati pūruṣaḥ /
tadā vivakṣyate 'khaṇḍajñānarūpī nirañjanaḥ // 68 //

When a person is free from all the extraneous conditions, then it can be said that he is pure and *indivisible intelligence.*

Emanation or Evolution

so'kāmayata puruṣaḥ sṛjate ca prajāḥ svayam /
avidyā bhāsate yasmāt tasmān mithyā svabhāvataḥ // 69 //

The Lord willed to create and himself created his creatures; from His will came out *Avidyā* (Ignorance), which is by nature false.

śuddhabrahmatvasambandho'vidyayā sahito bhavet /
brahmā tejoṁśato yāti yata ābhāsate nabhaḥ // 70 //

There takes place the conjunction between Pure Brahman and Avidyā, from the Tejas portion of which arises Brahmā, from which comes out Ākāśa.

tasmāt prakāśate vāyur vāyor agnis tato jalam /
prakāśate tataḥ pṛthvī kalpaneyaṁ sthitā sati // 71 //

From Ākāśa emanated air; from air came fire; from fire water; and from water came earth. This is the order of subtle emanation.

ākāsād vāyur ākāśapavanād agnisaṁbhavaḥ /
khavātāgner jalaṁ vyomavātāgmivārito mahī // 72 //

From ether, air; from air and ether combined came fire; from the triple compound of ether, air and fire came water; and from the combination of ether, air, fire and water was produced the (gross) earth.

khaṁ śabdalakṣaṇaṁ vāyuś cañcalaḥ sparśalakṣaṇaḥ /
syād rūpalakṣaṇaṁ tejaḥ salilaṁ rasalakṣaṇam //
gandhalakṣaṇikā pṛthvī nānyathā bhavati dhruvam // 73 //

The quality of ether is sound; of air which is ever in motion the quality is touch. Form is the quality of fire, and taste of water. And smell is the quality of earth. There is no gainsaying this.

syād ekaguṇam ākāśaṁ dviguṇo vāyur ucyate /
tathaiva triguṇaṁ tejo bhavantyāpaś caturguṇāḥ //
śabdaḥ sparśaś ca rūpaṁ ca raso gandhas tathaiva ca /
etatpañcaguṇā pṛthvī kalpakaiḥ kalpyate' dhunā // 74 //

Ākāśa has one quality; air two, fire three, water four, and earth five qualities, viz, sound, touch, taste, form and smell. This has been declared by the wise.

cakṣuṣā gṛhyate rūpaṁ gandho ghrāṇena gṛhyate /
raso rasanayā sparśas tvacā saṅgṛhyate param // 75 //
śrotreṇa gṛhyate śabdo niyataṁ bhāti nānyathā // 76 //

Form is perceived through eyes, smell through nose, taste through tongue, touch through skiṇ and sound through ear. These are verily the organs of perception.

caitanyāt sarvam utpannaṁ jagad etat carācaram /
asti cet kalpaneyaṁ syān nāsti ced asti cinmayam // 77 //

From Intelligence has come out all this universe, movable and immovable; whether or not its existence can be inferred, the "All-Intelligence" One does exist.

Absorption or Involution

pṛthvī śīrṇā jale magnā jalaṁ magnaṁ ca tejasi /
līnaṁ vāyau tathā tejo vyomni vāto layaṁ yayau //
avidyāyāṁ mahākāśo līyate parame pade // 78 //

The earth becomes subtle and is dissolved in water; water is resolved into fire; fire similarly merges in air; air gets absorption in ether; and ether is resolved in *Avidyā* (Ignorance), which merges into the Great Brahman.

vikṣepāvaraṇā śaktir durantā sukharūpiṇī /
jaḍarūpā mahāmāyā rajaḥsattvatamoguṇā // 79 //

There are two forces—*Vikṣepa* (manifestation) and *Āvaraṇa* (concealing) which are of great potentiality and power, and whose form is happiness. The great *Māyā,* which is non-intelligent and material, has three constituents: Sattva, Rajas and Tamas.

sā māyāvaraṇāśaktyāvṛtāvijñānarūpiṇī /
darśayej jagadākāraṁ taṁ vikṣepasvabhāvataḥ // 80 //

The non-intelligent form of Māyā covered by the *Āvaraṇa* force (concealment), manifests itself as the universe, owing to its power of manifestation.

tamoguṇādhikāvidyā yā sā durgā bhavet svayam /
īśvaras tadupahitaṁ caitanyaṁ tadabhūd dhruvam //
sattvādhikā ca yāvidyā lakṣmīḥ syād divyarūpiṇī /
caitanyaṁ tadupahitaṁ viṣṇur bhavati nānyathā // 81 //

When *Avidyā* has an excess of *Tamas,* then it manifests itself as Durgā; the Intelligence which presides over her is called Īśvara. When *Avidyā* has an excess of *Sattva,* it manifests itself as Lakṣmī of divine form; the Intelligence which presides over her is called Viṣṇu.

rajoguṇādhikāvidyā jñeyā sā vai sarasvatī /
yaś citsvarūpo bhavati brahmā tadupadhārakaḥ // 82 //

When *Avidyā* has an excess of *Rajas,* it manifests itself as Sarasvatī; the Intelligence which presides over her is known as Brahmā.

īśādyāḥ sakalā devā dṛśyante paramātmani /
śarīrādijaḍaṁ sarvaṁ sāvidyā tat tathā tathā // 83 //

Gods like Śiva, Brahmā, Viṣṇu, etc., are all seen in the great Spirit; bodies and all material objects are the various products of *Avidyā.*

evaṁrūpeṇa kalpante kalpakā viśvasambhavam /
tattvātattvaṁ bhavantīha kalpanānye na coditā // 84 //

The wise have thus explained the creation of the world. *Tattvas* (elements) and *non-Tattvas* (non-elements) are thus produced, not otherwise.

prameyatvādirūpeṇa sarvaṁ vastu prakāśyate /
viśeṣaśabdopādāne bhedo bhavati nānyathā // 85 //

All things manifest themselves as object of cognition etc. (endowed with qualities, etc.), and there arise various distinctions merely through words and names; but there is no real difference.

tathaiva vastu nāstyeva bhāsako vartate paraḥ /
svarūpatvena rūpeṇa svarūpaṁ vastu bhāsyate // 86 //

Therefore, the things do not exist; the great and glorious One that manifests them, alone exists; though things are false and unreal, yet, as the reflections of the real, they, for the time being, appear real.

ekaḥ sattāpūritānandarūpaḥ pūrṇo vyāpī vartate nāsti kiñcit /
etaj jñānaṁ yaḥ karotyeva nityaṁ muktaḥ sa syān
mṛtyusaṁsāraduḥkhāt // 87 //

The One Entity, blissful, entire and all-pervading, alone exists, and nothing else; he who constantly realises this knowledge is freed from death and the sorrow of the world- wheel.

yasyāropāpavādābhyāṁ yatra sarve layaṁ gatāḥ /
sa eko vartate nānyat taccittenāvadhāryate // 88 //

When, through the knowledge that all is illusory perception *(Āropa)* and by intellectual refutation *(Apavāda)* of other doctrines, this universe is resolved into the One, then, there exists that One and nothing else; then this is clearly perceived by the mind.

Karma Clothes the Jīva with Body

pitur annamayāt kośāj jāyate pūrvakarmaṇaḥ /
tac charīraṁ vidur duḥkhaṁ svaprāgbhogāya sundaram // 89 //

From the *Annamaya Kośa* (the physical vehicle) of the father, and in accordance with its past *Karma,* the human soul is re-incarnated; therefore, the wise consider this beautiful body as a punishment, for the suffering of the effects of past Karma.

māṁsāsthisnāyumajjādinirmitaṁ bhogamandiram /
kevalaṁ duḥkhabhogāya nāḍīsantatigulphitam // 90 //

This temple of suffering and enjoyment (i.e. human body), made up of flesh, bones, nerves, marrow, etc. and interspersed with blood vessels etc., is only for the sake of suffering.

pārmeṣṭhyam idaṁ gātraṁ pañcabhūtavinirmitam /
brahmāṇḍasañjñakaṁ duḥkhasukhabhogāya kalpitam // 91 //

This body, created by Brahmā, and composed of five elements and known as Brahmāṇḍa (the egg of Brahmā or microcosm) has been made for experiencing pleasure and suffering.

binduḥ śivo rajaḥ śaktir ubhayor milanāt svayam /
svapnabhūtāni jāyante svaśaktyā jaḍarūpayā // 92 //

From the direct association of sperm which is Śiva and ovum which is Śakti, and, through their inherent inter-action on each other, all creatures are born, which are unreal like a dream.

tatpañcīkaraṇāt sthūlānyasaṅkhyāni samāsataḥ /
brahmāṇḍasthāni vastūni yatra jīvo' sti karmabhiḥ //
tadbhūtapañcakāt sarvaṁ bhogāya jīvasañjñitā // 93 //

From the combination of all the five subtle elements, in this universe, innumerable gross objects are produced. The intelligence that is confined in them, through Karma, is called *Jīva.* All this world is derived from the five elements. The *Jīva* is the enjoyer of the fruits of action.

pūrvakarmānurodhena karomi ghaṭanām aham /
ajaḍaḥ sarvabhūtastho jaḍasthityā bhunakti tān // 94 //

In conformity with the effects of the past Karma of the *Jīvas,* I regulate all their destinies. *Jīva* is non-material, and is in all things; but it enters the material body to experience the fruits of *Karma.*

jaḍāt svakarmabhir baddho jīvākhyo vividho bhavet /
bhogāyotpadyate karma brahmāṇḍākhye punaḥ punaḥ // 95 //

Bound by own Karma, the *Jīvas* assume various forms. In this world, they come again and again to experience the consequences of their *Karma.*

jīvaś ca līyate bhogāvasāne ca svakarmaṇaḥ // 96 //

When the results of *Karma* have been experienced, *Jīva* is absorbed in *Paramabrahma.*

iti śrīśivasaṁhitāyāṁ yogaśāstre
īśvarapārvatīsaṁvāde prathamaḥ paṭalaḥ //1//

End of Chapter 1 on the Path of Harmony.

CHAPTER 2

Fundamentals of Yoga

Dvitīyaḥ Paṭalaḥ

The Microcosm

dehe'smin vartate meruḥ saptadvīpasamanvitaḥ /
saritaḥ sāgarāḥ śailāḥ kṣetrāṇi kṣetrapālakāḥ // 1 //

In this body, there exist Mount *Meru* surrounded by seven islands; rivers, seas, mountains, fields and tutelary deities.

ṛṣayo munayaḥ sarve nakṣatrāṇī grahās tathā /
puṇyatīrthāni pīṭhāni vartante pīṭhadevatāḥ // 2 //

There are in it seers and sages, all the stars and planets as well. There are sacred places of pilgrimage, shrines, and presiding deities of the shrines.

sṛṣṭisaṁhārakartārau bhramantau śaśibhāskarau /
nabho vāyuś ca vahniś ca jalaṁ pṛthvī tathaiva ca // 3 //

The sun and moon, agents of creation and destruction also move in it. Ether, air, fire, water and earth are also there.

The Nerve Centres

trailokye yāni bhūtāni tāni sarvāṇi dehataḥ /
meruṁ saṁveṣṭya sarvatra vyavahāraḥ pravartate// 4 //

All the beings that exist in the three worlds are also to be found in the body; surrounding *Meru* they are engaged in their respective functions.

jānāti yaḥ sarvam idaṁ sa yogī nātra saṁśayaḥ // 5 //

(But ordinary men do not know it.) He who knows all this is a Yogī; there is no doubt about it.

brahmāṇḍasañjñake dehe yathādeśaṁ vyavasthitaḥ /
meruśṛṅge sudhāraśmir bahir aṣṭakalāyutaḥ // 6 //

In this body, which is called Brahmāṇḍa (microcosm, literally the mundane egg), there is the nectar-rayed moon in its proper place, on the top of the spinal cord, with eight Kalās (in the shape of a semi-circle).

vartate' harniśaṁ so' pi sudhāṁ varṣatyadhomukhaḥ /
tato' mṛtaṁ dvidhābhūtaṁ yāti sūkṣmaṁ yathā ca vai // 7 //

This has its face *downwards*, and rains nectar day and night. The ambrosia further sub-divides itself into two subtle parts :

iḍāmārgeṇa puṣṭyarthaṁ yāti mandākinījalam /
puṣṇāti sakalaṁ deham iḍāmārgeṇa niścitam // 8 //

One of these, through the channel named Iḍā, goes over the body to *nourish* it, like the waters of the heavenly Gaṅgā. Certainly this ambrosia nourishes the whole body through the channel of Iḍā.

eṣa pīyūṣaraśmir hi vāmapārśve vyavasthitaḥ /
aparaḥ śuddhadugdhābho haṭhāt karṣati maṇḍalāt /
madhyamārgeṇa sṛṣṭyarthaṁ merau saṁyāti candramāḥ // 9 //

This nectar-rayed moon is on the left side. The other ray, brilliant as pure milk and fountain of great joy, enters through the middle path (called Suṣumṇā) into the spinal cord, in order to create this moon.

merumūle sthitaḥ sūryaḥ kalādvādaśasaṁyutaḥ /
dakṣiṇe pathi raśmibhir vahatyūrdhvaṁ prajāpatiḥ // 10 //

At the bottom of the Meru there is the sun having twelve Kalās. In the right- side path (Piṅgalā), the lord of creatures carries (the fluid) through its rays *upwards.*

pīyūṣaraśminiryāsaṁ dhātūṁś ca grasati dhruvam /
samīramaṇḍale sūryo bhramate sarvavigrahe // 11 //

It certainly swallows the vital secretions and ray-exuded nectar.

Together with the atmosphere, the sun moves through the whole body.

eṣā sūryaparāmūrtiḥ nirvāṇaṁ dakṣiṇe pathi /
vahate lagnayogena sṛṣṭisaṁhārakārakaḥ // 12 //

The right-side vessel, which is *Piṅgalā* is another form of the sun, and is the giver of Nirvāṇa. The Lord of creation and destruction (the sun) moves in this vessel through auspicious ecliptical signs.

The Nerves

sārdhalakṣatrayaṁ nāḍyaḥ santi dehāntare nṛṇām /
pradhānabhūtā nāḍyas tu tāsu mukhyāścaturdaśaḥ // 13 //

In the body of man there are 3,50,000 *Nāḍīs;* of them, the principal ones are fourteen:

suṣumṇeḍā piṅgalā ca gāndhārī hastijihvikā /
kuhūḥ sarasvatī pūṣā śaṅkhinī ca payasvinī // 14 //
vāruṇyalambusā caiva viśvodarī yaśasvinī /
etāsu tisro mukhyāḥ syuḥ piṅgaleḍā suṣumṇikā // 15 //

Suṣumṇā, Iḍā, Piṅgalā, Gāndhārī, Hastijihvikā, Kuhū, Sarasvatī, Pūṣā, Śaṅkhinī, Payasvinī, Vāruṇī, Alambusā, Viśvodarī, and Yaśasvinī. Among these Iḍā, Piṅgalā and Suṣumṇā are the chief.

tisṛṣvekā suṣumṇaiva mukhyā sā yogivallabhā /
anyāstadāśrayaṁ kṛtvā nāḍyaḥ santi hi dehinām // 16 //

Among these three, Suṣumṇā alone is the chief one. She is the beloved of Yogīs. Other Nāḍīs of the embodied ones depend on and are subordinate to it.

nāḍyas tu tā adhovaktrāḥ padmatantunibhāḥ sthitāḥ /
pṛṣṭhavaṁśaṁ samāśritya somasūryāgnirūpiṇī // 17 //

All these *Nāḍīs* have their mouths downwards, and are like thin threads of lotus. They are all supported by the vertebral column, and represent the sun, moon and fire.

tāsāṁ madhye gatā nāḍī citrā sā mama vallabhā /
brahmarandhrañca tatraiva sūkṣmāt sūkṣmataraṁ śubham // 18 //

The innermost of these three is *Citrā;* she is my beloved. In that alone there is the subtlest of all hollows called Brahmarandhra.

pañcavarṇojjvalā śuddhā suṣumṇāmadhyacāriṇī /
dehasyopādhirūpā sā suṣumṇāmadhyarūpiṇī // 19 //

Brilliant with five colours, pure, moving in the middle of Suṣumṇā, this Citrā is the vital part of body and centre of Suṣumṇā.

divyamārgam idaṁ proktam amṛtānandakārakam /
dhyānamātreṇa yogīndro duritaughaṁ vināśayet // 20 //

This has been called in the Śāstras the Heavenly Way; this is the giver of the joy of immortality; by contemplating it, a great Yogī destroys all sins.

The Pelvic Region

gudāt tu dvyaṅgulād ūrdhvaṁ meḍhrāt tu dvyaṅgulād adhaḥ /
caturaṅgulavistāram ādhāraṁ vartate samam // 21 //

Two digits above the rectum and two digits below the genital is the *Ādhāra* lotus, having a dimension of four digits.

tasminnādhārapadme ca karṇikāyāṁ suśobhanā /
trikoṇā vartate yoniḥ sarvatantreṣu gopitā // 22 //

In the pericarp of the *Ādhāra* lotus there is the triangular, beautiful *Yoni,* hidden and kept secret in all the Tantras.

tatra vidyullatākārā kuṇḍalī paradevatā /
sārdhatrikarā kuṭilā suṣumṇāmārgasaṁsthitā // 23 //

In it there is the supreme goddess *Kuṇḍalinī* of the form of lightning, in a coil. She has three coils and a half (like a serpent), and is positioned at the mouth of Suṣumṇā.

jagatsaṁsṛṣṭirūpā sā nirmāṇe satatodyatā /
vācām avācyā vāgdevī sadā devair namaskṛtā // 24 //

She represents the creative force of the world, and is always engaged in creation. She is the goddess of speech, whom speech cannot manifest, and who is praised by all gods.

iḍānāmnī tu yā nāḍī vāmamārge vyavasthitā /
suṣumṇāyāṁ samāśliṣya dakṣanāsāpuṭe gatā // 25 //

The *Nāḍī* called Iḍā is on the left side. Coiling round Suṣumṇā, it goes to the right nostril.

piṅgalānāma yā nāḍī dakṣamārge vyavasthitā /
madhyanāḍiṁ samāśliṣya vāmanāsāpuṭe gatā // 26 //

The *Nāḍī* called Piṅgalā is on the right side; coiling round the central *Nāḍī*, it enters the left nostril.

iḍāpiṅgalayor madhye suṣumṇā yā bhavet khalu /
ṣaṭsthāneṣu ca ṣaṭśaktiṁ ṣaṭpadmaṁ yogino viduḥ // 27 //

The *Nāḍi* which is between Iḍā and Piṅgalā is certainly Suṣumṇā. It has six stages, six forces,* six lotuses, known to the Yogīs.

pañcasthānaṁ suṣumṇāyā nāmāni syur bahūni ca /
prayojanavaśāt tāni jñātavyānīha śāstrataḥ // 28 //

The first five stages** of Suṣumṇā are known by various names; they will be revealed in this book as and when necessary.

anyāḥ santyaparā nāḍyo mūlādhārāt samutthitā /
rasanāmeḍhranayanaṁ pādāṅguṣṭhe ca śrotrakam //
kukṣikakṣāṅguṣṭhakarṇaṁ sarvāṅgaṁ pāyukukṣikam /
labdhvā tāṁ vai nivartante yathādeśasamudbhavāḥ//29//

The other *Nāḍīs,* rising from *Mūlādhāra,* go to the various parts of the body, e.g. tongue, genitals, eyes, feet, toes, ears, abdomen, armpit, fingers of hands, scrotum and anus. Having risen from their proper place, they stop at their respective destinations, as described above.

etābhya eva nāḍībhyaḥ śāstropaśāstrataḥ kramāt /
sārdhalakṣatrayaṁ jātaṁ yathābhāgaṁ vyavasthitam //30 //

From all these (fourteen) *Nāḍīs,* there arise gradually other branches and sub-branches, so that at last they become three hundred thousand and a half in number, and supply their respective places.

etā bhogavahā nāḍyo vāyusañcāradakṣakāḥ /
otaprotāḥ susaṁvyāpya tiṣṭhantyasmin kalevare // 31 //

These *Nāḍīs* are spread through the body crosswise and lengthwise; they are vehicles of sensation and keep watch over the movements of the air i.e., they regulate motor functions also.

* That is, the functions of the Cord, viz.: reflection, co-ordination, etc.

** The parts of which the Spinal Cord is composed are the Tāntrika stages, viz. Cervical, Dorsal, Lumbar, Sacral and Coccygeal.

The Abdominal Region

sūryamaṇḍalamadhyasthaḥ kalādvādaśasaṁyutaḥ /
vastideśe jvalad vahmir vartate cānnapācakaḥ //
eṣa vaiśvānaro'gnir vai mama tejoṁśasambhavaḥ /
karoti vividhaṁ pākaṁ prāṇināṁ deham āsthitaḥ // 32 //

In the abdomen there burns the fire—digester of food—situated in the middle of the sphere of the sun having twelve Kalās. Know this as the fire of Vaiśvānara; it is born from a portion of my own energy, and digests the various foods of creatures, being inside their bodies.

āyuḥpradāyako vahnir balaṁ puṣṭiṁ dadāti saḥ /
śarīrapāṭavañ cāpi dhvastarogasamudbhavaḥ // 33 //

This fire increases life, and gives strength and nourishment; makes the body full of energy; destroys all diseases; and gives health.

tasmād vaiśvānarāgniñ ca prajvālya vidhivat sudhīḥ /
tasmin annaṁ huned yogī pratyahaṁ guruśikṣayā // 34 //

A wise Yogī, having kindled this Vaiśvānara fire according to proper rites, should sacrifice food into it everyday in conformity with the teachings of his spiritual teacher.

brahmāṇḍasaṁjñake dehe sthānāni syur bahūni ca /
mayoktāni pradhānāni jñātavyānīha śāstrake // 35 //

This body called Brahmāṇḍa (microcosm) has many parts, but I have enumerated the most important of them in this book. (Surely) they ought to be known.

nānāprakāranāmāni sthānāni vividhāni ca /
vartante vigrahe tāni kathituṁ naiva śakyate // 36 //

Various are their names, and innumerable are the places in this human body; all of them cannot be enumerated here.

The Jīvātmā

itthaṁ prakalpite dehe jīvo vasati' sarvagaḥ /
anādivāsanāmālālaṅkṛtaḥ karmaśṛṅkhalaḥ // 37 //

In the body thus described, there dwells the Jīva, all- pervading, adorned with the garland of endless desires and chained (to the body) by *karma.*

nānāvidhaguṇopetaḥ sarvavyāpārakārakaḥ /
pūrvārjitāni karmāṇi bhunakti vividhāni ca // 38 //

The Jīva possessed of many qualities, being the agent of all events, tastes the fruit of his various *Karmas* amassed in the past life.

yadyat sandṛśyate loke sarvaṁ tatkarmasambhavam /
sarvakarmānusāreṇa jantur bhogān bhunakti vai // 39 //

Whatever is seen in the world (whether pleasure or pain) is born of one's *Karma.* All creatures enjoy or suffer, according to the results of their actions.

ye ye kāmādayo doṣāḥ sukhaduḥkhapradāyakāḥ /
te te sarve pravartante jīvakarmānusārataḥ // 40 //

The desires, etc., which cause pleasure or pain, act according to the past *Karma* of the Jīva.

puṇyoparaktacaitanye prāṇān prīṇāti kevalam /
bāhye puṇyamayaṁ prāpya bhojyavastu svayaṁ bhavet // 41 //

The Jīva that has accumulated an excess of good and virtuous actions receives a happy life; and in the world he gets pleasant and good things to enjoy, without any trouble.

tataḥ karmabalāt puṁsaḥ sukhaṁ vā duḥkham eva ca /
pāpoparaktacaitanyaṁ naiva tiṣṭhati niścitam //
na tadbhinno bhavet so'pi tadbhinno na tu kiñcana /
māyopahitacaitanyāt sarvaṁ vastu prajāyate // 42 //

In proportion to the force of his *Karma,* man suffers misery or enjoys pleasure. The Jīva that has accumulated an excess of evil never stays in peace—it is not separate from its *Karmas;* except Karma, there is nothing in this world. From the Intelligence veiled by *Māyā,* all things have been evolved.

yathākāle' pi bhogāya jantūnāṁ vividhodbhavaḥ /
yathā doṣavaśāc chuktau rajatāropaṇaṁ bhavet //
tathā svakarmadoṣād vai brahmaṇyāropyate jagat // 43 //

As at a proper time, various creatures are born to enjoy (or suffer) the consequences of their *Karma;* as through mistake a pearl-shell is taken for silver; so through the defect of one's own *Karmas,* a man superimposes the material universe on Brahman.

savāsanābhramotpannonmūlanātisamarthanam /
utpannaṁ ced īdṛṣam syāj jñānam mokṣaprasādhanam // 44 //

From desire all these delusions arise; they can be eradicated with great difficulty; when the salvation-giving knowledge of the unreality of the world arises, then are desires destroyed.

sākṣād viśeṣadṛṣṭis tu sākṣātkāriṇi vibhrame /
kāraṇam nānyathā yuktyā satyaṁ satyaṁ mayoditam // 45 //

Being engrossed in the manifested (objective world), the illusion arises about that which is the manifestor—the subject. There is no other (cause of this illusion). Verily, verily, I tell you the truth.

sākṣātkāribhrame sākṣāt sākṣātkāriṇi nāśayet /
so hi nāstīti saṁsāre bhramo naiva nivartate // 46 //

The illusion of the manifested (objective world) is destroyed when the Maker of the Manifest becomes manifest. This illusion does not cease so long as one thinks, "Brahma is not."

mithyājñānanivṛttis tu viśeṣadarśanād bhavet /
anyathā na nivṛttiḥ syād dṛśyate rajatabhramaḥ // 47 //

By looking closely and deeply into the matter, this false knowledge vanishes. It cannot be removed otherwise; the illusion of silver remains.

yāvan notpadyate jñānaṁ sākṣātkāre nirañjane /
tāvat sarvāṇi bhūtāni dṛśyante vividhāni ca // 48 //

As long as knowledge does not arise about the stainless (i.e. pure) Manifestor of the universe, so long all things appear separate and many.

yadā karmārjitaṁ dehaṁ nirvāṇe sādhanaṁ bhavet /
tadā śarīravahanaṁ saphalaṁ syān na cānyathā // 49 //

When this body, obtained through *Karma,* is made the means of obtaining Nirvāṇa (divine beatitude), then only the carrying of the burden of the body becomes fruitful, not otherwise.

yādṛśī vāsanā mūlā vartate jīvasaṅginī /
tādṛśaṁ vahate jantuḥ kṛtyākṛtyavidhau bhramam // 50 //

Of whatever nature is the original desire *(Vāsanā)*, that clings to and accompanies the Jīva (through various incarnations); similar is the illusion which it suffers, according to its deeds and misdeeds.

saṁsārasāgaraṁ tartuṁ yadīcched yogasādhakaḥ /
kṛtvā varṇāśramaṁ karma phalavarjaṁ tadācaret // 51 //

If a practitioner of Yoga wishes to cross the ocean of the world, he should perform all the duties of his *Varṇāśrama* (the condition of life), renouncing all the fruits of his acts.

viṣayāsaktapuruṣā viṣayeṣu sukhepsavaḥ /
vācābhiruddhanirvāṇāḥ vartante pāpakarmaṇi // 52 //

Persons attached to sensual objects and desirous of sensual pleasures, stop short of Nirvāṇa through much talk, and fall into sinful deeds.

ātmānam ātmanā paśyan na kiñcid iha paśyati /
tadā karmaparityāge na doṣo' sti mataṁ mama // 53 //

When a person does not see anything else here, having seen the Self by the self, then there is no sin (for him if he) renounces all ritual works. This is my opinion.

kāmādayo vilīyante jñānād eva na cānyathā /
abhāve sarvatattvānāṁ svayaṁ tattvaṁ prakāśate // 54 //

All desires and the rest are dissolved through Gnosis only, and not otherwise. When all (minor) Tattvas (principles) cease to exist, then the Tattva (Brahman) itself becomes manifest.

iti śrīśivasaṁhitāyām yogaśāstre
īśvarapārvatīsaṁvāde dvitīyaḥ paṭalaḥ //2//

End of Chapter 2 on Fundamentals of Yoga.

CHAPTER 3

On Yoga Practice

Tṛtīyaḥ Paṭalaḥ

The Vāyus

hṛdyasti paṅkajaṁ divyaṁ divyaliṅgena bhūṣitam /
kādiṭhāntākṣaropetaṁ dvādaśārṇavibhūṣitam // 1 //

In the heart, there is a brilliant lotus with twelve petals adorned with brilliant signs. It has the letters from k to ṭh (i.e. k, kh, g, gh, ṅ, c, ch, j, jh, ñ, ṭ, ṭh), the twelve beautiful letters.

prāṇo vasati tatraiva vāsanābhir alaṅkṛtaḥ /
anādikarmasaṁśliṣṭaḥ prokto' haṅkārasaṁyutaḥ // 2//

Prāṇa lives there, adorned with various desires, accompanied by impressions of past actions, that have no beginning, and said to be joined with egoism *(Ahaṅkāra).*

Note: The heart is in the centre where there is the seed *yaṁ.*

prāṇasya vṛttibhedena nāmāni vividhāni ca /
vartante tāni sarvāṇi kathituṁ naiva śakyate // 3 //

From its different functions *Prāṇa* receives different names; all of them cannot be stated here:

prāṇo'pānaḥ samānaś codāno vyānaś ca pañcamaḥ /
nāgaḥ kūrmaś ca kṛkaro devadatto dhanañjayaḥ // 4 //

Prāṇa, Apāna, Samāna, Udāna, Vyāna, Nāga, Kūrma, Kṛkara, Devadatta, and *Dhanañjaya.*

daśanāmāni mukhyāni mayoktānīha śāstrake /
kurvanti te'tra kāryāṇi preritāni svakarmabhiḥ // 5 //

These are the ten principal names, described by me in this Śāstra; they perform all the functions, incited thereto by their own actions.

atrāpi vāyavaḥ pañca mukhyāḥ syur daśataḥ punaḥ /
tatrāpi śreṣṭhakartārau prāṇāpānau mayoditau // 6 //

Again, out of these ten, the first five are the leading ones; even among these, *Prāṇa* and *Apāna* are the highest agents, in my opinion.

hṛdi prāṇo gude' pānaḥ samāno nābhimaṇḍale /
udānaḥ kaṇṭhadeśastho vyānaḥ sarvaśarīragaḥ // 7 //

The seat of *Prāṇa* is heart; of *Apāna,* anus; of *Samāna,* the region about navel; of *Udāna,* throat; while *Vyāna* moves all over the body.

nāgādivāyavaḥ pañca te kurvanti ca vigrahe /
udgāronmīlanaṁ kṣuttṛḍjṛmbhā hikkā ca pañcamaḥ // 8 //

The five remaining *Vāyus, Nāga,* etc., perform the following functions in the body: Eructation, opening the eyes, hunger and thirst, gaping or yawning, and, lastly, hiccup.

anena vidhinā yo vai brahmāṇḍaṁ vetti vigraham /
sarvapāpavinirmuktaḥ sa yāti paramāṁ gatiṁ // 9 //

He who in this way knows the microcosm of the body, being absolved from all sins, reaches the highest state.

The Guru

adhunā kathayiṣyāmi kṣipraṁ yogasya siddhaye /
yaj jñātvā nāvaśīdanti yogino yogasādhane // 10 //

Now I shall tell you, how easily to attain success in Yoga, by knowing which Yogīs never fail in the practice of Yoga.

bhaved vīryavatī vidyā guruvaktrasamudbhavā /
anyathā phalahīnā syān nirvīryāpyatiduḥkhadā // 11 //

Only the knowledge imparted by a Guru, through his lips, is powerful and useful; otherwise it becomes fruitless, weak and very painful.

guruṁ santoṣya yatnena ye vai vidyām upāsate /
avalambena vidyāyās tasyāḥ phalam avāpnuyāt // 12 //

He who is devoted to any knowledge, while pleasing his Guru with all attention, readily obtains the fruit of that knowledge.

guruḥ pitā gurur mātā gurur devo na saṁśayaḥ /
karmaṇā manasā vācā tasmāt sarvaiḥ prasevyate // 13 //

There is not the least doubt that Guru is father, Guru is mother, and Guru is God even; and as such, he should be served by all with their thought, word and deed.

guruprasādataḥ sarvaṁ labhyate śubham ātmanaḥ /
tasmāt sevyo gurur nityam anyathā na śubhaṁ bhavet // 14 //

By Guru's favour everything good relating to one's self is obtained. So Guru ought to be served daily; else there can be nothing auspicious.

pradakṣiṇatrayaṁ kṛtvā spṛṣṭvā savyena pāṇinā /
aṣṭāṅgena namaskuryād gurupādasaroruham // 15 //

Let him salute his Guru, with eight times touching the ground, after walking three times round him, and touching with his right hand his lotus- feet.

The Adhikārī

śraddhayātmavatāṁ puṁsāṁ siddhir bhavati niścitā /
anyeṣāṁ ca na siddhiḥ syāt tasmāt yatnena sādhayet // 16 //

A person who has control over himself attains success verily through faith; none other can succeed. Therefore, Yoga should be practised faithfully with care and perseverance.

na bhavet saṅgayuktānāṁ tathā'viśvāsinām api /
gurupūjāvihīnānāṁ tathā ca bahusaṅginām //
mithyāvādaratānāṁ ca tathā niṣṭhurabhāṣiṇām /
gurusantoṣahīnānāṁ na siddhiḥ syāt kadācana // 17 //

Those who are addicted to sensual pleasures or keep bad company, who are disbelievers, who are devoid of respect for their Guru, who resort to promiscuous assemblies, who are addicted to false and vain controversies, who are cruel in their speech, and who do not give satisfaction to their Guru never attain success.

phaliṣyatīti viśvāsaḥ siddheḥ prathamalakṣaṇam /
dvitīyaṁ śraddhayā yuktaṁ tṛtīyaṁ gurupūjanam //
caturthaṁ samatābhāvaṁ pañcamendriyanigraham /
ṣaṣṭhaṁ ca pramitāhāraṁ saptamaṁ naiva vidyate // 18 //

The first condition of success is the firm belief that it (Vidyā) will succeed and be fruitful; the second condition is having faith in it; the third is respect for the Guru; the fourth is the spirit of universal equality; the fifth is the restraint of the organs of sense; the sixth is moderate eating. There is no seventh condition.

yogopadeśaṁ samprāpya labdhvā yogavidaṁ gurum /
gurūpadiṣṭavidhinā dhiyā niścitya sādhayet // 19 //

Having received instructions in Yoga, and obtained a Guru who knows Yoga, let him practise with earnestness and faith, according to the method taught by the teacher.

The Place etc.

suśobhane maṭhe yogī padmāsanasamanvitaḥ /
āsanopari saṁviśya pavanābhyāsam ācaret // 20 //

Let a Yogī go to a beautiful and pleasant place of retirement or a cell, assume the posture *Padmāsana,* and sitting on a seat (made of *Kuśa* grass) begin to practise the regulation of breath.

samakāyaḥ prāñjaliśca praṇamya ca gurūn sudhīḥ /
dakṣe vāme ca vighneśaṁ kṣetrapālāmbikāṁ punaḥ // 21 //

A wise beginner should keep his body firm and inflexible, his hands joined as if in supplication, and salute the Gurus on the left side. He should also pay salutations to Gaṇeśa on the right side, and again to the Guardians of the worlds and goddess Ambikā, who are on the left side.

Prāṇāyāma

tatas' ca dakṣāṅguṣṭhena nirudhya piṅgalāṁ sudhīḥ /
iḍayā pūrayed vāyuṁ yathāśaktyā tu kumbhayet //
tatas tyaktvā piṅgalayā śanair eva na vegataḥ // 22 //

Then let the wise practitioner close with his right thumb *Piṅgalā* (the right nostril), inspire air through Iḍā (the left nostril), and keep the air confined—suspend his breathing—as long as he can, and afterwards let him breathe out slowly, and not forcibly, through the right nostril.

punaḥ piṅgalayāpūrya yathāśaktyā tu kumbhayet /
iḍayā recayed vāyuṁ na vegena śanaiḥ śanaiḥ // 23 //

Again, let him draw breath through the right nostril, and stop breathing as long as his strength permits; then let him expel the air through the left nostril, not forcibly, but slowly and gently.

idaṁ yogavidhānena kuryād viṁśati kumbhakān /
sarvadvandvavinirmuktaḥ pratyahaṁ vigatālasaḥ // 24 //

According to the above method of Yoga, let him practise twenty Kumbhakas (retention of breath). He should practise this daily without neglect or idleness, and free from all pairs of opposites (of love and hatred, and doubt and contentment etc.).

prātaḥkāle ca madhyāhne sūryāste cārdharātrake /
kuryād evaṁ catur vāraṁ kāleṣveteṣu kumbhakān // 25 //

These *Kumbhakas* should be practised four times—(1) once *early* in the morning at sunrise, (2) then at *midday,* (3) then at *sunset,* and (4) the final at *midnight.*

itthaṁ māsatrayaṁ kuryād anālasyo dine dine /
tato nāḍīviśuddhiḥ syād avilambena niścitam // 26 //

When this has been practised daily, for three months, with regularity, the *Nāḍīs* (vessels)of the body will readily and surely be purified.

yadā tu nāḍīśuddhiḥ syād yoginas tattvadarśinaḥ /
tadā vidhvastadoṣaś ca bhaved ārambhasambhavaḥ // 27 //

When thus the Nāḍīs of the truth-knowing Yogī are purified, then his defects being all destroyed, he enters the first stage in the practice of Yoga called *ārambha.*

cihnāni yogino dehe dṛśyante nāḍiśuddhitaḥ /
kathyante tu samastānyaṅgāni saṅkṣepato mayā // 28 //

Certain signs are perceived in the body of the Yogī whose Nāḍīs have been purified. I shall describe, in brief, all those various signs.

samakāyaḥ sugandhiś ca sukāntiḥ svarasādhakaḥ /
ārambhaghaṭakaś caiva yathā paricayas tadā //
niṣpattiḥ sarvayogeṣu yogāvasthā bhavanti tāḥ // 29 //

The body of the person practising regulation of breath becomes harmoniously developed, emits sweet scent, looks beautiful and lovely and has a sonorous voice. In all kinds of Yoga, there are four stages : 1. Ārambha- avasthā (the state of beginning); 2. Ghaṭa-avasthā (the state of co-operation of Self and Higher Self); 3. Paricaya-avasthā (knowledge); 4. Niṣpatti-avasthā (the final consummation).

ārambhaḥ kathito' smābhir adhunā vāyusiddhaye /
aparaḥ kathyate paścāt sarvaduḥkhaughanāśanaḥ // 30 //

We have already described the beginning or Ārambha- avasthā; the rest will be described hereafter. They destroy all sin and sorrow.

prauḍhavahniḥ subhogī ca sukhī sarvāṅgasundaraḥ /
sampūrṇahṛdayo yogī sarvotsāhabalānvitaḥ //
jāyate yogino' vaśyam etat sarvaṁ kalevare // 31 //

The following qualities are surely always found in the body of every Yogī : Strong appetite, good digestion, cheerfulness, handsome figure, great courage, mighty enthusiasm and full strength.

atha varjyaṁ pravakṣyāmi yogavighnakaraṁ param /
yena saṁsāraduḥkhābdhiṁ tīrtvā yāsyanti yoginaḥ // 32 //

Now I tell you the great obstacles to Yoga which must be avoided, as by their removal the Yogīs cross easily this sea of worldly sorrow.

The Things to be Renounced

āmlaṁ rūkṣaṁ tathā tīkṣṇaṁ lavaṇaṁ sārṣapaṁ kaṭum /
bahulaṁ bhramaṇaṁ prātaḥsnānaṁ tailaṁ vidāhakam //
steyaṁ hiṁsāṁ janadveṣaṁ cāhaṅkāramanārjavam /
upavāsam asatyaṁ ca mohaṁ ca prāṇipīḍanam //
strīsaṅgam agnisevāṁ ca bahvālāpaṁ priyāpriyam /
atīvabhojanaṁ yogī tyajed etāni niścitam // 33 //

The Yogī should renounce the following: 1 acids, 2 astringents, 3 pungent substances, 4 salt, 5 mustard, and 6 bitter things; 7 much walking, 8 early bathing (before sunrise) and 9 things roasted in oil; 10 theft, 11 killing (of animals), 12 enmity towards any person, 13 pride, 14 duplicity, and 15 crookedness; 16 fasting, 17 untruth, 18 infatuation, 19 cruelty towards animals; 20 companionship of women, 21 worship of (or handling or sitting near) fire, and 22 talking too much whether pleasant or unpleasant, and lastly, 23 overeating.

The Means

upāyaṁ ca pravakṣyāmi kṣipraṁ yogasya siddhaye /
gopanīyaṁ sādhakānāṁ yena siddhir bhavet khalu // 34 //

Now I will tell you the means by which success in Yoga is quickly obtained; it must be kept secret by the practitioner so that success may come with certainty.

ghṛtaṁ kṣīraṁ ca miṣṭhānnaṁ tāmbūlaṁ cūrṇavarjitam /
karpūraṁ nistuṣaṁ miṣṭaṁ sumaṭhaṁ sūkṣmarandhrakam //
siddhāntaśravaṇaṁ nityaṁ vairāgyagṛhasevanam /
nāmasaṅkīrtanaṁ viṣṇoḥ sunādaśravaṇaṁ param //
dhṛtiḥ kṣamā tapaḥ śaucaṁ hrīr matir gurusevanam /
sadaitāni paraṁ yogī niyamāni samācaret // 35 //

A great Yogī should always practise the following observances : He should use 1 clarified butter, 2 milk, 3 sweet food, 4 betel without lime, 5 camphor; 6 kind words, 7 pleasant monastery or retired cell, having a small door; 8 hear discourses on truth, and 9 always discharge his household duties with Vairāgya (without attachment); 10 sing the name of Viṣṇu; 11 and hear sweet music, 12 have patience; 13 constancy, 14 forgiveness, 15 austerities, 16 purifications, 17 modesty, 18 devotion, and 19 service of the Guru.

anile'rkapraveśe ca bhoktavyaṁ yogibhiḥ sadā /
vāyau praviṣṭe śaśini śayanaṁ sādhakottamaiḥ // 36 //

When the air enters the sun, it is the proper time for the Yogī to take his food (i.e., when the breath flows through Piṅgalā or right nostril); when the air enters the moon, he should go to sleep (i.e., when the breath flows through Iḍā or the left nostril).

sadyo bhukte' pi kṣudhite nābhyāsaḥ kriyate budhaiḥ /
abhyāsakāle prathamaṁ kuryāt kṣīrājyabhojanam // 37 //

Yoga (e.g. *Prāṇāyāma*) should not be practised just after the meals, nor when one is very hungry; before beginning the practice, some milk and butter should be taken.

tato' bhyāse sthirībhūte na tādṛṅniyamagrahaḥ /
abhyāsinā vibhoktavyaṁ stokaṁ stokaṁ anekadhā //
pūrvoktakāle kuryāt tu kumbhakān prativāsare // 38 //

When one is well-established in his practice, then he need not observe these restrictions. The practitioner should eat in small quantities at a time, though frequently; and should practise *kumbhaka* daily at the stated times.

tato yatheṣṭā śaktiḥ syād yogino vāyudhāraṇe /
yatheṣṭaṁ dhāraṇād vāyoḥ kumbhakaḥ sidhyati dhruvam //
kevale kumbhake siddhe kiṁ na syād iha yoginaḥ // 39 //

When the Yogī can regulate the air and stop the breath (whenever and how long) he likes, then certainly he gets success in Kumbhaka, and from the success in Kumbhaka only, what things can the Yogī not have here ?

The First Stage

svedaḥ sañjāyate dehe yoginaḥ prathamodyame /
yadā sañjāyate svedo mardanaṁ kārayet sudhīḥ //
anyathā vigrahe dhātur naṣṭo bhavati yoginaḥ // 40 //

In the first stage of *Prāṇāyāma,* the body of the Yogī begins to perspire. When it perspires, he should rub it well; otherwise the body of the Yogī loses its *Dhātu* (humors).

The Second and Third Stages

dvitīye hi bhavet kampo dārdurī madhyame matā /
tato' dhikatarābhyāsād gaganecarasādhakaḥ // 41 //

In the second stage, there takes place trembling of the body; in the third, jumping about like a frog; and when the practice becomes greater, the adept walks in the air.

Vāyusiddhi

yogī padmāsanastho' pi bhuvam utsṛjya vartate /
vāyusiddhis tadā jñeyā saṁsāradhvāntanāśinī // 42 //

When the Yogī, though remaining in *Padmāsana,* can rise in the air and leave the ground, then know that he has gained *Vāyu-Siddhi* (mastery over air), which destroys the darkness of the world.

tāvatkālaṁ prakurvīta yogoktaniyamagraham /
alpanidrā purīṣaṁ ca stokaṁ mūtraṁ ca jāyate // 43 //

But so long (as he does not gain it), let him practise observing all the rules and restrictions laid down above. From the perfection of *Prāṇāyāma,* follows decrease of sleep, excrements and urine.

arogitvam adīnatvaṁ yoginas tattvadarśinaḥ /
svedo lālā kṛmiś caiva sarvathaiva na jāyate // 44 //

The truth-perceiving Yogī becomes free from disease, and sorrow or affliction; he never gets (putrid) perspiration, saliva and intestinal worms.

kaphapittānilāś caiva sādhakasya kalevare /
tasmin kāle sādhakasya bhojyeṣvaniyamagrahaḥ // 45 //

When in the body of the practitioner, there is not any increase of phlegm, wind, or bile, then he may with impunity be irregular in his diet and the rest.

atyalpaṁ bahudhā bhuktvā yogī na vyathate hi saḥ /
athābhyāsavaśād yogī bhūcarīṁ siddhim āpnuyāt //
yathā dardurajantūnāṁ gatiḥ syāt pāṇitāḍanāt // 46 //

No injurious results then would follow, were the Yogī to take a large quantity of food, or very little. Through the strength of constant practice, the Yogī obtains *Bhūcarī-siddhi.* He moves as a frog jumps over the ground, when frightened away by the clapping of hands.

santyatra bahavo vighnā dāruṇā durnivāraṇāḥ /
tathāpi sādhayed yogī prāṇaiḥ kaṇṭhagatair api // 47 //

Verily, there are many hard and almost insurmountable obstacles in Yoga. Yet a Yogī should go on with his practice at all hazards, even were his life to come to the throat.

tato rahasyupāviṣṭaḥ sādhakaḥ saṁyatendriyaḥ /
praṇavaṁ prajaped dīrghaṁ vighnānāṁ nāśahetave // 48 //

Then let the practitioner, sitting in a solitary place and restraining his senses, utter by inaudible repetition, the long praṇava OM, in order to destroy all obstacles.

pūrvārjitāni karmāṇi prāṇāyāmena niścitam /
nāśayet sādhako dhīmān ihalokodbhavāni ca // 49 //

The wise practitioner surely destroys all his *Karma,* whether acquired in this life or in the past, through the regulation of breath.

pūrvārjitāni pāpāni puṇyāni vividhāni ca /
nāśayet ṣoḍaśa prāṇāyāmena yogipuṅgavaḥ // 50 //

The great Yogī destroys by sixteen *Prāṇāyāmas* the various merits and sins accumulated earlier.

pāpatūlacayānāho pradahet pralayāgninā /
tataḥ pāpavinirmuktaḥ paścāt puṇyāni nāśayet // 51 //

This *Prāṇāyama* destroys sin, as fire burns away a heap of cotton; it makes the Yogī free from sin; next it destroys the merits.

prāṇāyāmena yogīndro labdhaiśvaryāṣṭakāni vai /
pāpapuṇyodadhiṁ tīrtvā trailokyacaratām iyāt // 52 //

The mighty Yogī having attained, through *Prāṇāyāma,* the eight psychic powers, and having crossed the ocean of merits and sins, moves about freely through the three worlds.

Increase of Duration

tato' bhyāsakrameṇaiva ghaṭikātritayaṁ bhavet /
yena syāt sakalā siddhir yoginaḥ svepsitā dhruvam // 53 //

Then gradually he should make himself able to practise for three Ghaṭis (one hour and a half at a time. He should be able to restrain breath for that period). Through this, the Yogī undoubtedlly obtains all the cherished powers.

Siddhis or Perfections

vāksiddhiḥ kāmacāritvaṁ dūradṛṣṭis tathaiva ca /
dūrāśrutiḥ sūkṣmadṛṣṭiḥ parakāyapraveśanam //
viṇmūtralepane svarṇam adṛśyakaraṇam tathā /
bhavantyetāni sarvāṇi khecaratvaṁ ca yoginām // 54 //

The Yogī acquires the following powers: Vāksiddhi (prophesying), transporting himself everywhere at will *(Kāmacāritva)*, clairvoyance *(Dūradṛṣṭi)*, clairaudience *(Dūraśruti)*, subtle-sight *(Sūkṣmadṛṣṭi)*, and the power of entering another's body *(Parakāyapraveśana)*, turning base metals into gold by rubbing them with his excrements and urine, the power of becoming invisible, and, lastly, ability of moving in the air.

The Ghaṭa Avasthā

yadā bhaved ghaṭāvasthā pavanābhyāsane parā /
tadā saṁsāracakre' smin nāsti yanna sa dhārayet // 55 //

When, by the practice of *Prāṇāyāma,* the Yogī reaches the state of *Ghaṭa* (water-jar), then for him there is nothing in this circle of universe which he cannot accomplish.

prāṇāpānau nādabindū jīvātmaparamātmanau /
militvā ghaṭate yasmāt tasmād vai ghaṭa ucyate // 56 //

Ghaṭa is said to be that state in which *Prāṇa* and *Apāna Vāyus, Nāda* and *Bindu, Jīvātmā* and *Paramātmā* combine and co-operate.

yāmamātraṁ yadā dhartuṁ samarthaḥ syāt tadādbhutaḥ /
pratyāhāras tadaiva syān nāntarā bhavati dhruvam // 57 //

When he gets the power of holding breath for three hours, then certainly the wonderful state of *Pratyāhāra* is reached without fail.

yaṁ yaṁ jānāti yogīndras taṁ tam ātmeti bhāvayet /
yair indriyair yadvidhānas tadindriyajayo bhavet // 58 //

Whatever object the Yogī perceives, let him consider it to be the spirit. When the modes of action of various senses are known, then they can be conquered.

yāmamātraṁ yadā pūrṇam bhaved abhyāsayogataḥ /
ekavāraṁ prakurvīta tadā yogī ca kumbhakam //
daṇḍāṣṭakaṁ yadā vāyur niścalo yogino bhavet /
svasāmarthyāt tadāṅguṣṭhe tiṣṭhed vā tūlavat sudhīḥ // 59 //

When, through great practice, the Yogī can perform one *Kumbhaka* for full three hours, when for eight *Daṇḍas* (= 3 hours) the breathing of the Yogī is suspended, then that wise one can balance himself on his thumb and becomes as light as cotton.

Paricaya Avasthā

tataḥ paricayāvasthā yogino' bhyāsato bhavet /
yadā vāyuś candrasūryaṁ tyaktvā tiṣṭhati niścalam //
vāyuḥ paricito vāyuḥ suṣumṇāvyomni sañcaret // 60 //

After this, through exercise, the Yogī reaches the *Paricaya Avasthā.* When the air leaving the sun and the moon (right and left nostrils), remains unmoved and steady in the ether of *Suṣumṇā,* then it is in the *Paricaya* state.

kriyāśaktiṁ gṛhītvaiva cakrān bhittvā suniścitam /
yadā paricayāvasthā bhaved abhyāsayogataḥ //
trikūṭaṁ karmaṇāṁ yogī tadā paśyati niścitaṁ // 61 //

When he, by the practice of Yoga, acquires power of action *(Kriyāśakti)* and pierces through the six *Cakras,* and reaches the sure condition of *Paricaya,* then the Yogī, verily, sees the three-fold effect of *Karma.*

tataś ca karmakūṭāni praṇavena vināśayet /
sa yogī karmabhogāya kāyavyūhaṁ samācaret // 62 //

Then, let the Yogī destroy the multitude of *Karmas* by *Praṇava (Om);* let him accomplish *Kāyavyūha* (a mystical process), in order to enjoy or suffer the consequences of all his actions in one life (without the necessity of re-birth).

asmin kāle mahāyogī pañcadhā dhāraṇaṁ caret /
yena bhūrādisiddhiḥ syāt tato bhūtabhayāpahā // 63 //

At that time let the great Yogī practise the five-fold *Dhāraṇā* (forms of concentration on Viṣṇu) by which command over the five elements is obtained, and fear of injuries from anyone of them is removed. (Earth, Water, Fire, Air, Ākāśa cannot harm him.)

Note: He should perform 5 Kumbhakas at each centre or Cakra.

ādhāre ghaṭikāḥ pañca liṅgasthāne tathaiva ca /
tadūrdhvaṁ ghaṭikāḥ pañca nābhihṛnmadhyake tathā //
bhrūmadhyordhvaṁ tathā pañca ghaṭikā dhārayet sudhīḥ /
tathā bhūrādinā naṣṭo yogīndro na bhavet khalu // 64 //

Let the wise Yogī practise *Dhāraṇā* thus : five *Ghaṭīś* (2 hours) in the Ādhāra Lotus (Mūlādhāra); five Ghaṭīs in the seat of *Liṅga* (Svādhiṣṭhāna); five *Ghaṭīs* in the region above it (in the navel, Maṇipūra); and the same in the heart (Anāhata); five *Ghaṭīs* in the throat (Viśuddha) and, lastly let him hold *Dhāraṇā* for five *Ghaṭīs* in the space between the two eyebrows (Ājñācakra). By this practice the elements cease to cause any harm to the great Yogī.

medhāvī sarvabhūtānāṁ dhāraṇāṁ yaḥ samabhyaset /
śatabrahmamṛtenāpi mṛtyus tasya na vidyate // 65 //

The wise Yogī, who thus continually practises concentration *(Dhāraṇā),* never dies through hundreds of cycles of the great Brahmā.

Niṣpatti

tato' bhyāsakrameṇaiva niṣpattir yogino bhavet /
anādikarmabījāni yena tīrtvā ' mṛtaṁ pibet // 66 //

After this, through gradual exercise, the Yogī reaches the *Niṣpatti-avasthā* (the state of consummation). The Yogī, having destroyed all the seeds of Karma accumulated since beginningless time drinks the water of immortality.

yadā niṣpattir bhavati samādheḥ svena karmaṇā /
jīvanmuktasya śāntasya bhaved dhīrasya yoginaḥ //
yadā niṣpattisampannaḥ samādhiḥ svecchayā bhavet /
gṛhītvā cetanāṁ vāyuḥ kriyāśaktiṁ ca vegavān //
sarvāṁś cakrān vijitvā ca jñānaśaktau vilīyate // 67 //

When the *Jīvanmukta* (liberated while still living) tranquil Yogī has obtained, through practice, the consummation of Samādhi (meditation), and when this state of consummated Samādhi can be voluntarily evoked, then the forceful vital air having taken hold of *Cetanā* (conscious intelligence)and the faculty of action conquers all the Cakras and merges itself in the faculty of cognition.

idānīṁ kleśahānyarthaṁ vaktavyaṁ vāyusādhanam /
yena saṁsāracakre' smin bhogahānir bhaved dhruvam // 68 //

Now we shall describe the methods of breath control in order to remove the troubles (which await the Yogī), through which vanish all sufferings and enjoyments in this cycle of births and deaths.

rasanāṁ tālumūle yaḥ sthāpayitvā vicakṣaṇaḥ /
pibet prāṇānilaṁ tasya yogānāṁ saṅkṣayo bhavet // 69 //

When a skilful Yogī, by placing the tongue at the root of the palate, can drink the *Prāṇa Vāyu* (vital air), then there occurs complete dissolution of all Yogas (i.e., he is no longer in need of Yoga).*

kākacañcvā pibet vāyuṁ śītalaṁ yo vicakṣaṇaḥ /
prāṇāpānavidhānajñaḥ sa bhaven muktibhājanaḥ // 70 //

When a skilful Yogī, knowing the laws of the action of *Prāṇa* and *Apāna,* can drink the cool air through the contraction of the mouth, in the form of a crow-bill, then he becomes entitled to liberation.

sarasaṁ yaḥ pibed vāyuṁ pratyahaṁ vidhinā sudhīḥ /
naśyanti yoginas tasya śramadāhajarāmayāḥ // 71 //

That wise Yogī, who daily drinks the ambrosial air, according to proper rules, destroys fatigue, burning (fever), decay and old age, and injuries.

rasanām ūrdhvagāṁ kṛtvā yaś candre salilaṁ pibet /
māsamātreṇa yogīndro mṛtyuṁ jayati niścitam // 72 //

Pointing the tongue upwards, when the Yogī can drink the nectar flowing from the moon (situated between the two eyebrows), within a month he certainly would conquer death.

rājadantabilaṁ gāḍhaṁ sampīḍya vidhinā pibet /
dhyātvā kuṇḍalinīṁ devīṁ ṣaṇmāsena kavir bhavet// 73//

* Some texts read 'rogāṇāṁ' instead of 'yogānāṁ' in which case, it will mean "freedom from all diseases."

When having firmly closed the glottis by the proper yogic method, and contemplating on the goddess Kuṇḍalinī, he drinks (the moon fluid of immortality), he becomes a sage or poet within six months.

kākacañcvā pibed vāyuṁ sandhyayor ubhayor api /
kuṇḍalinyā mukhe dhyātvā kṣayarogasya śāntaye // 74 //

He should drink the air through the crow-bill, in both twilights i.e., in morning and evening, contemplating that it goes to the mouth of Kuṇḍalinī, for the cure of consumption.

aharniśaṁ pibed yogī kākacañcvā vicakṣaṇaḥ /
pibet prāṇānilaṁ tasya rogāṇāṁ saṅkṣayo bhavet //
dūraśrutir dūradṛṣṭis tathā syād darśanaṁ khalu // 75 //

When the wise Yogī drinks the fluid day and night through the crow-beak, his diseases are destroyed: he acquires certainly the powers of clairaudience and clairvoyance.

dantair dantān samāpīḍya pibed vāyuṁ śanaiḥ śanaiḥ /
ūrdhvajihvaḥ sumedhāvī mṛtyuṁ jayati so ' cirāt // 76 //

When firmly closing the teeth (by pressing the upper on the lower jaw), and placing the tongue upwards, the wise Yogī drinks the fluid very slowly, within a short period he conquers death.

ṣaṇmāsamātram abhyāsaṁ yaḥ karoti dine dine /
sarvapāpavinirmukto rogān nāśayate hi saḥ // 77 //

One who daily continues this exercise for six months only, is freed from all sins, and destroys all diseases.

saṁvatsarakṛtābhyāsād bhairavo bhavati dhruvam /
aṇimādiguṇān labdhvā jitabhūtagaṇaḥ svayam // 78 //

If he continues this exercise for a year, he becomes a Bhairava; he obtains the powers of *Aṇimā* &c., and conquers all elements.

rasanām ūrdhvagāṁ kṛtvā kṣaṇārdhaṁ yadi tiṣṭhati /
kṣaṇeṅa mucyate yogī vyādhimṛtyujarādibhiḥ // 79 //

If the Yogī can remain for half a second with his tongue drawn upwards, he becomes free from disease, death, and old age etc.

rasanāṁ prāṇasaṁyuktāṁ pīḍyamānāṁ vicintayet /
na tasya jāyate mṛtyuḥ satyaṁ satyaṁ mayoditam // 80 //

Verily, verily, I tell you the truth that the person never dies who contemplates by pressing the tongue, combined with the vital fluid or Prāṇa.

evam abhyāsayogena kāmadevo ' dvitīyakaḥ /
na kṣudhā na tṛṣā nīdrā naiva mūrchā prajāyate // 81 //

Through this exercise and Yoga, he becomes Kāmadeva without a rival. He feels neither hunger, nor thirst, nor sleep, nor swoon.

anenaiva vidhānena yogīndro' vanimaṇḍale /
bhavet svacchandacārī ca sarvāpatparīvarjitaḥ // 82 //

Acting upon these methods the great Yogī becomes in the world perfectly independent; and freed from all obstacles, he can go everywhere.

na tasya punarāvṛttir modate sa surair api /
puṇyapāpair na lipyeta etadācaraṇena saḥ // 83 //

By practising thus, he is never reborn, nor is he tainted by virtue and vice, but enjoys (for ages) with gods.

The Postures

caturaśītyāsanāni santi nānāvidhāni ca /
tebhyaś catuṣkam ādāya mayoktāni bravīmyaham //
siddhāsanaṁ tataḥ padmāsanaṁ cograṁ ca svastikam // 84 //

There are eighty- four postures, of various modes. Out of them, four ought to be adopted, which I mention below: 1 Siddhāsana, 2 Padmāsana, 3 Ugrāsana, 4 Svastikāsana.

Siddhāsana

yoniṁ sampīḍya yatnena pādamūlena sādhakaḥ /
meḍhropari pādamūlaṁ vinyased yogavit sadā //
ūrdhvaṁ nirīkṣya bhrūmadhyaṁ niścalaḥ saṁyatendriyaḥ /
viśeṣo' vakrakāyaśca rahasyudvegavarjitaḥ //
etat siddhāsanaṁ jñeyaṁ siddhānāṁ siddhidāyakam // 85 //

Siddhāsana that gives success to the practitioner is as follows : Pressing with care by the heel the perineum, the other heel the

Yogī should place on the genitals; he should fix his gaze upwards on the space between the two eyebrows, should be steady, and restrain his senses. His body particularly must be straight and without any bend. The place should be a solitary one, free from noise.

yenābhyāsavaśāc chīghraṁ yoganiṣpattim āpnuyāt /
siddhāsanaṁ sadā sevyaṁ pavanābhyāsinā param // 86 //

He who wishes to attain quick consummation of Yoga by exercise, should adopt Siddhāsana posture, and practise regulation of the breath.

yena saṁsāram utsṛjya labhate paramāṁ gatim /
nātaḥ parataraṁ guhyam āsanaṁ vidyate bhuvi //
yenānudhyānamātreṇa yogī pāpād vimucyate // 87 //

Through this posture the Yogī, leaving the world, attains the highest end. Throughout the world there is no posture more secret than this. By assuming and contemplating in this posture, the Yogī is freed from sin.

Padmāsana

uttānau caraṇau kṛtvā ūrusaṁsthau prayatnataḥ /
ūrumadhye tathothānau pāṇī kṛtvā tu tādṛśau //
nāsāgre vinyased dṛṣṭiṁ dantamūlaṁ ca jihvayā /
uttolya cibukaṁ vakṣe utthāpya pavanaṁ śanaiḥ //
yathāśaktyā samākṛṣya pūrayed udaraṁ śanaiḥ /
yathāśaktyaiva paścāt tu recayed anirodhataḥ //
idaṁ padmāsanaṁ proktaṁ sarvavyādhivināśanam // 88 //

I describe now Padmāsana which wards off (or cures) all diseases: Having crossed the legs, carefully place the feet on the opposite thighs(i.e., the left foot on the right thigh, and vice versa); cross both the hands and place them similarly on the thighs; fix the sight on the tip of the nose; pressing the tongue against the root of the teeth, (the chin should be elevated, the chest expanded) then draw the air slowly, fill the chest with all your might, and expel it slowly, in an unobstructed stream.

durlabhaṁ yena kenāpi dhīmatā labhyate param // 89 //

It cannot be practised by everybody; only the wise attains success in it.

anuṣṭhāne kṛte prāṇaḥ samaś calati tatkṣaṇāt /
bhaved abhyāsane samyak sādhakasya na saṁśayaḥ // 90 //

By performing and practising this posture, undoubtedly the vital airs of the practitioner at once become completely equable, and flow harmoniously through the body.

padmāsane sthito yogī prāṇāpānavidhānataḥ /
pūrayet sa vimuktaḥ syāt satyaṁ satyaṁ vadāmyaham // 91 //

Sitting in Padmāsana posture, and knowing the action of *Prāṇa* and *Apāna,* when the Yogī performs the regulation of breath, he is emancipated. I tell you the truth. Verily, I tell you the truth.

Ugrāsana

prasārya caraṇadvandvaṁ parasparam asaṁyutam /
svapāṇibhyāṁ dṛḍhaṁ dhṛtvā jānūpari śiro nyaset //
āsanogram idaṁ proktaṁ bhaved aniladīpanam /
dehāvasādaharaṇaṁ paścimottānasañjñakam //
ya etad āsanaṁ śreṣṭhaṁ pratyahaṁ sādhayet sudhīḥ /
vāyuḥ paścimamārgeṇa tasya sañcarati dhruvam // 92 //

Stretch out both the legs and keep them apart; firmly take hold of the head by the hands, and place it on the knees. This is called Ugrāsana (the stern- posture). It excites the motion of the air, destroys the dullness and uneasiness of the body, and is also called *Paścima- uttāna* (the posterior crossed posture). That wise man who daily practises this noble posture can certainly induce the flow of the air *per viam posteriori.*

etad abhyāsaśīlānāṁ sarvasiddhiḥ prajāyate /
tasmād yogī prayatnena sādhayet siddhisādhakaḥ // 93 //

Those who practise this obtain all the *Siddhis;* therefore, one desirous of attaining powers, should practise this diligently.

gopanīyaṁ prayatnena na deyaṁ yasya kasyacit /
yena śīghraṁ marutsiddhir bhaved duḥkhaughanāśinī // 94 //

This should be kept secret with the greatest care, and not be given indiscriminately to. Through it, *Vāyu-siddhi* is easily obtained, and it destroys a multitude of miseries.

Svastikāsana

jānūrvor antare samyag dhṛtvā pādatale ubhe /
samakāyaḥ sukhāsīnaḥ svastikaṁ tat pracakṣate // 95 //

Place the soles of the feet completely under the thighs; keep the body straight; and sit at ease. This is called Svastikāsana.

anena vidhinā yogī mārutaṁ sādhayet sudhīḥ /
dehe na kramate vyādhis tasya vāyuś ca siddhyati // 96 //

In this way, the wise Yogī should practise the regulation of the air. No disease can attack his body, and he obtains *Vāyusiddhi.*

sukhāsanam idaṁ proktaṁ sarvaduḥkhapraṇāśanam /
svastikaṁ yogibhir gopyaṁ svastīkaraṇam uttamam // 97 //

This is also called Sukhāsana, the easy posture. This health-giving, good Svastikāsana should be kept secret by the Yogī.

iti śrīśivasaṁhitāyāṁ yogaśāstre
īśvarapārvatīsaṁvāde tṛtīyaḥ paṭalaḥ //3//

End of Chapter 3 On Yoga Practice.

Chapter 4

Yoni-Mudrā

Caturthaḥ Paṭalaḥ

ādau pūrakayogena svādhāre pūrayen manaḥ /
gudameḍhrāntare yonis tāmākuñcya pravartayet // 1 //

First with a strong inspiration fix the mind in the Ādhāra Lotus. Then engage in contracting the Yoni, which is situated in the perineal space.

brahmayonigataṁ dhyātvā kāmaṁ kandhūkasannibham/
sūryakoṭipratīkāśaṁ candrakoṭisuśītalam //
tasyordhvaṁ tu śikhā sūkṣmā cidrūpā paramā kalā /
tayā sahitam ātmānam ekībhūtaṁ vicintayet // 2 //

There let him contemplate that the God of Love resides in that Brahmayoni and that he is beautiful like Bandhūka flower *(Pentapetes Phoenicia)*, brilliant as tens of millions of suns, and cool as tens of millions of moons. Above this (Yoni) is a very small and subtle flame, whose form is intelligence. Then let him imagine that union takes place there between himself and that flame (Śiva and Śakti).

gacchati brahmamārgeṇa liṅgatrayakrameṇa vai /
amṛtaṁ taddhi svargasthaṁ paramānandalakṣaṇam //
śvetaraktaṁ tejasāḍhyaṁ sudhādhārāpravarṣiṇam /
pītvā kulāmṛtaṁ divyaṁ punar eva viśet kulam // 3 //

(Then imagine that) there go up through the Suṣumṇā Nāḍī, the three bodies in their due order (i.e., etheric, astral and mental bodies). There is emitted in every Cakra the nectar, the characteristic of which is great bliss. Its colour is whitish rosy (pink). It is full of splendour, showering down in jets the immortal fluid. Let him drink this wine of immortality which is divine, and then again enter the Kula (i.e., perineal space).

Note: While these subtle bodies go up, they drink at every stage this nectar, called Kulāmṛta.

punar eva kulaṁ gacchen mātrāyogena nānyathā /
sā ca prāṇasamākhyātā hyasmiṁs tantre mayoditā // 4 //

Then let him go again to the Kula through the practice of Mātrā Yoga (i.e., Prāṇāyāma). This Yoni has been called by me in this Tantra as equal to life.

punaḥ pralīyate tasyāṁ kālāgnyādiśivātmakam /
yonimudrā parā hyeṣā bandhas tasyāḥ prakīrtitaḥ /
tasyās tu bandhamātreṇa tan nāsti yan na sādhayet // 5 //

Again let him be absorbed in that Yoni, where dwells the fire of death—the nature of Śiva, etc. Thus has been described by me the method of practising the great Yoni-Mudrā. From success in its practice, there is nothing which cannot be accomplished.

chinnarūpās tu ye mantrāḥ kīlitāḥ stambhitāś ca ye /
dagdhāḥ mantrāḥ śikhāhīnāḥ malinās tu tiraskṛtāḥ //
mandā bālās tathā vṛddhāḥ prauḍhā yauvanagarvitāḥ /
aripakṣe sthitā ye ca nirvīryāḥ sattvavarjitāḥ /
tathā sattvena hīnāś ca khaṇḍitāḥ śatadhākṛtāḥ //
vidhānena ca saṁyuktāḥ prabhavanty acireṇa tu /
siddhimokṣapradāḥ sarve guruṇā viniyojitāḥ //
dīkṣayitvā vidhānena abhiṣicya sahasradhā /
tato mantrādhikārārtham eṣā mudrā prakīrtitā // 6 //

Even those Mantras which are deformed *(Chinna)* or paralyzed *(Kīlita)*, scorched *(Stambhita)* by fire, or whose flame has become attenuated, or which are dark, and ought to be abandoned, or which are evil, or too old, or which are proud of their budding youth, or have gone over to the side of the enemy, or weak and essenceless without vitality, or which have been divided into hundreds of parts, even they become fertile through time and method. All these can give powers and emancipation when properly given to a disciple by a Guru, after having initiated him according to proper rites, and bathed him a thousand times. This Yoni-mudrā has been described in order that the student may deserve (to be initiated into the mysteries of) and receive the Mantras.

brahmahatyāsahasrāṇi trailokyam api ghātayet /
nāsau lipyati pāpena yonimudrānibandhanāt // 7 //

He who practises Yoni-Mudrā is not polluted by sin, were he to murder a thousand Brāhmaṇas or kill all the inhabitants of the three worlds.

guruhā ca surāpī ca steyī ca gurutalpagaḥ /
etaiḥ pāpair na badhyeta yonimudrānibandhanāt // 8 //

Were he to kill his teacher or drink wine or commit theft or violate the bed of his preceptor, he is not stained by these sins by virtue of this Mudrā.

tasmād abhyāsanam nityaṁ kartavyaṁ mokṣakāṅkṣibhiḥ /
abhyāsāj jāyate siddhir abhyāsān mokṣam āpnuyāt // 9 //

Therefore, those who wish for emancipation should practise this daily. Through *practice* success is obtained; through practice one gains liberation.

saṁvidaṁ labhate' bhyāsād yogo' bhyāsāt pravartate /
mudrāṇāṁ siddhir abhyāsād abhyāsād vāyusādhanam //
kālavañcanam abhyāsāt tathā mṛtyuñjayo bhavet // 10 //

Perfect consciousness is gained through *practice.* Yoga is attained through *practice;* success in Mudrās comes by practice; through practice is gained success in Prāṇāyāma. Death can be cheated of its prey through practice; and man becomes the conqueror of death by practice.

vāksiddhiḥ kāmacāritvaṁ bhaved abhyāsayogataḥ /
yonimudrā paraṁ gopyā na deyā yasyakasyacit /
sarvathā naiva dātavyā prāṇaiḥ kaṇṭhagatair api // 11 //

Through practice one gets the power of *Vāk* (prophecy), and the power of going everywhere through mere exertion of will. This Yoni-Mudrā should be kept in great secrecy, and not be given to anyone. Even when threatened with death, it should not be revealed or given to others.

The Awakening of Kuṇḍalinī

adhunā kathayiṣyāmi yogasiddhikaraṁ param /
gopanīyaṁ susiddhānāṁ yogaṁ paramadurlabham // 12 //

Now I shall tell you the best means of attaining success in Yoga. The practitioners should keep it secret. It is the most inaccessible Yoga.

suptā guruprasādena yadā jāgarti kuṇḍalī /
tadā sarvāṇi padmāni bhidyante granthayo'pi ca // 13 //

When the sleeping goddess Kuṇḍalinī is awakened through the grace of Guru, then all the lotuses and the knots are readily pierced through and through.

tasmāt sarvaprayatnena prabodhayitum īśvarīm /
brahmarandhramukhe suptāṁ mudrābhyāsaṁ samācaret // 14 //

Therefore, in order that the goddess, who is asleep at the mouth of Brahmarandhra (the innermost hollow of Suṣumṇā), be awakened, the Mudrās should be practised with greatest care.

mahāmudrā mahābandho mahāvedhaś ca khecarī /
jālandharo mūlabandho viparītakṛtis tathā //
uḍḍīyānaṁ ca vajrolī daśamaṁ śakticālanam /
idaṁ hi mudrādaśakaṁ mudrāṇām uttamottamam // 15 //

Out of the many Mudrās, the following ten are the best: (1) Mahāmudrā, (2) Mahābandha, (3) Mahāvedha, (4) Khecarī, (5) Jālandhara, (6) Mūlabandha, (7) Viparītakaraṇa, (8) Uḍḍīyāna, (9) Vajrolī, and (10) Śakticālana.

Mahāmudrā

atha mahāmudrākathanam :
mahāmudrāṁ pravakṣyāmi tantre' smin mama vallabhe /
yāṁ prāpya siddhāḥ siddhiṁ ca kapilādyāḥ purā gatāḥ // 16 //

My dearest, I shall now describe to you Mahāmudrā, from whose knowledge the ancient sages, Kapila and others, obtained success in Yoga.

apasavyena saṁpīḍya pādamūlena sādaram /
gurūpadeśato yoniṁ gudameḍhrāntarālagām //

savyaṁ prasāritaṁ pādaṁ dhṛtvā pāṇiyugena vai /
navadvārāṇi saṁyamya cibukaṁ hṛdayopari //
cittaṁ cittapathe dattvā prabhaved vāyusādhanam /
mahāmudrā bhaved eṣā sarvatantreṣu gopitā //
vāmāṅgena samabhyasya dakṣāṅgenābhyaset punaḥ /
prāṇāyāmaṁ samaṁ kṛtvā yogī niyatamānasaḥ // 17 //

In accordance with the instructions of the Guru, press gently the perineum with the heel of the left foot. Stretching the right foot out, hold it fast by the two hands. Having closed the nine gates (of the body), place the chin on the chest. Then concentrate the vibrations of the mind and inspire air and retain it by Kumbhaka (so long as one can comfortably keep it). This is the Mahāmudrā, held secret in all the Tantras. The steady-minded Yogī, having practised it on the left side, should then practise it on the right side; and in all cases must be firm in Prāṇāyāma, the regulation of his breath.

anena vidhinā yogī mandabhāgyo'pi sidhyati /
sarvāsām eva nāḍīnāṁ cālanaṁ bindumāraṇam //
jīvanan tu kaṣāyasya pātakānāṁ vināśanam /
sarvarogopaśamanaṁ jaṭharāgnivivardhanam //
vapuṣā kāntim amalāṁ jarāmṛtyuvināśanam /
vāñchitārthaphalaṁ saukhyam indriyāṇāṁ ca māraṇam //
etad uktāni sarvāṇi yogārūḍhasya yoginaḥ /
bhaved abhyāsato' vaśyaṁ nātra kāryā vicāraṇā // 18 //

In this way, even the most unfortunate Yogī might obtain success. By this means all the Nāḍīs of the body are roused and stirred into activity; life is increased and its decay is checked; and all sins are destroyed. All diseases are healed; and the gastric fire is increased. It gives faultless beauty to the body, and destroys decay and death. All fruits of desires and pleasures are obtained, and the senses are conquered. The Yogī fixed in meditation acquires all the above-mentioned things through practice. There should be no hesitation in doing so.

gopanīyā prayatnena mudreyaṁ surapūjite /
yāṁ tu prāpya bhavāmbodheḥ pāraṁ gacchanti yoginaḥ // 19 //

O one worshipped by the gods, know that this Mudrā is to be kept secret with greatest care. Obtaining this, the Yogī crosses the ocean of the world.

mudrā kāmadudhā hyeṣā sādhakānāṁ mayoditā /
guptācāreṇa kartavyā na deyā yasyakasyacit // 20 //

This Mudrā, described by me, is the giver of all desires to the practitioner; it should be practised in secrecy, and ought never to be given to anybody.

Mahābandha

atha mahābandhakathanam :
tataḥ prasāritaḥ pādo vinyasya tam' urūpari /
gudayoniṁ samākuñcya kṛtvā cāpānam ūrdhvagam //
yojayitvā samānena kṛtvā prāṇam adhomukham /
bandhayed ūrdhvagatyarthaṁ prāṇāpānena yaḥ sudhīḥ //
kathito'yaṁ mahābandhaḥ siddhimārgapradāyakaḥ /
nāḍījālād rasavyūho mūrdhānaṁ yāti yoginaḥ //
ubhābhyāṁ sādhayet padbhyām ekaikaṁ suprayatnataḥ // 21 //

Then (after Mahāmudrā), having extended the (right) foot, place it on the (left) thigh; contract the perineum, and draw *Apāna Vāyu* upwards and join it with *Samāna Vāyu;* bend *Prāṇa Vāyu* downwards, and then let the wise Yogī bind them in trinity in the navel (i.e., *Prāṇa* and *Apāna* should be joined with *Samāna* in the navel). I have told you now the Mahābandha, which shows the way to emancipation. By this, all the fluids in the Nāḍīs of the body of the Yogī are propelled towards the head. This should be practised with great care, alternately with both feet.

bhaved abhyāsato vāyuḥ suṣumṇāmadhyasaṅgataḥ /
anena vapuṣaḥ puṣṭir dṛḍhabandho' sthipañjare //
sampūrṇahṛdayo yogī bhavantyetāni yoginaḥ /
bandhenānena yogīndraḥ sādhayet sarvam īpsitam // 22 //

Through this practice, the wind enters the middle of Suṣumṇā; the body is invigorated by it; the bones are firmly knitted; the heart of the Yogī becomes full (of cheerfulness). By this Bandha, the great Yogī accomplishes all his desires.

Mahāvedha

atha mahāvedhakathanam :
apānaprāṇayor aikyaṁ kṛtvā tribhuvaneśvari /
mahāvedhasthito yogī kukṣim āpūrya vāyunā /
sphicau santāḍayed dhīmān vedho' yaṁ kīrtito mayā // 23 //

O goddess of the three worlds, when the Yogī, while performing Mahābandha, causes the union of *Prāṇa* and *Apāna Vāyus* and filling in the viscera with air drives it slowly towards the nates, it is called Mahāvedha.

vedhenānena saṁvidhya vāyunā yogipuṅgavaḥ /
granthiṁ suṣumṇāmārgeṇa brahmagranthiṁ bhinattyasau // 24 //

The best of the Yogīs having, through the help of the *Vāyu,* pierced with this perforator the knot which is in the path of Suṣumṇā, should then pierce the knot of Brahma.

yaḥ karoti sadābhyāsaṁ mahāvedhaṁ sugopītam /
vāyusiddhir bhavet tasya jarāmaraṇanāśinī // 25 //

He who practises this Mahāvedha with great secrecy, obtains *Vāyu-siddhi* (victory over the wind). It destroys old age and death.

cakramadhye sthitā devāḥ kampanti vāyutāḍanāt /
kuṇḍalyapi mahāmāyā kailāse sā vilīyate // 26 //

The gods residing in the Cakras tremble owing to the gentle influx and eflux of air in Prāṇāyāma; the great goddess, Kuṇḍalī Mahāmāyā, is also absorbed in mount Kailāsa.

mahāmudrāmahābandhau niṣphalau vedhavarjitau /
tasmād yogī prayatnena karoti tritayaṁ kramāt // 27 //

Mahāmudrā and Mahābandha become fruitless if they are not followed by Mahāvedha; therefore, the Yogī should practise all these three successively with great care.

etat trayaṁ prayatnena caturvāraṁ karoti yaḥ /
ṣaṇmāsābhyantaraṁ mṛtyuṁ jayatyeva na saṁśayaḥ // 28 //

He who practises these three daily four times with great care, undoubtedly conquers death within six months.

etattrayasya māhātmyaṁ siddho jānāti netaraḥ /
yaj jñātvā sādhakāḥ sarve siddhiṁ samyag labhanti vai // 29 //

Only a Siddha knows the importance of these three and no one else; knowing these, all the practitioners obtain success.

gopanīyā prayatnena sādhakaiḥ siddhim īpsubhiḥ /
anyathā ca na siddhiḥ syān mudrāṇām eṣa niścayaḥ // 30 //

This should be kept in great secrecy by practitioners desirous of obtaining power; otherwise, it is certain that the coveted powers can never be obtained through the practice of Mudrās.

Khecarī

atha khecarīmudrākathanam :
bhruvor antargatāṁ dṛṣṭiṁ vidhāya sudṛḍhāṁ sudhīḥ /
upaviśyāsane vajre nānopadravavarjitaḥ //
lambikordhvaṁ sthite garte rasanāṁ viparītagām /
saṁyojayet prayatnena sudhākūpe vicakṣaṇaḥ /
mudraiṣā khecarī proktā bhaktānām anurodhataḥ // 31 //

The wise Yogī, sitting in *Vajrāsana* posture, in a place free from all disturbance, should firmly fix his gaze on the spot in the middle of the two eyebrows; and reversing the tongue, fix it in the hollow under the epiglottis, placing it with great care at the mouth of the well of nectar(i.e. closing up the air passage). This Mudrā, described by me at the request of my devotees, is the Khecarī-Mudrā.

siddhīnāṁ jananī hyeṣā mama prāṇādhikapriyā /
nirantarakṛtābhyāsāt pīyūṣaṁ pratyahaṁ pibet //
tena vigrahasiddhiḥ syān mṛtyumātaṅgakesarī // 32 //

O my beloved, know this to be the source of all success. Always practising it let him drink the ambrosia daily. By this he obtains *Vigraha-siddhi* (perfect body), and conquers death even as a lion overpowers an elephant.

apavitraḥ pavitro vā sarvāvasthāṁ gato' pi vā /
khecarī yasya śuddhā tu sa śuddho nātra saṁśayaḥ // 33 //

Whether pure or impure, in whatever condition one may be, if success be obtained in Khecarī, he becomes pure. There is no doubt in it.

kṣaṇārdhaṁ kurute yas tu tīrtvā pāpamahārṇavam /
divyabhogān prabhuktvā ca satkule sa prajāyate // 34 //

He who practises it even for a moment crosses the great ocean of sins, and having enjoyed the pleasures of Deva-world is born in a noble family.

mudraiṣā khecarī yastu svasthacitto hyatandritaḥ /
śatabrahmagatenāpi kṣaṇārdhaṁ manyate hi saḥ // 35 //

He who practises this Khecarī-Mudrā calmly and without laziness counts as half a second the period of hundred Brahmās.

gurūpadeśato mudrāṁ yo vetti khecarīm imām /
nānāpāparato dhīmān sa yāti paramāṁ gatim // 36 //

He who knows this Khecarī-Mudrā according to the instructions of his Guru, obtains the highest end, even though immersed in great sins.

sā prāṇasadṛśi mudrā yasminkasmin na dīyate /
pracchādyate prayatnena mudreyaṁ surapūjite // 37 //

O one adored by gods, this Mudrā, dear as life, should not be given to this and that; it should be kept concealed with great care.

Jālandhara Bandha

atha jālandharabandhaḥ :
baddhvā galaśirājālaṁ hṛdaye cibukaṁ nyaset /
bandho jālandharaḥ prokto devānām api durlabhaḥ //
nābhisthavahnir jantūnāṁ sahasrakamalacyutam /
pibet pīyūṣavistāraṁ tadarthaṁ bandhayed imam // 38 //

Having contracted the muscles of the throat press the chin on the chest. This is said to be the Jālandhara-Mudrā. Even gods reckon it as inaccessible. The fire in the region of the navel (i.e., the gastric fire) drinks the nectar which exudes out of the thousand-petalled lotus. [In order to prevent the nectar to be thus consumed] he should practise this Bandha.

bandhenānena pīyūṣaṁ svayaṁ pibati buddhimān /
amaratvaṁ ca samprāpya modate bhuvanatraye // 39 //

Through this Bandha, the wise Yogī himself drinks the nectar, and, obtaining immortality, enjoys the three worlds.

jālandharo bandha eṣa siddhānāṁ siddhidāyakaḥ /
abhyāsaḥ kriyate nityaṁ yoginā siddhim icchatā // 40 //

This Jālandhara-Bandha is the giver of success to the practitioner; a Yogī desirous of success should practise it daily.

Mūlabandha

atha mūlabandhaḥ :
pādamūlena saṁpīḍya gudamārgaṁ suyantritam /
balād apānam ākṛṣya kramād ūrdhvaṁ sucārayet /
kalpito' yaṁ mūlabandho jarāmaraṇanāśanaḥ // 41 //

Pressing well the anus with the heel, forcibly draw upwards the *Apāna Vāyu* slowly by practice. This is described as the Mūlabandha—the destroyer of old age and death.

apānaprāṇayor aikyaṁ prakarotyadhikalpitam /
bandhenānena sutarāṁ yonimudrā prasiddhyati // 42 //

If, in the course of the practice of this Mudrā, the Yogī can unite *Apāna* with *Prāṇa Vāyu,* then it becomes of course the Yoni-Mudrā.

siddhāyāṁ yonimudrāyāṁ kiṁ na sidhyati bhūtale /
bandhasyāsya prasādena gagane vijitālasaḥ /
padmāsane sthito yogī bhuvam utsṛjya vartate // 43 //

He who has accomplished Yoni-Mudrā, what can he not accomplish in this world! Sitting in *Padmāsana* posture, free from idleness, the Yogī, leaving the ground, moves through the air by virtue of this Mudrā.

sugupte nirjane deśe bandham enaṁ samabhyaset /
saṁsārasāgaraṁ tartuṁ yadīcched yogipuṅgavaḥ // 44 //

44. If the wise Yogī is desirous of crossing the ocean of Saṁsāra, let him practise this Bandha in secret, in a retired place.

Viparītakaraṇī

atha viparītakaraṇīmudrā :
bhūtale svaśiro dattvā khe nayec caraṇadvayam /
viparītakṛtiś caiṣā sarvatantreṣu gopitā // 45 //

Placing the head on the ground, let him stretch out his legs upwards, moving them round and round. This is *Viparītakaraṇī*, kept secret in all the Tantras.

etad yaḥ kurute nityam abhyāsaṁ yāmamātrataḥ /
mṛtyuṁ jayati sa yogī pralaye nāpi sīdati // 46 //

A Yogī who practises it daily for three hours, conquers death, and is not destroyed even in Pralaya.

kurute' mṛtapānaṁ yaḥ siddhānāṁ samatām iyāt /
sa sevyaḥ sarvalokānāṁ bandham enaṁ karoti yaḥ // 47 //

He who drinks nectar becomes equal to Siddhas; he who practises this Bandha becomes fit for worship by all the worlds.

Uḍḍīyāna Bandha

nābher ūrdhvam adhaścāpi tānaṁ paścimam ācaret /
uḍḍyānabandha eṣa syāt sarvaduḥkhaughanāśanaḥ //
udare paścimaṁ tānaṁ nābher ūrdhvaṁ tu kārayet /
uḍyānākhyo' tra bandho' yaṁ mṛtyumātaṅgakesarī // 48 //

When the intestines above and below the navel are brought to the left side, it is called Uḍḍīyāna Bandha—the destroyer of all sins and sorrows. The left side viscera of the abdominal cavity should be brought above the navel. This is Uḍḍīyāna Bandha, the lion overpowering the elephant of death.

nityaṁ yaḥ kurute yogī caturvāraṁ dine dine /
tasya nābhes tu śuddhiḥ syād yen siddho bhaven marut // 49 //

The Yogī, who always practises it four times a day, purifies thereby his navel, through which the winds are purified.

ṣaṇmāsam abhyasan yogī mṛtyuṁ jayati niścitam /
tasyodarāgnir jvalati rasavṛddhiḥ prajāyate // 50 //

By practising it for six months, the Yogī certainly conquers death; the gastric fire is kindled; and there takes place an increase of the fluids of the body.

anena sutarāṁ siddhir vigrahasya prajāyate /
rogāṇāṁ saṁkṣayaś cāpi yogino bhavati dhruvam//51//

Through this, consequently, *Vvigrahasiddhi* is also obtained. All the diseases of the Yogī are certainly destroyed by it.

guror labdhvā prayatnena sādhayet tu vicakṣaṇaḥ /
nirjane susthite deśe bandhaṁ paramadurlabham // 52 //

Having learnt the method from a Guru, the wise Yogī should practise it with great care. This most inacessible Mudrā should be practised in a solitary and undisturbed place.

Śakticālana

atha śakticālanamudrā :
ādhārakamale suptāṁ cālayet kuṇḍalīṁ dṛḍhām /
apānavāyum āruhya balād ākṛṣya buddhimān /
śakticālanamudreyaṁ sarvaśaktipradāyinī // 53 //

Let the wise Yogī forcibly and firmly draw up the goddess Kuṇḍalī sleeping in the *Ādhāra* Lotus, by means of the *Apāna Vāyu*. This is Śakticālana Mudrā, the giver of all powers.

śakticālanam evaṁ hi pratyahaṁ yaḥ samācaret /
āyurvṛddhir bhavet tasya rogāṇāṁ ca vināśanam // 54 //

He who practises this Śakticālana daily, gets increase of life and destruction of diseases.

vihāya nidrāṁ bhujagī svayam ūrdhve bhavet khalu /
tasmād abhyāsanaṁ kāryaṁ yoginā siddhim icchatā // 55 //

Leaving sleep, the serpent (i.e. Kuṇḍalī) herself goes up; therefore let the Yogī desirous of power practise this.

yaḥ karoti sadābhyāsaṁ śakticālanam uttamam /
yena vigrahasiddhiḥ syād aṇimādiguṇapradā /
gurūpadeśavidhinā tasya mṛtyubhayaṁ kutaḥ // 56 //

He who practises always this best Śakticālana according to the instructions of his Guru, obtains *Vigraha-Siddhi,* which gives the powers of *Aṇimā,* etc., and has no fear of death.

muhūrtadvayaparyantaṁ vidhinā śakticālanam /
yaḥ karoti prayatnena tasya siddhir adūrataḥ /
yuktāsanena kartavyaṁ yogibhiḥ śakticālanam // 57 //

He who practises Śakticālana properly for two seconds, and with care, is very near to success. This Mudrā should be practised by the Yogī in the proper posture.

etat tu mudrādaśakaṁ na bhūtaṁ na bhaviṣyati /
ekaikābhyāsane siddhiḥ siddho bhavati nānyathā // 58 //

These are the ten Mudrās whose equal there never was nor ever shall be. Through the practice of any one of them, a person becomes a Siddha and obtains success.

iti śrīśivasaṁhitāyāṁ yogaśāstre
īśvarapārvatī 'saṁvāde caturthaḥ paṭalaḥ //4//

End of Chapter 4 on Yoni-Mudrā.

CHAPTER 5

Kinds of Yoga

Pañcamaḥ Paṭalaḥ

śrīdevyuvāca:
brūhi me vākyam īśāna paramārthadhiyaṁ prati /
ye vighnāḥ santi lokānāṁ vada me priya śaṅkara // 1 //

Pārvatī said:

O Lord, O beloved Śaṅkara, tell me, for the sake of those whose minds search after the supreme end, the obstacles and hindrances in the path.

īśvara uvāca:
śṛṇu devi pravakṣyāmi yathā vighnāḥ sthitāḥ sadā /
muktiṁ prati narāṇām ca bhogaḥ paramabandhanaḥ//2//

Śiva said:

Listen, O Goddess, I shall tell thee all the obstacles that stand in the path to the attainment of emancipation. Enjoyments *(bhoga)* are the greatest of all impediments.

Bhoga (Enjoyment)

atha bhogarūpayogavighnakathanam :
nārī śayyāsanaṁ vastraṁ dhanam asya viḍambanam /
tāmbūlaṁ bhakṣyayānāni rājyaiśvaryavibhūtayaḥ /
haimaṁ raupyaṁ tathā tāmraṁ ratnaṁ cāgurudhenavaḥ /
pāṇḍityaṁ vedaśāstrāṇi nṛtyaṁ gītaṁ vibhūṣaṇam /
vaṁśīvīṇāmṛdaṅgāś ca gajendraś cāśvavāhanam /
dārāpatyāni viṣayā vighnā ete prakīrtitāḥ /
bhogarūpā ime vighnā dharmarūpān imān śṛṇu // 3 //

Woman, bed, seat, dress, and riches are the obstacles. Betels, dainty dishes, carriages, kingdoms, lordliness and powers; gold, silver, as well as copper, gems, aloe wood, and kine; *learning* the Vedas and the Śāstras; dancing, singing and ornaments; harp, flute and drum; riding on elephants and horses; wives and children; worldly enjoyments—all these are so many impediments. These are the obstacles which arise from *Bhoga* (enjoyment). Hear now the impediments which arise from the practice of ritualistic religion.

Dharma (Rituals and Observances)

atha dharmarūpayogavighnakathanam :
snānaṁ pūjāvidhir homaṁ tathā mokṣamayī sthitiḥ /
vratopavāsaniyamamaunam indriyanigrahaḥ /
dhyeyo dhyānaṁ tathā mantro dānaṁ khyātir diśāsu ca /
vāpīkūpataḍāgādiprāsādārāmakalpanā /
yajñaṁ cāndrāyaṇaṁ kṛcchraṁ tīrthāni vividhāni ca /
dṛśyante ca ime vighnā dharmarūpeṇa saṁsthitāḥ // 4 //

Ablutions, worships of deities, fire sacrifice, hankering after *Mokṣa,* vows and penances, fasts, religious observances, silence, ascetic practices, contemplation and the object of contemplation, *mantras,* and alms- giving, world-wide fame,constructing tanks, wells, ponds, convents and groves; sacrifices, austerities etc., cāndrāyaṇa, and pilgrimages: all these are impediments in the form of religious acts.

Jñāna (Knowledge as Obstacle)

atha jñānarūpavighnakathanam :
yat tu vighnaṁ bhavej jñānaṁ kathayāmi varānane /
gomukhaṁ svāsanaṁ kṛtvā dhautiprakṣālanaṁ ca tat /
nāḍīsañcāravijñānaṁ pratyāhāranirodhanam /
kukṣisañcālanam kṣipraṁ praveśa indriyādhvanā /
nāḍīkarmāṇi kalyāṇi bhojanaṁ śrūyatāṁ mama // 5 //

Now I shall describe, O Pārvatī, the obstacles which arise from knowledge: Sitting in the *Gomukha* posture and practising Dhauti (washing the intestines by Haṭha Yoga), knowledge of the distribution of the *Nāḍīs* (the vessels of the human body), learning of *Pratyāhāra* (withdrawal of senses), trying to awaken the Kuṇḍalinī-power by moving quickly the belly (a process of Haṭha

Yoga), entering into the path of the *Indriyas*, and knowledge of the action of the *Nāḍīs:* these are the obstacles. Now listen to the mistaken notions of diet, O Pārvatī.

navadhāturasaṁ chindhi śuṇṭhikās tāḍayet punaḥ /
ekakālaṁ samādhiḥ syāl liṅgabhūtam idaṁ śṛṇu // 6 //

That *Samādhi* (trance) can be at once induced by drinking certain new chemical essences and by eating certain kinds of food, is a mistake. Now hear about the mistaken notion of the influence of company.

saṅgamaṁ gaccha sādhūnāṁ saṅkocaṁ bhaja durjanāt /
praveśanirgame vāyor gurulakṣaṃ vilokayet // 7 //

"Keep the company of the virtuous, and avoid that of the vicious" (is a mistaken notion). Measuring of the heaviness and lightness of the inspired and expired air (is an erroneous idea).

piṇḍasthaṁ rūpasaṁsthaṁ ca rūpasthaṁ rūpavarjitam /
brahmaitasmin matāvasthā hṛdayaṁ ca praśāmyati /
ityete kathitā vighnā jñānarūpe vyavasthitāḥ // 8 //

Brahman is in the body or is the maker of form, or has a form, or has no form, or is everything—all these consoling doctrines are obstacles. Such notions are impediments in the shape of Jñāna (knowledge).

Four Kinds of Yoga

atha caturvidhayogakathanam :
mantrayogo haṭhaścaiva layayogas tṛtīyakaḥ /
caturtho rājayogaḥ syāt sa dvidhābhāvavarjitaḥ // 9 //

Yoga is of four kinds : First Mantra-Yoga, second Haṭha-Yoga, third Laya-Yoga, fourth Rāja-Yoga, which discards duality.

Sādhakas (Aspirants)

caturdhā sādhako jñeyo mṛdumadhyādhimātrakāḥ /
adhimātratamaḥ śreṣṭho bhavābdhau laṅghanakṣamaḥ // 10 //

Know that aspirants are of four kinds : mild, moderate, ardent and the most ardent, the best one who can cross the ocean of the world.

Mild Aspirant

atha mṛdusādhakalakṣaṇam :
mandotsāhī susaṁmūḍho vyādhistho gurudūṣakaḥ /
lobhī pāpamatiś caiva bahvāśī vanitāśrayaḥ //
capalaḥ kātaro rogī parādhīno' tiniṣṭhuraḥ /
mandācāro mandavīryo jñātavyo mṛdumānavaḥ //
dvādaśābde bhavet siddhir etasya yatnataḥ param /
mantrayogādhikārī sa jñātavyo guruṇā dhruvam // 11 //

Men of small enterprise, oblivious, sickly and fault finders with their teachers; avaricious, sinful, gourmands, and attached helplessly to their wives; fickle, timid, diseased, not independent, and cruel; those whose characters are bad and who are weak: know all the above to be mild Sādhakas. With great efforts such men succeed in twelve years; the teacher should know them as fit for Mantra-Yoga.

Moderate Aspirant

samabuddhiḥ kṣamāyuktaḥ puṇyākāṅkṣī priyaṁvadaḥ /
madhyasthaḥ sarvakāryeṣu sāmānyaḥ syān na saṁśayaḥ //
etaj jñātvaiva gurubhir dīyate muktito layaḥ // 12 //

Liberal-minded, merciful, desirous of virtue, sweet in their speech; those who never go to extremes in any undertaking—these are the middling. These are to be initiated by the teacher in Laya-Yoga.

Ardent Aspirant

atha adhimātrasādhakalakṣaṇam :
sthirabuddhir laye yuktaḥ svādhīno vīryavān api /
mahāśayo dayāyuktaḥ kṣamāvān satyavān api //
śūro vayaḥsthaḥ śraddhāvān gurupādābjapūjakaḥ /
yogābhyāsarataś caiva jñātavyaś cādhimātrakaḥ //
etasya siddhiḥ ṣaḍvarṣe bhaved abhyāsayogataḥ /
etasmai dīyate dhīro haṭhayogaś ca sāṅgataḥ // 13 //

Steady-minded, knowing Laya-Yoga, independent, full of energy, magnanimous, full of sympathy, forgiving, truthful, courageous, full of faith, worshippers of the lotus-feet of their Gurus, engaged always in the practice of Yoga—know such men to be Adhimātra. They obtain success in the practice of Yoga within six years, and ought to be initiated in Haṭha-Yoga and its branches.

The Most Ardent Aspirants

atha adhimātratamasādhakalakṣaṇam :
mahāvīryānvitotsāhī manojñaḥ śauryavān api /
śāstrajño' bhyāsaśīlaś ca nirmohaś ca nirākulaḥ //
navayauvanasampanno mitāhārī jitendriyaḥ /
nirbhayaś ca śucir dakṣo dātā sarvajanāśrayaḥ //
adhikārī sthiro dhīmān yathecchāvasthitaḥ kṣamī /
suśīlo dharmacārī ca guptaceṣṭaḥ priyaṁvadaḥ //
śāstraviśvāsasampanno devatāgurupūjakaḥ /
janasaṅgaviraktaś ca mahāvyādhivivarjitaḥ //
adhimātravratajñaś ca sarvayogasya sādhakaḥ /
tribhiḥ saṁvatsaraiḥ siddhir etasya nātra saṁśayaḥ //
sarvayogādhikārī sa nātra kāryā vicāraṇā // 14 //

Those who have the largest amount of energy, are enterprising, engaging, heroic, who know the Śāstras, and are persevering, free from the effects of blind emotions, and, not easily confused, who are in the prime of their youth, moderate in their diet, rulers of their senses, fearless, clean, skilful, charitable, a help to all; competent, firm, talented, contented, forgiving, good- natured, religious, who keep their endeavours secret, of sweet speech, peaceful, who have faith in scriptures and are worshippers of God and Guru, who are averse to fritter away their time in society, and are free from any grievous malady, who are acquainted with the duties of their kind, and are the practitioners of every kind of Yoga—undoubtedly, they obtain success in three years; they are entitled to be initiated in all kinds of Yoga without any hesitation.

Invocation of One's Shadow (Pratīkopāsana)

atha pratīkopāsanam :
pratīkopāsanā kāryā dṛṣṭādṛṣṭaphalapradā /
punāti darśanād atra nātra kāryā vicāraṇā // 15 //

The invocation of Pratīka (shadow) gives to the devotee results seen as well as unseen; undoubtedly, by its very sight, a man becomes pure.

gāḍhātape svapratibimbiteśvaraṁ nirīkṣya visphāritalocanadvayam/
yadā nabhaḥ paśyati svapratīkaṁ nabho'ṅgaṇe taṭkṣaṇam eva paśyati//16//

In a clear sun-lit sky, behold with a steady gaze your own divine reflection; whenever this is seen even for a single second in the sky, you behold God at once in the sky.

pratyahaṁ paśyate yo vai svapratīkaṁ nabho'ṅgaṇe /
āyurvṛddhir bhavet tasya na mṛtyuḥ syāt kadācana // 17 //

He who daily sees his shadow in the sky, will get his years increased and will never die an accidental death.

yadā paśyati sampūrṇam svapratīkaṁ nabho'ṅgaṇe /
tadā jayam avāpnoti vāyuṁ nirjitya sañcaret // 18 //

When the shadow is seen fully reflected in the field of the sky, then he obtains victory, and conquering Vāyu, he goes everywhere.

How to invoke

At the time of rising sun, or by moon, let him steadily fix his gaze on the neck of the shadow he throws; then, after some time, let him look into the sky; if he sees a full grey shadow in the sky, it is auspicious.

yaḥ karoti sadābhyāsaṁ cātmānaṁ vindate param /
pūrṇānandaikapuruṣaṁ svapratīkaprasādataḥ // 19 //

He who always practises this attains the all-blissful supreme Being, the highest soul, through the grace of his shadow.

yātrākāle vivāhe ca śubhe karmaṇi saṅkaṭe /
pāpakṣaye puṇyavṛddhau pratīkopāsanaṁ caret // 20 //

At the time of commencing travel, marriage, or auspicious rite, or when in trouble, it is of great use. This invocation of the shadow destroys sins and increases virtue.

nirantarakṛtābhyāsād antare paśyati dhruvam /
tadā muktim avāpnoti yogī niyatamānasaḥ // 21 //

By practising it always, he begins at last to see it in his heart, and the persevering Yogī gets liberation.

aṅguṣṭhābhyām ubhe śrotre tarjanībhyāṁ dvilocane /
nāsārandhre ca madhyābhyām anāmābhyāṁ mukhaṁ dṛḍham //
nirudhya mārutaṁ yogī yadaiva kurute bhṛśam /
tadā lakṣaṇam ātmānaṁ jyotīrūpaṁ sa paśyati // 22 //

Let him close the ears with his thumbs, the eyes with index fingers, the nostrils with the middle fingers, and with the remaining four fingers let him press together the upper and lower lips. The Yogī, by having thus firmly confined the air, sees his soul in the shape of light.

tat tejo dṛśyate yena kṣaṇamātraṁ nirākulam /
sarvapāpavinirmuktaḥ sa yāti paramāṁ gatim // 23 //

When one sees, without obstruction, this light for even a moment, he becoming free from sin, reaches the highest state.

nirantarakṛtābhyāsād yogī vigatakalmaṣaḥ /
sarvadehādi vismṛtya tadabhinnaḥ svayaṁ gataḥ // 24 //

The Yogī, free from sin, and practising this continually, forgets his physical, subtle and causal bodies, and becomes one with that soul.

yaḥ karoti sadābhyāsaṁ guptācāreṇa mānavaḥ /
sa vai brahmavilīnaḥ syāt pāpakarmarato yadi // 25 //

He who practises this in secrecy, is absorbed in Brahman, even though he has been engaged in sinful acts.

Mystic Sounds

gopanīyaḥ prayatnena sadyaḥ pratyayakārakaḥ /
nirvāṇadāyako loke yogo' yaṁ mama vallabhaḥ //
nādaḥ sañjāyate tasya krameṇābhyāsataś ca vai // 26 //

This should be kept secret; it at once produces conviction; it gives Nirvāṇa to mankind. This is my most beloved Yoga. From practising this gradually, the Yogī begins to hear the mystic sound (Nāda).

mattabhṛṅgaveṇuvīṇāsadṛśaḥ prathamo dhvaniḥ /
evam abhyāsataḥ paścāt saṁsāradhvāntanāśanam //
ghaṇṭānādasamaḥ paścāt dhvanir megharavopamaḥ /
dhvanau tasmin mano dattvā yadā tiṣṭhati nirbhayaḥ //
tadā sañjāyate siddhir layasya mama vallabhe // 27 //

The first sound is like the hum of the honey-intoxicated bee, next that of a flute, then of a harp; after this, by the gradual practice of Yoga, the destroyer of the darkness of the world, he hears the sounds of ringing bells; then sounds like roar of thunder. When one fixes his full attention on this sound, being free from fear, he gets absorption, O my beloved!

tatra nāde yadā cittaṁ ramate yogino bhṛśam /
vismṛtya sakalaṁ bāhyaṁ nādena saha śāmyati // 28 //

When the mind of the Yogī is well absorbed in this sound, then forgetting all external things, it calms down along with the sound.

etad abhyāsayogena jitvā samyag guṇān bahūn /
sarvārambhaparityāgī cidākāśe vilīyate // 29 //

By this practice of Yoga he conquers all the three qualities (i.e., Sattva, Rajas & Tamas); and being free from all states, he is absorbed in *Cidākāśa* (the ether of intelligence).

A Secret

nāsanaṁ siddhasadṛśam na kumbhasadṛśaṁ balam /
na khecarīsamā mudrā na nādasadṛśo layaḥ // 30 //

There is no posture like *Siddhāsana,* no power like that of *Kumbha,* no *Mudrā* like *Khecarī,* and no absorption like that of *Nāda* (the mystic sound).

idānīṁ kathayiṣyāmi muktasyānubhavam priye /
yaj jñātvā labhate muktiṁ pāpayukto' pi sādhakaḥ // 31 //

Now I shall describe to thee, O dear, the foretaste of salvation, knowing which even a sinful aspirant may obtain salvation.

samabhyarceśvaraṁ samyak kṛtvā ca yogam uttamaṁ /
gṛhṇīyāt susthito bhūtvā guruṁ santoṣya buddhimān // 32 //

Having adored God properly, and having completely performed the best Yoga, and being in a calm and steady state and posture, let the wise Yogī initiate himself into this Yoga by pleasing his Guru.

jīvādi sakalaṁ vastuṁ dattvā yogavidaṁ gurum /
santoṣyātiprayatnena yogo' yaṁ gṛhyate budhaiḥ // 33 //

Having given all his cattle and property to the Guru who knows Yoga, and having satisfied him with great care, let the wise man receive this initiation.

viprān santoṣya medhāvī nānāmaṅgalasaṁyutaḥ /
mamālaye śucir bhūtvā pragṛhṇīyāc chubhātmakam // 34 //

Having pleased the Brāhmaṇas by giving them all kinds of good things, let a wise man receive this auspicious Yoga in my house (i.e., the temple of Śiva) with purity of heart.

saṁnyasyānena vidhinā prāktanaṁ vigrahādikam /
bhūtvā divyavapur yogī gṛhṇīyād vakṣyamāṇakam // 35 //

Having renounced by the above methods all his previous bodies (the results of his past Karma), and being in his spiritual (or luminous) body, let the Yogī receive what is being said now.

padmāsanasthito yogī janasaṅgavivarjitaḥ /
vijñānanāḍīdvitayam aṅgulībhyāṁ nirodhayet // 36 //

Sitting in Padmāsana posture in a solitary place, let the Yogī press the two *Vijñāna Nāḍīs* (the vessels of consciousness) with his two fingers.

siddhes tadāvirbhavati sukharūpī nirañjanaḥ /
tasmin pariśramaḥ kāryo yena siddho bhavet khalu // 37 //

By obtaining success in this, he becomes all happiness and unstained; therefore, let him endeavour with all his might, in order to ensure success.

yaḥ karoti sadābhyāsaṁ tasya siddhir na dūrataḥ /
vāyusiddhir bhavet tasya kramād eva na saṁśayaḥ // 38 //

He who practises this always, obtains success within a short time; he gets also Vāyu-Siddhi in course of time.

sakṛd yaḥ kurute yogī pāpaughaṁ nāśayed dhruvam /
tasya syān madhyame vāyoḥ praveśo nātra saṁśayaḥ // 39 //

The Yogī, who does it even once, verily destroys all sins; and undoubtedly in him *Vāyu* enters the middle channel.

etad abhyāsaśīlo yaḥ sa yogī devapūjitaḥ /
aṇimādiguṇān labdhvā vicared bhuvanatraye // 40 //

The Yogī who practises this with perseverance is worshipped even by gods; he receives the psychic powers of *Aṇimā, Laghimā* etc., and can go everywhere, throughout the three worlds, at pleasure.

yo yathāsyānilābhyāsāt tadbhavet tasya vigrahaḥ /
tiṣṭhed ātmani medhāvī saṁyutaḥ krīḍate bhṛśam // 41 //

According to the strength of one's practice in commanding *Vāyu,* he gets command over his body; the wise, dwelling in the spirit, enjoys the world in the present body.

etad yogaṁ paraṁ gopyaṁ na deyaṁ yasya kasyacit /
yaḥ pramāṇaiḥ samāyuktas tameva kathyate dhruvam // 42 //

This Yoga is a great secret, and not to be given to every body; it might be revealed to him only, in whom all the qualifications of a Yogī are perceived.

Various Kinds of Dhāraṇā

yogī padmāsane tiṣṭhet kaṇṭhakūpe yadā smaran /
jihvāṁ kṛtvā tālumūle kṣutpipāsā nivartate // 43 //

Let the Yogī seat himself in Padmāsana, and fix his attention on the cavity of the throat; let him place his tongue at the base of the palate; by this he will get rid of hunger and thirst.

kaṇṭhakūpād adhaḥ sthāne kūrmanāḍyasti śobhanā /
tasmin yogī mano dattvā cittasthairyaṁ labhed bhṛśam // 44 //

Below the cavity of the throat, there is a beautiful *Nāḍī* (vessel) called *Kūrma;* when the Yogī fixes his attention on it, he acquires stability of *Citta* (mind).

śiraḥ kapāle rudrākṣam vivaraṁ cintayed yadā /
tadā jyotiḥ prakāśaḥ syād vidyutpuñjasamaprabhaḥ /
etac cintanamātreṇa pāpānāṁ saṁkṣayo bhavet /
durācāro' pi puruṣo labhate paramaṁ padam // 45 //

When the Yogī constantly thinks that he has got a third eye—the eye of Śiva—in the middle of his forehead, he then perceives a fire brilliant like lightning. By contemplating on this light, all sins are destroyed, and even the most wicked person obtains the highest end.

aharniśaṁ yadā cintāṁ tatkaroti vicakṣaṇaḥ /
siddhānāṁ darśanaṁ tasya bhāṣaṇaṁ ca bhaved dhruvam // 46 //

If the experienced Yogī thinks of this light day and night, he sees the Siddhas (adepts), and can certainly converse with them.

tiṣṭhan gacchan svapan bhuñjan dhyāyec chūnyam aharniśam /
tadākāśamayo yogī cidākāśe vilīyate // 47 //

He who contemplates on *Śūnya* (void or vacuum or space), while walking or standing, dreaming or waking, becomes altogether etherial, and is absorbed in the *Cidākāśa*.

etaj jñānaṁ sadā kāryaṁ yoginā siddhim icchatā /
nirantarakṛtābhyāsān mama tulyo bhaved dhruvam //
etaj jñānabalād yogī sarveṣāṁ vallabho bhavet // 48 //

The Yogī, desirous of success, should always obtain this knowledge; by constant practice, he becomes equal to me; through the force of this knowledge, he becomes the beloved of all.

sarvān bhūtān jayaṁ kṛtvā nirāśīr aparigrahaḥ /
nāsāgre dṛśyate yena padmāsanagatena vai //
manaso maraṇaṁ tasya khecaratvaṁ prasiddhyati // 49 //

Having conquered all the elements, and being free from all desires and worldly possessions, when the Yogī sitting in Padmāsana, fixes his gaze on the tip of the nose, his mind becomes dead and he obtains the spiritual power called *Khecarī*.

jyotiḥ paśyati yogīndraḥ śuddhaṁ śuddhācalopamam /
tatrābhyāsabalenaiva svayaṁ tadrakṣako bhavet // 50 //

The great Yogī beholds light, pure as the the holy mountain (Kailāsa); and through the force of his practice in it, he becomes the lord and guardian of the light.

uttānaśayane bhūmau suptvā dhyāyan nirantaram /
sadyaḥ śramavināśāya svayaṁ yogī vicakṣaṇaḥ //
śiraḥpāścātyabhāgasya dhyāne mṛtyuñjayo bhavet /
bhrūmadhye dṛṣṭimātreṇa hyaparaḥ parikīrtitaḥ // 51 //

Stretching himself on the ground, let him contemplate on this light; by so doing all his weariness and fatigue are destroyed. By contemplating on the back part of his head, he becomes the conqueror of death. We have described before the effect of fixing one's attention on the space between the two eyebrows (so it need not be enumerated here).

caturvidhasya cānnasya rasas tredhā vibhajyate /
tatra sāratamo liṅgadehasya pariposakaḥ //
saptadhātumayaṁ piṇḍam ekaḥ puṣṇāti madhyagaḥ // 52 //

The four kinds of food (i.e., that which is chewed, that which is sucked, that which is licked and that which is drunk), which a man takes, are transformed into a fluid which is divided into three parts. The best part (or the finest extract of food) goes to nourish the *Liṅga Śarīra* or subtle body (the seat of force). The second or middle part goes to nourish this gross body composed of seven *Dhātus* (humours).

yāti viṇmūtrarūpeṇa tṛtīyaḥ saptato bahiḥ /
ādyabhāgadvayaṁ nāḍyaḥ proktās tāḥ sakalā api /
poṣayanti vapur vāyum āpādatalamastakam // 53 //

The third or the most inferior part goes out of the body in the shape of excrement and urine. The first two essences of food are found in the *Nāḍīs,* and being carried by them, they nourish the body from head to foot.

nāḍībhir ābhiḥ sarvābhir vāyuḥ sañcarate yadā /
tadaivānnaraso dehe sāmyeneha pravartate // 54 //

When the *Vāyu* moves through all the *Nāḍīs,* then, owing to this *Vāyu* (oxygen ?), the fluids of the body get extraordinary force and energy.

caturdaśānāṁ tatreha vyāpāre mukhyatā matā /
tā anugratvahīnāś ca prāṇasañcāranāḍikāḥ // 55 //

The most important of these *Nāḍīs* are fourteen, distributed in different parts of the body and performing various functions. They are either weak or strong, and *Prāṇa* (vitality) flows through them.

THE SIX CAKRAS

Mūlādhāra Cakra

gudād dvayaṅgulataś cordhvaṁ meḍhraikāṅgulatas tvadhaḥ /
evaṁ cāsti samaṁ kandaṁ samantāc caturaṅgulam // 56 //

Two fingers above rectum and two fingers below Liṅga, four fingers in width is a space like a bulbous root.

paścimābhimukhīḥ yoniṛ gudameḍhrāntarālagā /
tatra kandaṁ samākhyātaṁ tatrāste kuṇḍalī sadā //
saṁveṣṭya sakalāṁ nāḍīḥ sārddhatrikuṭilākṛtiḥ /
mukhe niveśya sā pucchaṁ suṣumṇāvivare sthitā // 57 //

In this space is the *Yoni* having its face towards the back; that space is called the root; there dwells the goddess *Kuṇḍalinī*. It surrounds all the *Nāḍīs,* and has three coils and a half; and holding its tail in its own mouth, it rests in the hole of *Suṣumṇā.*

suptā nāgopamā hyeṣā sphurantī prabhayā svayā /
ahivat sandhisaṁsthānā vāgdevī bījasañjñikā // 58 //

It sleeps there like a serpent, and is luminous by its own light. Like a serpent it lives between the joints; it is the goddess of speech, and is called the seed *(Bīja).*

jñeyā śaktir iyaṁ viṣṇor nirbharā svarṇabhāsvarā /
sattvaṁ rajas tamaś ceti guṇatrayaprasūtikā // 59 //

Full of energy, and like burning gold, know this Kuṇḍalinī to be the power *(Śakti)* of *Viṣṇu;* it is the mother of the three qualities—Sattva (rhythm), Rajas (energy) and Tamas (inertia).

tatra bandhūkapuṣpābhaṁ kāmabījaṁ prakīrtitam /
kalahemasamaṁ yoge prayuktākṣararūpiṇam // 60 //

There, beautiful like a *Bandhūka* flower, is placed the seed of love (Klīṁ); it is brilliant like burnished gold, and is described in Yoga as eternal.

suṣumṇāpi ca saṁśliṣṭā bījaṁ tatra varaṁ sthitam /
śaraccandranibhaṁ tejas svayam etat sphurat sthitam //
sūryakoṭipratīkāśaṁ candrakoṭisuśītalam /
etat trayaṁ militvaiva devī tripurabhairavī //
bījasañjñaṁ paraṁ tejas tadeva parikīrtitam // 61 //

Suṣumṇā also embraces it, and the beautiful seed is there; there it rests shining brilliantly like the autumnal moon, with the luminosity of millions of suns, and the coolness of millions of moons. Goddess Tripura Bhairavī has these three (fire, sun, and moon) taken together, and collectively she is called Bīja. It is also called the great energy.

kriyāvijñānaśaktibhyāṁ yutaṁ yatparito bhramat /
uttiṣṭhat praviśat tvaṁbhaḥ sūkṣamaṁ śoṇaśikhāyutam //
yonisthaṁ tatparaṁ tejaḥ svayaṁbhūliṅgasañjñitam // 62 //

It *(Bīja)* is endowed with the powers of action (motion) and sensation, and circulates throughout the body. It is subtle, and has a flame of fire; sometimes it rises up, and at other times it falls down into the water. This is the great energy which rests in the perineum, and is called *Svayambhū-liṅga* (the self-born).

ādhārapadmam etaddhi yonir yasyāsti kandataḥ /
parisphurad vādisāntaṁ caturvarṇdṁ caturdalam // 63 //

All this is called the *Ādhāra-padma* (the support lotus), and the four petals of it are designated by the letters v, ś, ṣ, s. (व, श, ष, स).

kulābhidhaṁ suvarṇābhaṁ svayaṁbhūliṅgasaṅgatam /
dviraṇḍo yatra siddho' sti ḍākinī yatra devatā //
tatpadmamadhyagā yonis tatra kuṇḍalinī sthitā /
tasyā ūrdhve sphurat tejaḥ kāmabījaṁ bhraman matam //
yaḥ karoti sadā dhyānaṁ mūlādhāre vicakṣaṇaḥ /
tasya syād dārdurī siddhir bhūmityāgakrameṇa vai // 64 //

Near this *Svayambhū-liṅga* is a golden region called *Kula* (family); its presiding adept is called *Dviraṇḍa,* and its presiding goddess called *Ḍākinī.* In the centre of that lotus is the *Yoni* where resides *Kuṇḍalinī;* the circulating bright energy above that is called *Kāmabīja* (the seed of love). A wise man who always contemplates on this *Mūlādhāra* obtains *Dārdurī-siddhi* (frog-jump power); and by degrees he can altogether leave the ground (i.e., rise in the air).

vapuṣaḥ kāntir utkṛṣṭā jaṭharāgnivivardhanam /
ārogyaṁ ca paṭutvaṁ ca sarvajñatvaṁ ca jāyate // 65 //

The brilliance of the body is increased; the gastric fire becomes powerful; and freedom from disease, cleverness, and omniscience ensue.

bhūtaṁ bhavyaṁ bhaviṣyaṁ ca vetti sarvaṁ sakāraṇam /
aśrutānyapi śāstrāṇi sarahasyaṁ bhaved dhruvam // 66 //

He knows what has been, what is happening, and what is to be, together with their causes; he masters the unheard of sciences together with their mysteries.

vaktre sarasvatī devī sadā nṛtyati nirbharam /
mantrasiddhir bhavet tasya japād eva na saṁśayaḥ // 67 //

On his tongue always dances the Goddess of Learning; he obtains *Mantra-siddhi* (success in Mantras), through constant recitation only.

jarāmaraṇaduḥkhaughān nāśayati guror vacaḥ /
idaṁ dhyānaṁ sadā kāryaṁ pavanābhyāsinā param /
dhyānamātreṇa yogīndro mucyate sarvakilviṣāt // 68 //

Guru's blessing destroys old age, death, and innumerable troubles. A practitioner of Prāṇāyāma should always meditate upon it; by its mere contemplation, a great Yogī is freed from all sins.

mūlapadmaṁ yadā dhyāyed yogī svayaṁbhūliṅgasañjñakam /
tadā tatkṣaṇamātreṇa pāpaughaṁ nāśayed dhruvam // 69 //

When the Yogī contemplates this Mūlādhāra lotus—the *Svayaṁbhū-liṅga*—then, undoubtedly, at that very moment, all his sins are destroyed.

yad yat kāmayate citte tat tat phalam avāpnuyāt /
nirantarakṛtābhyāsāt taṁ paśyati vimuktidam //
bāhyād ābhyantaraṁ śreṣṭhaṁ pūjanīyaṁ prayatnataḥ /
tataḥ śreṣṭhatamaṁ hyetan nānyad asti mataṁ mama // 70 //

Whatever the mind desires, he gets; by habitual exercise he sees him who gives salvation, who is the best both inside and outside and who is to be worshipped with great care. Better than him, I know none.

ātmasaṁsthaṁ śivaṁ tyaktvā bahiḥsthaṁ yaḥ samarcayet /
hastasthaṁ piṇḍam utsṛjya bhramate jīvitāśayā // 71 //

He who, leaving Śiva (God) who is inside, worships that which is outside (i.e., worships external forms), is like one who throws away the sweetmeat in his hand, and wanders away in search of food.

ātmaliṅgārcanaṁ kuryād anālasyo dine dine /
tasya syāt sakalā siddhir nātra kāryā vicāraṇā // 72 //

Let one thus meditate daily, without negligence, on his own *Svayaṁbhū-liṅga* and have no doubt that from this will come all powers.

nirantarakṛtābhyāsāt ṣaṇmāsaiḥ siddhim āpnuyāt /
tasya vāyupraveśo' pi suṣumṇāyāṁ bhaved dhruvam // 73 //

By habitual exercise he gets success in six months; and undoubtedly his *Vāyu* enters the middle channel *(Suṣumṇā).*

manojayaṁ ca labhate vāyubinduvidhāraṇāt /
aihikāmuṣmikī siddhir bhaven naivātra saṁśayaḥ // 74 //

He conquers the mind, and can restrain his breath and his semen; then he gets success in this as well as the other world without doubt.

Svādhiṣṭhāna Cakra

atha svādhiṣṭhānacakravivaraṇam :
dvitīyantu sarojaṁ ca liṅgamūle vyavasthitam /
bādilāntaṁ ca ṣaḍvarṇaṁ paribhāsvaraṣaḍdalaṁ //
svādhiṣṭhānābhidham tat tu paṅkajaṁ śoṇarūpakam /
bālākhyo yatra siddho' sti devī yatrāsti rākiṇī // 75 //

The second Cakra is situated at the base of the organ of generation. It has six petals designated by the letters b, bh, m, y, r, l. Its stalk is called Svādhiṣṭhāna; the colour of the lotus is blood-red; its presiding adept is called Bāla; and its goddess, Rākiṇī.

yo dhyāyati sadā divyaṁ svādhiṣṭhānāravindakam /
tasya kāmāṅganāḥ sarvā bhajante kāmamohitāḥ // 76 //

He who daily contemplates on this *Svādhiṣṭhāna lotus,* becomes an object of love and adoration to all beautiful women.

vividhaṁ cāśrutaṁ śāstram niḥśaṅko vai bhaved dhruvam /
sarvarogavinirmukto loke carati nirbhayaḥ // 77 //

He fearlessly recites the various Śāstras and sciences unknown to him before; becomes free from all diseases; and moves throughout the universe fearlessly.

maraṇaṁ khādyate tena sa kenāpi na khādyate /
tasya syāt paramā siddhir aṇimādiguṇapradā //

vāyuḥ sañcarate dehe rasavṛddhir bhaved dhruvam /
ākāśapaṅkajagalat pīyūṣam api varddhate // 78 //

Death is eaten by him; he is eaten by none; he obtains the highest psychic powers like Aṇimā, Laghimā, etc. Vāyu moves equably throughout his body; the humours of his body also are increased; the ambrosia exuding from the etherial lotus also increases in him.

Maṇipūra Cakra

atha maṇipūracakravivaraṇam :
tṛtīyaṁ paṅkajaṁ nābhau maṇipūrakasañjñakam /
daśāraṇḍādiphāntāraiḥ śobhitaṁ hemavarṇakam // 79 //

The third Cakra, called Maṇipūra, is situated near the navel; it is of golden colour, having ten petals designated by the letters ḍ, ḍh, ṇ, t, th, d, dh, n, p, ph.

rudrākhyo yatra siddho' sti sarvamaṅgaladāyakaḥ /
tatrasthā lākinīnāmnī devī paramadhārmikā // 80 //

Its presiding adept is called Rudra, the giver of all auspicious things, and the presiding goddess of this place is called the most sacred Lākinī.

tasmin dhyānaṁ sadā yogī karoti maṇipūrake /
tasya pātālasiddhiḥ syān nirantarasukhāvahā //
īpsitaṁ ca bhavel loke duḥkharogavināśanam /
kālasya vañcanaṁ cāpi paradehapraveśanam // 81 //

When a Yogī contemplates on the Maṇipūra lotus, he gets the power called *Pātāla Siddhi,* the giver of constant happiness. He becomes lord of desires; destroys sorrows and diseases; cheats death; and can enter the body of another.

jāmbūnadādikaraṇam siddhānāṁ darśanaṁ bhavet /
oṣadhīdarśanaṁ cāpi nidhīnāṁ darśanaṁ bhavet // 82 //

He can make gold, etc., see the adepts (clairvoyantly), discover medicines for diseases, and see hidden treasures.

Anāhata Cakra

atha anāhatacakravivaraṇam :
hṛdaye' nāhataṁ nāma caturthaṁ paṅkajaṁ bhavet /
kādiṭhāntārṇasaṁsthānaṁ dvādaśārasamanvitam //
atiśoṇaṁ vāyubījaṁ prasādasthānam īritam // 83 //

In the heart is the fourth Cakra, Anāhata. It has twelve petals designated by the letters k, kh, g, gh, ṅ, c, ch, j, jh, ñ, ṭ, ṭh. Its colour is deep blood-red; it has the seed of *Vāyu,* yaṁ, and is a very pleasant spot.

padmasthaṁ tatparaṁ tejo bāṇaliṅgaṁ prakīrtitam /
yasya smaraṇamātreṇa dṛṣṭādṛṣṭaphalaṁ labhet // 84 //

In this lotus is a flame called *bāṇaliṅga;* by contemplating on this, one gets seen and unseen rewards.

siddhaḥ pinākī yatrāste kākinī yatra devatā /
etasmin satataṁ dhyānaṁ hṛtpāthoje karoti yaḥ /
kṣubhyante tasya kāntā vai kāmārtā divyayoṣitaḥ // 85 //

Its presiding adept is Pinākī; and Kākinī is its goddess. He who always contemplates on this lotus of the heart is eagerly desired by celestial maidens.

jñānaṁ cāpratimaṁ tasya trikālaviṣayaṁ bhavet /
dūraśrutir dūradṛṣṭiḥ svecchayā khagatāṁ vrajet // 86 //

He gets immeasurable knowledge; knows the past, present and future time; has clairaudience, clairvoyance and can walk in the air, whenever he likes.

siddhānāṁ darśanaṁ cāpi yoginīdarśanaṁ tathā /
bhavet khecarasiddhiś ca khecarāṇāṁ jayas tathā // 87 //

He sees the adepts, and the goddess known as Yoginī; obtains the power known as *Khecarī;* and conquers all who move in the air.

yo dhyāyati paraṁ nityaṁ bāṇaliṅgaṁ dvitīyakam /
khecarī bhūcarī siddhir bhavet tasya na saṁśayaḥ // 88 //

He who meditates daily on the hidden *Bāṇaliṅga,* undoubtedly obtains the psychic powers called *Khecarī* (moving in the air) and *Bhūcarī* (going at will all over the world).

etad dhyānasya māhātmyaṁ kathituṁ naiva śakyate /
brahmādyāḥ sakalā devā gopayanti parantvidam // 89 //

I cannot fully describe the importance of the meditation on this lotus; even gods Brahmā etc. keep the method of its contemplation secret.

Viśuddha Cakra

atha viśuddhacakravivaraṇam :
kaṇṭhasthānasthitaṁ padmaṁ viśuddhaṁ nāma pañcamaṃ /
suhemābhaṁ svaropetaṁ ṣoḍaśasvarasaṁyutam /
chagalāṇḍo'sti siddho'tra śākinī cādhidevatā // 90 //

This lotus situated in the throat, is the fifth Cakra called Viśuddha. Its colour is like brilliant gold, and it is adorned with sixteen petals and is the seat of the vowel sounds (i.e., its sixteen petals are designated by the sixteen vowels: *a, ā, i, ī, u, ū, ṛ, ṝ, ḷ, ḹ, e, ai, o, au, ȧ, aḥ*. Its presiding adept is called *Chagalāṇḍa*, and its presiding goddess is called Śākinī.

dhyānaṁ karoti yo nityaṁ sa yogīśvarapaṇḍitaḥ /
kintvasya yogino'nyatra viśuddhākhye saroruhe //
caturvedā vibhāsante sarahasyā nidheriva // 91 //

He who always meditates on it, is truly the lord of Yogīs, and deserves to be called wise; by the meditation of this Viśuddha lotus, a Yogī at once understands the four *Vedas* and their mysteries.

rahaḥsthāne sthito yogī yadā krodhavaśo bhavet /
tadā samastaṁ trailokyaṁ kampate nātra saṁśayaḥ // 92 //

When the Yogī, fixing his mind on this secret spot, feels angry, then undoubtedly all three worlds begin to tremble.

ihasthāne mano yasya daivād yāti layaṁ yadā /
tadā bāhyaṁ parityajya svāntare ramate dhruvam // 93 //

Even if by chance, the mind of the Yogī is absorbed in this place, then he becomes withdrawn from the external world, and enjoys certainly the inner world.

tasya na kṣatir āyāti svaśarīrasya śaktitaḥ /
saṁvatsarasahasre'pi vajrātikaṭhinasya vai // 94 //

His body never grows weak; and he retains his full strength for a thousand years, the body having become harder than adamant.

yadā tyajati tad dhyānaṁ yogīndro'vanimaṇḍale /
tadā varṣasahasrāṇi manyate tat kṣaṇaṁ kṛtī // 95 //

When the Yogī leaves off this meditation, then to him in this world thousands of years appear as so many moments.

Ājñā Cakra

atha ājñācakravivaraṇam :
ājñāpadmaṁ bhruvor madhye hakṣopetam dvipatrakam /
śuklābhaṁ tanmahākālaḥ siddho devyatra hākinī // 96 //

The two-petalled Cakra, called Ājñā, is situated between the two eyebrows, and has the letters *h,* and *kṣ;* it is white in lustre; its presiding adept is *Mahākāla* (Great Time); its presiding goddess is *Hākinī.*

śaraccandranibhaṁ tatrākṣarabījaṁ vijṛṁbhitam /
pumān paramahaṁso'yaṁ yaj jñātvā nāvasīdati // 97 //

Within that petal, there is the eternal Bīja (the syllable ṭhaṁ), brilliant as the autumnal moon. A wise anchorite, by knowing this, is never pulled down.

etad eva paraṁ tejaḥ sarvatantreṣu gopitam /
cintayitvā parāṁ siddhiṁ labhate nātra saṁśayaḥ // 98 //

This is the great light held secret in all the *Tantras;* by meditating on this, one obtains the highest success; there is no doubt of it.

turīyaṁ tritayaṁ liṅgaṁ tadahaṁ muktidāyakaḥ /
dhyānamātreṇa yogīndro matsamo bhavati dhruvam // 99 //

I am the giver of salvation; I am the third *Liṅga* in the *Turīya* (the state of ecstasy, also the name of the thousand-petalled lotus). By meditating on this, a Yogī becomes certainly like me.

iḍā hi varaṇā khyātā piṅgalāsīti hocyate /
vārāṇasī tayor madhye viśvanātho' tra bhāṣitaḥ // 100 //

The two Nāḍīs called Iḍā and Piṅgalā are the real Varaṇā and Asī. The space between them is called Vārāṇasī (Banaras, the holy city of Śiva). There it is said that Viśvanātha (the Lord of the universe) dwells.

etatkṣetrasya māhātmyam ṛṣibhis tattvadarśibhiḥ /
śāstreṣu bahudhā proktaṁ paraṁ tattvaṁ subhāṣitam // 101 //

The greatness of this holy place has been declared in the scriptures by the truth-perceiving sages. Its great secret has been very eloquently dwelt upon by them.

The Thousand-Petalled Lotus

atha sahasrāracakravivaraṇam :
suṣumṇā meruṇā yātā brahmarandhraṁ yato' sti vai /
tataś caiṣā parāvṛtya tadājñāpadmadakṣiṇe //
vāmanāsāpuṭaṁ yāti gaṅgeti parigīyate // 102 //

Suṣumṇā goes along the spinal cord up to where *Brahmarandhra* (the hole of Brahma) is situated. Thence by a certain flexure, it goes to the right side of the Ājñā lotus, whence it proceeds to the left nostril, and is called Gaṅgā.

brahmarandhraṁ hi yatpadmaṁ sahasrāraṁ vyavasthitam /
tatra kande hi yā yonis tasyāṁ candro vyavasthitaḥ /
trikoṇākāratas tasyāḥ sudhā kṣarati santatam //
iḍāyām amṛtaṁ tatra samaṁ sravati candramāḥ /
amṛtaṁ vahati dhārā dhārārūpaṁ nirantaram //
vāmanāsāpuṭaṁ yāti gaṅgetyuktā hi yogibhiḥ // 103 //

The lotus which is situated in *Brahmarandhra* is called *Sahasrāra* (the thousand-petalled). In the space in its centre, dwells the moon. From that triangular place, elixir is continually exuding. This moon-fluid of immortality unceasingly flows through *Iḍā*. The elixir flows in a stream , a continuous stream. Going to the left nostril, it receives from the Yogīs the name "Gaṅgā".

ājñāpaṅkajadakṣāṁsād vāmanāsāpuṭaṁ gatā /
udagvaheti tatreḍā varaṇā samudāhṛtā // 104 //

From the right-side portion of Ājñā lotus and going to the left nostril flows *Iḍā*. It is here called Varaṇā (the northward-flowing Gaṅgā).

tato dvayor hi madhye tu vārāṇasīti cintayet /
tadākārā piṅgalāpi tadājñākamalāntare //
dakṣanāsāpuṭe yāti proktāsmābhir asīti vai // 105 //

Let a Yogī meditate on the space between the two (*Iḍā* and *Piṅgalā*) as *Vārāṇasī* (Banaras). *Piṅgalā* also comes in the same way from the left side portion of the Ājñā lotus, and goes to the right nostril, and has been called by us *Asī*.

mūlādhāre hi yat padmaṁ catuṣpatraṁ vyavasthitam /
tatra madhye hi yā yonis tasyāṁ sūryo vyavasthitaḥ // 106 //

The lotus which is situated in Mūlādhāra has four petals. In the space between them, dwells the sun.

tatsūryamaṇḍaladvārād viṣaṁ kṣarati santatam /
piṅgalāyāṁ viṣaṁ tatra samarpayati tāpanaḥ // 107 //

From that sphere of the sun, poison exudes continuously. The Sun passes on that poison to Piṅgalā.

viṣaṁ tatra vahantī yā dhārārūpaṁ nirantaram /
dakṣanāsāpuṭe yāti kalpiteyaṁ tu pūrvavat // 108 //

The venom (sun-fluid of mortality) which flows there continuously in a stream goes to the right nostril, as the moon-fluid of immortality goes to the left.

ājñāpaṅkajavāmāṁsād dakṣanāsāpuṭaṁ gatā /
udagvahā piṅgalāpi purāsīti prakīrtitā // 109 //

Rising from the left side of the Ājñā lotus and going to the right nostril, this northward flowing Piṅgalā has been called of yore Asī.

ājñāpadmam idaṁ proktaṁ yatra devo maheśvaraḥ /
pīṭhatrayaṁ tataś cordhvaṁ niruktaṁ yogacintakaiḥ //
tad bindunādaśaktyākhyaṁ bhālapadme vyavasthitam // 110 //

The two-petalled Ājñā-lotus has been thus described where dwells God Maheśvara. Yogīs describe three more sacred stages above this. They are called *Bindu, Nāda* and *Śakti,* and are situated in the lotus of the forehead.

yaḥ karoti sadā dhyānam ājñāpadmasya gopitam /
pūrvajanmakṛtaṁ karma vinaśyed avirodhataḥ // 111 //

He who always contemplates on the hidden Ājñā lotus, at once destroys all the *Karmas* of his past life without any opposition.

iha sthito yadā yogī dhyānaṁ kuryān nirantaram /
tadā karoti pratimāpūjājapam anarthavat // 112 //

Remaining in this place, when a Yogī meditates constantly, then to him all forms, worships and prayers appear worthless.

yakṣarākṣasagandharvā apsarogaṇakinnarāḥ /
sevante caraṇau tasya sarve tasya vaśānugāḥ // 113 //

Yakṣas, Rākṣasas, Gandharvas, Apsarās, and Kinnaras, all serve at his feet. They become obedient to his command.

karoti rasanāṁ yogī praviṣṭāṁ viparītagām /
lambikordhveṣu garteṣu dhṛtvā dhyānam bhayāpaham //
asmin sthāne mano yasya kṣaṇārdhaṁ vartate'calam /
tasya sarvāṇi pāpāni saṁkṣayaṁ yānti tatkṣaṇāt // 114 //

By reversing the tongue and placing it in the long hollow of the palate, let the Yogī enter into meditation, that destroys all fears. All his sins, whose mind remains steady here even for a second, are at once destroyed.

yāni yāni hi proktāni pañcapadme phalāni vai /
tāni sarvāṇi sutarām etaj jñānād bhavanti hi // 115 //

All the fruits which have been described above as resulting from meditation on the other five lotuses, are obtained through the knowledge of this one Ājñā lotus alone.

yaḥ karoti sadābhyāsam ājñāpadme vicakṣaṇaḥ /
vāsanāyāḥ mahābandhaṁ tiraskṛtya pramodate // 116 //

The wise one, who continually practises meditation on this Ājñā lotus, becomes free from the mighty chain of desires, and enjoys happiness.

prāṇaprayāṇasamaye tat padmaṁ yaḥ smaran sudhīḥ /
tyajet prāṇaṁ sa dharmātmā paramātmani līyate // 117 //

When at the time of death, a Yogī meditates on this lotus, leaving this life, that holy one is absorbed in Paramātmā.

tiṣṭhan gacchan svapan bhuñjan yo dhyānaṁ kurute naraḥ /
pāpakarmavikurvāṇo na hi majjati kilviṣe // 118 //

He who meditates on this, standing or walking, sleeping or eating, is not touched by sins, even if it were possible for him to do sinful deeds.

yogī bandhād vinirmuktaḥ svīyayā prabhayā svayam /
dvidaladhyānamāhātmyaṁ kathituṁ naiva śakyate //
brahmādidevatāś caiva kiñcin matto vidanti te // 119 //

A Yogī becomes free from the chain by his own exertion. The importance of the meditation on the two-petalled lotus cannot be fully described. Even the gods like Brahmā, etc., have learnt only a portion of its grandeur from me.

ata ūrdhvaṁ tālumūle sahasrāraṁ saroruham /
asti yatra suṣumṇāyā mūlaṁ savivaraṁ sthitam // 120 //

Above this, at the base of the palate, is the thousand-petalled lotus, in that part where the hole of that *Suṣumṇā* is.

tālumūle suṣumṇā sā adhovaktrā pravartate /
mūlādhāreṇa yonyagrāt sarvanāḍyaḥ samāśritāḥ //
tā bījabhūtās tattvasya brahmamārgapradāyikāḥ // 121 //

From the base or root of the palate, *Suṣumṇā* extends downwards, till it reaches *Mūlādhāra* and the perineum: all Nāḍīs surround it, or are supported by it. These *Nāḍīs* are the seeds of mystery, or the sources of all principles which constitute a man, and show the road to Brahma (i.e. give salvation).

tālumūle ca yat padmaṁ sahasrāraṁ puroditam /
tatkande yonir ekāsti paścimābhimukhī matā // 122 //

The lotus which is at the root of the palate is called *Sahasrāra* (the thousand-petalled); in its centre, there is a Yoni (seat or power-centre) which has its face downwards.

tasyā madhye suṣumṇāyā mūlaṁ savivaraṁ sthitam /
brahmarandhraṁ tadevoktam āmūlādhārapaṅkajam // 123 //

In that is the root of *Suṣumṇā,* together with its hole; this is called *Brahmarandhra* (the hole of Brahma), extending up to the Mūlādhāra Padma.

tatas tadrandhre tacchaktiḥ suṣumṇā kuṇḍalī sadā /
suṣumṇāyāṁ sadā śaktiś citrā syān mama vallabhe //
tasyāṁ mama mate kāryā brahmarandhrādikalpanā // 124 //

In that hole of *Suṣumṇā* there dwells as its inner force the Kuṇḍalinī. In *Suṣumṇā* there is also a constant current of the energy called *Citrā;* its actions or modifications should be called, in my opinion, *Brahmarandhra,* etc.

yasyāḥ smaraṇamātreṇa brahmajñatvaṁ prajāyate /
pāpakṣayaś ca bhavati na bhūyaḥ puruṣo bhavet // 125 //

By simply remembering this, one obtains the knowledge of Brahman; all sins are destroyed; and one is never born again as man.

praveśitaṁ calāṅguṣṭhaṁ mukhe svasya niveśayet /
tenātra na vahatyeva dehacārī samīraṇaḥ // 126 //

Let him thrust the moving thumb into his mouth; by this the air, which flows through the body, is stopped.

tena saṁsāracakre' smin bhramatītyeva sarvadā /
tadarthaṁ na pravartante yoginaḥ prāṇadhāraṇe /
tata evākhilā nāḍyaḥ viruddhā cāṣṭaveṣṭanā /
iyaṁ kuṇḍalinī śaktī randhram tyajati nānyathā // 127 //

Owing to this *(Vāyu)* man wanders in the cycle of birth and death; the Yogīs, therefore, do not desire to keep up this circulation; all the *Nāḍīs* are bound by eight knots; only this *Kuṇḍalinī* can pierce these knots and pass out of the *Brahmarandhra,* and show the way to salvation.

yadā pūrṇāsu nāḍīṣu sanniruddhānilās tadā /
bandhatyāgena kuṇḍalyā mukhaṁ randhrād bahir bhavet // 128 //

When the air is confined fully in all the Nāḍīs, then Kuṇḍalinī leaves these knots and forces its way out of the Brahmarandhra.

suṣumṇāyāṁ sadaivāyaṁ vahet prāṇasamiraṇaḥ /
mūlapadmasthitā yonir vāmadakṣiṇakoṇataḥ //
iḍāpiṅgalayor madhye suṣumṇā yonimadhyagā // 129 //

Then the vital air continually flows in Suṣumṇā. On the right and left side of Mūlādhāra, are situated *Iḍā* and *Piṅgalā.* Suṣumṇā passes through the middle of it.

brahmarandhraṁ tu tatraiva suṣumṇādhāramaṇḍale /
yo jānāti sa muktaḥ syāt karmabandhād vicakṣaṇaḥ // 130 //

The hollow of Suṣumṇā in the sphere of Ādhāra is called Brahmarandhra. The wise one who knows this is emancipated from the chain of Karma.

brahmarandhramukhe tāsāṁ saṅgamaḥ syād asaṁśayaḥ /
tasmin snāne snātakānāṁ muktiḥ syād avirodhataḥ // 131 //

All these three Nāḍīs meet certainly at the mouth of Brahmarandhra; by bathing at this place one certainly obtains salvation.

The Sacred Triveṇī

gaṅgāyamunayor madhye vahatyeṣā sarasvatī /
tāsāṁ tu saṅgame snātvā dhanyo yāti parāṁ gatim // 132 //

Between Gaṅgā and Yamunā flows this Sarasvatī; by bathing at their junction the fortunate one obtains salvation.

iḍā gaṅgā purā proktā piṅgalā cārkaputrikā /
madhyā sarasvatī proktā tāsāṁ saṅgo' tidurlabhaḥ // 133 //

We have said before that *Iḍā* is Gaṅgā and *Piṅgalā* is the daughter of the Sun (Yamunā); in the middle Suṣumṇā is Sarasvatī; the place where all three join is a most inaccessible one.

sitāsite saṅgame yo manasā snānam ācaret /
sarvapāpavinirmukto yāti brahma sanātanam // 134 //

He who performs mental bathing at the junction of the White *(Iḍā)* and the Black *(Piṅgalā)* becomes free from all sins, and reaches the eternal Brahma.

triveṇyāṁ saṅgame yo vai pitṛkarma samācaret /
tārayitvā pitṝn sarvān sa yāti paramāṁ gatim // 135 //

He who performs the funeral rites of his ancestors at the junction of these three rivers *(Triveṇī)* procures salvation for his ancestors and himself reaches the highest end.

nityaṁ naimittikaṁ kāmyaṁ pratyahaṁ yaḥ samācaret /
manasā cintayitvā tu so' kṣayaṁ phalam āpnuyāt // 136 //

He who daily performs the three kind of duties (i.e., the regular, occasional and optional ones) by mentally meditating on this place, receives the unfading reward.

sakṛd yaḥ kurute snānaṁ svarge saukhyaṁ bhunakti saḥ /
dagdhvā pāpān aśeṣān vai yogī śuddhamatiḥ svayam // 137 //

He who once bathes at this sacred place enjoys heavenly felicity; all his sins are burned, and he becomes a pure-minded Yogī.

apavitraḥ pavitro vā sarvāvasthāṁ gato'pi vā /
snānācaraṇamātreṇa pūto bhavati nānyathā // 138 //

Whether pure or impure, in whatever state one might be, by performing ablution at this mystic place, he becomes undoubtedly holy.

mṛtyukāle plutaṁ dehaṁ triveṇyāḥ salīle yadā /
vicintya yas tyajet prāṇān sa tadā mokṣam āpnuyāt // 139 //

At the time of death let him bathe himself in the water of this *Triveṇī* (the confluence of three rivers); he who dies thinking of this, reaches salvation then and there.

nātaḥ paratarаṁ guhyaṁ triṣu lokeṣu vidyate /
goptavyaṁ tat prayatnena na vyākhyeyaṁ kadācana // 140 //

There is no greater secret than this throughout the three worlds. This should be kept secret with great care. It ought never to be revealed.

brahmarandhre mano dattvā kṣaṇārdhaṁ yadi tiṣṭhati /
sarvapāpavinirmuktaḥ sa yāti paramāṁ gatim // 141 //

If the mind becomes steadily fixed even for half a second at the *Brahmarandhra,* one becomes free from sins and reaches the highest end.

asmin līnaṁ mano yasya sa yogī mayi līyate /
aṇimādiguṇān bhuktvā svecchayā puruṣottamaḥ // 142 //

The holy Yogī whose mind is absorbed in this, is absorbed in me after having enjoyed the powers called *Aṇimā, Laghimā* etc.

etadrandhradhyānamātreṇa martyaḥ saṁsāre'smin vallabho me bhavet saḥ /
pāpān jitvā muktimārgādhikārī jñānaṁ dattvā tārayatyadbhutaṁ vai // 143 //

The man knowing this *Brahmarandhra,* becomes my beloved in this world; conquering sins, he becomes entitled to salvation; by spreading knowledge, he saves thousands of people.

caturmukhāditridaśair agamyaṁ yogivallabham /
prayatnena sugopyaṁ tad brahmarandhraṁ mayoditam // 144 //

The Four-faced and other gods can hardly obtain this knowledge. It is the most invaluable treasure of Yogīs; this mystery of the *Brahmarandhra* should be kept a great secret.

The Moon of Mystery

purā mayoktā yā yoniḥ sahasrāre saroruhe /
tasyā'dho vartate candras taddhyānaṁ kriyate budhaiḥ // 145 //

I have said before that there is an energy-centre (Yoni) in the middle of *Sahasrāra;* below that is the moon; let the wise meditate on this.

yasya smaraṇamātreṇa yogīndro' vanimaṇḍale /
pūjyo bhavati devānāṁ siddhānāṁ sammato bhavet // 146 //

By meditating on this a Yogī becomes adorable in this world, and is respected by gods and adepts.

śiraḥkapālavivare dhyāyed dugdhamahodadhim /
tatra sthitvā sahasrāre padme candraṁ vicintayet // 147 //

In the sinus of the forehead let him meditate on the Ocean of Milk; from that place let him meditate on the Moon, which is in Sahasrāra.

śiraḥkapālavivare dviraṣṭakalayā yutaḥ /
pīyūṣabhānuhaṁsākhyaṁ bhāvayet taṁ nirañjanam /
nirantarakṛtābhyāsāt tridinaiḥ paśyati dhruvam /
dṛṣṭimātreṇa pāpaughaṁ dahatyeva sa sādhakaḥ // 148 //

In the sinus of the forehead there is the nectar-containing Moon, having sixteen digits (*Kalās,* i.e., full). Let him meditate on this stainless one. By constant practice, he sees it in three days. By merely seeing it, the practitioner burns all his sins.

anāgataṁ ca sphurati cittaśuddhir bhavet khalu /
sadyaḥ kṛtvāpi dahati mahāpātakapañcakam // 149 //

The future reveals itself to him; his mind becomes pure; and though he might have committed the five great sins, by a moment's contemplation of this he destroys them.

ānukūlyaṁ grahā yānti sarve naśyantyupadravāḥ /
upasargāḥ śamaṁ yānti yuddhe jayam avāpnuyāt /
khecarībhūcarīsiddhir bhavet kṣīrendudarśanāt /
dhyānād eva bhavet siddhi nātra kāryā vicāraṇā /
satatābhyāsayogena siddho bhavati nānyathā /
satyaṁ satyaṁ punaḥ satyaṁ mama tulyo bhaved dhruvam /
yogaśāstre' pyabhiratam yogināṁ siddhidāyakam // 150 //

All the heavenly bodies (planets, etc.)become auspicious; all dangers are destroyed; all accidents are warded off; success is obtained in war; *Khecarī* and *Bhucarī* powers are acquired by the seeing of the moon which is in the head. By mere contemplation on it all these results ensue; there is no doubt of it. By constant practice of Yoga one verily becomes an adept. Verily, verily, again most verily, he becomes certainly my equal. The continual study of the science of Yoga gives success to the Yogīs.

The Mystic Mount Kailāsa

atha rājayogakathanam :
ata ūrdhvaṁ divyarūpaṁ sahasrāraṁ saroruham /
brahmāṇḍākhyasya dehasya bāhye tiṣṭhati muktidam // 151 //

Above this (i.e., the lunar sphere) is the brilliant thousand-petalled lotus. It is outside this microcosm of the body; it is the giver of salvation.

kailāso nāma tasyaiva maheśo yatra tiṣṭhati /
nakulākhyo' vināśī ca kṣayavṛddhivivarjitaḥ // 152 //

Its name is verily *Kailāsa,* where dwells the great Lord (Śiva), who is called Nakula and is without destruction and without increase or decrease.

sthānasyāsya jñānamātreṇa nṛṇām saṁsāre'smin saṁbhavo naiva bhūyaḥ /
bhūtagrāmaṁ santatābhyāsayogāt kartuṁ hartuṁ syāc ca śaktiḥ samagrā//153//

Men, as soon as they discover this most secret place, become free from re-births in this universe. By the practice of this Yoga one gets the power of creating or destroying this aggregate of elements.

sthāne pare haṁsanivāsabhūte, kailāsanāmnīha niviṣṭacetāḥ /
yogī hṛtavyādhir adhaḥkṛtādhir vā"yuś ciraṁ jīvati mṛtyumuktaḥ//154//

When the mind is steadily fixed at this place, which is the residence of the Great Swan and is called Kailāśa, then that Yogī, devoid of diseases and subduing all accidents, lives a long life, free from death.

cittavṛttir yadā līnā kulākhye parameśvare /
tadā samādhisāmyena yogī niścalatāṁ vrajet // 155 //

When the mind of the Yogī is absorbed in the Great God called Kula, then having attained fullness of *Samādhi,* the Yogī gets steadfastness.

nirantarakṛte dhyāne jagadvismaraṇaṁ bhavet /
tadā vicitrasāmarthyaṁ yogino bhavati dhruvam // 156 //

By constant meditation one forgets the world; then really the Yogī obtains wonderful power.

tasmād galitapīyūṣaṁ pibed yogī nirantaram /
mṛtyormṛtyuṁ vidhāyāśu kulaṁ jitvā saroruhe /
atra kuṇḍaliśaktir layaṁ yāti kulābhidhā /
tadā caturvidhā sṛṣṭir līyate paramātmani // 157 //

Let the Yogī continually drink the nectar which flows out of it; by this he gives deathblow to death, and conquers the *Kula.* Here the *Kula Kuṇḍalinī* force is absorbed; after this the fourfold creation is absorbed in Paramātman.

Rāja-Yoga

yaj jñātvā prāpya viṣayaṁ cittavṛttir vilīyate /
tasmin pariśramaṁ yogī karoti nirapekṣakaḥ // 158 //

By this knowledge, the modifications of the mind are suspended, however active they may be; therefore, let the Yogī untiringly and unselfishly try to obtain this knowledge.

cittavṛttir yadā līnā tasmin yogī bhaved dhruvam /
tadā vijñāyate' khaṇḍajñānarūpo nirañjanaḥ // 159 //

When the modifications of the mind are suspended, then one certainly becomes a Yogī; then is known the blemishless Supreme Being having the form of indivisible Gnosis.

brahmāṇḍabāhye sañcintya svapratīkaṁ yathoditam /
tam āveśya mahac chūnyaṁ cintayed avirodhataḥ // 160 //

Let him meditate on his own reflection in the sky as beyond the Cosmic Egg in the manner previously described. Through that let him contemplate on the Great Void unceasingly.

ādyantamadhyaśūnyaṁ tat koṭisūryasamaprabham /
candrakoṭipratīkāśam abhyasya siddhim āpnuyāt // 161 //

The Great Void having no beginning , middle , or end, has the brilliance of tens of millions of suns, and the coolness of tens of millions of moons. By meditating continually on this, one obtains success.

etad dhyānaṁ sadā kuryād anālasyaṁ dine dine /
tasya syāt sakalā siddhir vatsarān nātra saṁśayaḥ // 162 //

Let him practise actively this Dhyāna everyday; within a year he will obtain all success undoubtedly.

kṣaṇārdhaṁ niścalaṁ tatra mano yasya bhaved dhruvam /
sa eva yogī sadbhaktaḥ sarvalokeṣu pūjitaḥ // 163 //

He whose mind is absorbed in that even for a second, is certainly a Yogī, and a good devotee, and is reverenced in all worlds.

tasya kalmaṣasaṁghātas tatkṣaṇād eva naśyati // 164 //

All his sins are at once verily destroyed.

yaṁ dṛṣṭvā na pravartate mṛtyusaṁsāravartmani /
abhyaset taṁ prayatnena svādhiṣṭhānena vartmanā // 165 //

By seeing it one never returns to the path of this mortal universe; let the Yogī, therefore, practise this with great care by the path of *Svādhiṣṭhāna,* (i.e., meditating on the Svādhiṣṭhāna Cakra).

etad dhyānasya māhātmyaṁ mayā vaktuṁ na śakyate /
yaḥ sādhayati jānāti so' smākam api sammataḥ // 166 //

I cannot describe the greatness of this meditation. He who practises, knows. He becomes respected by me.

dhyānād eva vijānāti vicitraphalasaṁbhavam /
aṇimādiguṇopeto bhavatyeva na saṁśayaḥ // 167 //

By meditation one at once knows the wonderful effects of this Yoga (i.e., of the contemplation of the void); undoubtedly he attains the psychic powers like *Aṇimā, Laghimā,* etc.

rājayogo mayākhyātaḥ sarvatantreṣu gopitaḥ /
rājādhirājayogo'yaṁ kathayāmi samāsataḥ // 168 //

Thus have I described the Rāja-Yoga; it is kept secret in all the Tantras; now I shall describe to you briefly the Rājādhirāja Yoga.

Rājādhirāja Yoga

svastikaṁ cāsanaṁ kṛtvā sumaṭhe jantuvarjite /
guruṁ sampūjya yatnena dhyānam etat samācaret // 169 //

Sitting in *Svastikāsana,* in a beautiful monastery, free from all men and animals, having paid respects to his Guru, let the Yogī practise this meditation.

nirālambo bhavej jīvo jñātvā vedāntayuktitaḥ /
nirālambaṁ manaḥ kṛtvā na kiñcic cintayet sudhīḥ // 170 //

Knowing through the arguments of Vedānta the Jīva should be free from attachment; let him make his mind also free from attachment; and let him not think of anything else.

etad dhyānān mahāsiddhir bhavatyeva na saṁśayaḥ /
vṛttihīnaṁ manaḥ kṛtvā pūrṇarūpaḥ svayaṁ bhavet // 171 //

Undoubtedly, by this meditation the highest success *(mahā-siddhi)* is obtained, by making the mind functionless; he himself becomes perfect in form.

sādhayeṭ satataṁ yo vai sa yogī vigataspṛhaḥ /
ahaṁ nāma na ko'pyasti sarvadātmaiva vidyate // 172 //

He who practises this always, is the real passionless Yogī; he never uses the word " I," but always finds himself full of Ātman.

ko bandhaḥ kasya vā mokṣa ekaṁ paśyet sadā hi saḥ /
etat karoti yo nityaṁ sa mukto nātra saṁśayaḥ // 173 //

What is bondage; what is emancipation? To him ever all is *one;* undoubtedly, he who practises this always, is really emancipated.

sa eva yogī sadbhaktaḥ sarvalokeṣu pūjitaḥ /
aham asmīti yan matvā jīvātmaparamātmanoḥ /
ahaṁ tvam etad ubhayaṁ tyaktvākhaṇḍaṁ vicintayet /
adhyāropāpavādābhyāṁ yatra sarvaṁ vilīyate /
tad bījam āśrayed yogī sarvasaṅgavivarjitaḥ // 174 //

He is the Yogī; he is the true devotee; he is worshipped in all the worlds, who contemplates Jīvātmā and Paramātmā as related to each other as "I" and "Am,"who renounces "I"and "thou" and meditates on the indivisible; the Yogī free from all attachment takes shelter in that meditation in which, through the knowledge of superimposition and negation, all is dissolved.

aparokṣaṁ cidānandaṁ pūrṇaṁ tyaktvā bhramākulāḥ /
parokṣaṁ cāparokṣaṁ ca kṛtvā mūḍhā bhramanti vai // 175 //

Leaving that Brahman, who is immediately known, who is knowledge, who is bliss, and who is absolute consciousness, the deluded wanders about, vainly discussing the manifested and the unmanifested.

carācaram idaṁ viśvaṁ parokṣaṁ yaḥ karoti ca /
aparokṣaṁ paraṁ brahma tyaktaṁ tasmin pralīyate // 176 //

He who meditates on this universe of moving and non-moving things, that is really unmanifest, but abandons the supreme Brahman—directly manifest—is verily absorbed in this universe.

jñānakāraṇam ajñānaṁ yathā notpadyate bhṛśam /
abhyāsaṁ kurute yogī sadā saṅgavivarjitaḥ // 177 //

The Yogī, free from all attachment, constantly exerts himself in keeping up this practice that leads to Gnosis, so that there may not be again the upheaval of Ignorance.

sarvendriyāṇi saṁyamya viṣayebhyo vicakṣaṇaḥ /
viṣayebhyaḥ suṣuptyeva tiṣṭhet saṅgavivarjitaḥ // 178 //

The wise one, by restraining all his senses from their objects, and being free from all company, remains in the midst of these objects, as if in deep sleep, i.e., does not perceive them.

evam abhyasato nityaṁ svaprakāśaṁ prakāśate /
śrotur buddhau samarpyārthaṁ nivartante guror giraḥ /
tadabhyāsavaśād ekaṁ svato jñānaṁ pravartate // 179 //

Thus constantly practising the meditation the Self-luminous becomes manifest; here end all the teachings of the Guru after having imparted the truth to the hearer (i.e. they can help the student no further). Henceforth he must help himself; they can no more increase his reason or power; so by the mere force of his own practice he must gain the Gnosis.

yato vāco nivartante aprāpya manasā saha /
sādhanād amalaṁ jñānaṁ svayaṁ sphurati tad dhruvam // 180 //

That Gnosis from which speech and mind turn back baffled, is only to be obtained through practice; for then this pure Gnosis bursts forth of itself.

haṭhaṁ vinā rājayogo rājayogaṁ vinā haṭhaḥ /
tasmāt pravartate yogī haṭhe sadgurumārgataḥ // 181 //

Haṭha Yoga cannot be obtained without Rāja Yoga, nor can Rāja Yoga be attained without Haṭha Yoga. Therefore, let the Yogī first learn Haṭha Yoga from the instructions of a wise Guru.

sthite dehe jīvati ca yogaṁ na śriyate bhṛśam /
indriyārthopabhogeṣu sa jīvati na saṁśayaḥ // 182 //

He who, while living in this physical body, does not practise Yoga, is living merely for the sake of sensual enjoyments.

abhyāsapākaparyantaṁ mitānnaśaraṇaṁ bhavet /
anyathā sādhanaṁ dhīmān kartuṁ pārayatīha na // 183 //

From the time he begins till the time he gains perfect mastery, let the Yogī eat moderately and abstemiously; otherwise, however clever, he cannot gain success.

atīva sādhusaṁlāpaṁ vadet saṁsadi buddhimān /
karoti piṇḍarakṣārthaṁ bahvālāpavivarjitaḥ /
tyajyate tyajyate saṅgaḥ sarvathā tyajyate bhṛśam /
nānyathā labhen muktiṁ satyaṁ satyaṁ mayoditam // 184 //

The wise Yogī in an assembly should utter words of highest good, but should not talk much; he eats a little to keep up his physical frame; let him renounce the company of men; verily, let him renounce all company; otherwise he cannot attain *Mukti* (salvation); verily, I tell you the truth.

guptaiva kriyate'bhyāsaḥ saṅgaṁ tyaktvā tadantare /
vyavahārāya kartavyo bāhye saṅgo na rāgataḥ /
sve sve karmaṇi vartante sarve te karmasaṁbhavāḥ /
nimittamātraṁ karaṇe na doṣo'sti kadācana // 185 //

Let him practise this in secrecy, free from the company of men, in a retired place. For the sake of appearances, he should remain in society, but should not have his heart in it. He should not renounce the duties of his profession, caste or rank; but let him perform these merely, as an instrument of the Lord, without any thought of the event. By thus doing there is no sin.

evaṁ niścitya sudhiyā gṛhastho'pi yadācaret /
tadā siddhim avāpnoti nātra kāryā vicāraṇā // 186 //

Even a householder *(Gṛhastha)*, by wisely following this method, may obtain success; there is no doubt of it.

pāpapuṇyavinirmuktaḥ parityaktāṅgasādhakaḥ /
yo bhavet sa vimuktaḥ syād gṛhe tiṣṭhan sadā gṛhī /
na pāpapuṇyair lipyeta yogayukto sadā gṛhī /
kurvannapi sadā pāpān svakārye lokasaṅgrahe // 187 //

Remaining in the midst of the family, always doing the duties of a householder, he who is free from merits and demerits, and has restrained his senses, attains salvation. The householder practising Yoga is not touched by sins; if to protect mankind he does any sin, he is not polluted by it.

The Mantra—*oṁ aiṁ klīṁ strīṁ*

adhunā sampravakṣyāmi mantrasādhanam uttamam /
aihikāmuṣmikaṁ saukhyaṁ yena syād avirodhataḥ // 188 //

Now I shall tell you the best of practices, the Japa of *Mantra:* from this one gains happiness in this as well in the world beyond this.

yasmin mantre vare jñāte yogasiddhir bhavet khalu /
yoginaḥ sādhakendrasya sarvaiśvaryasukhapradā // 189 //

By knowing this highest of the *Mantras,* a Yogī certainly attains success *(Siddhi):* this gives all power and pleasure to the one-pointed Yogī.

mūlādhāre'sti yat padmaṁ caturdalasamanvitam /
tanmadhye vāgbhavaṁ bījaṁ visphurantaṁ taḍitprabham// 190//

In the four-petalled Mūlādhāra lotus is the Bīja of speech, brilliant as lightning (i.e., the syllable *aiṁ*).

hṛdaye kāmabijaṁ tu bandhūkakusumaprabham /
ājñāravinde śaktyākhyaṁ candrakoṭisamaprabham //
bījatrayam idaṁ gopyaṁ bhuktimuktiphalapradam /
etan mantratrayaṁ yogī sādhayet siddhisādhakaḥ // 191 //

In the heart is the Bīja of love, beautiful as a *Bandhūka* flower (klīṁ). In the space between the two eyebrows (i.e., in the Ājñā lotus)is the Bīja of Śakti (strīṁ), brilliant as tens of millions of moons. These three seeds should be kept secret; they give enjoyment and emancipation. Let the Yogī repeat these three Mantras and try to attain success.

N.B.: The mystical names of these Bīja *Mantras* are not given in the text. The whole Mantra is: Oṁ , aiṁ, klīṁ , strīṁ.

etan mantraṁ guror labdhvā na drutaṁ na vilaṁbitam /
akṣarākṣarasandhānaṁ niḥsandigdhamanā japet // 192 //

Let him learn this *Mantra* from his Guru; let him repeat it neither too fast nor too slowly, keeping the mind free from all doubts, and understanding the mystic relation between the letters of the *Mantra.*

tadgataś caikacittaś ca śāstroktavidhinā sudhīḥ /
devyās tu purato lakṣaṁ hutvā lakṣatrayaṁ japet // 193 //

A wise Yogī, intently fixing his attention on this *Mantra,* performing all the duties peculiar to his caste, should perform one hundred thousand *Homas* (fire sacrifices)and then repeat this *Mantra* three hundred thousand times in the presence of Goddess Tripurā.

karavīraprasūnaṁ tu guḍakṣīrājyasaṁyutam /
kuṇḍe yonyākṛte dhīmān japānte juhuyāt sudhīḥ // 194 //

At the end of this sacred repetition *(Japa),* let the wise Yogī again perform *Homa,* in a triangular hollow, with sugar, milk, butter and a flower of *Karavīra* (oleander).

anuṣṭhāne kṛte dhīmān pūrvasevā kṛtā bhavet /
tato dadāti kāmān vai devī tripurabhairavī // 195 //

By this performance of Homa-Japa-Homa, Goddess Tripura-Bhairavī, who has been propitiated by the above *Mantra,* becomes pleased, and grants all the desires of the Yogī.

guruṁ santoṣya vidhival labdhvā mantravarottamam /
anena vidhinā yukto mandabhāgyo'pi siddhyati // 196 //

Having satisfied the Guru and having received this highest of *Mantras,* in proper way, and performing its recitation in the way laid down, with mind concentrated, even one most heavy-burdened with past Karmas attains success.

lakṣam ekaṁ japed yas tu sādhako vijitendriyaḥ /
darśanāt tasya kṣubhyante yoṣito madanāturāḥ //
patanti sādhakasyāgre nirlajjā bhayavarjitāḥ // 197 //

The Yogī, who having controlled his senses, recites this *Mantra* one hundred thousand times, gains the power of attracting others.

japtena ced dvilakṣeṇa ye yasmin viṣaye sthitāḥ /
āgacchanti yathā tīrthaṁ vimuktakulavigrahāḥ //
dadati tasya sarvasvaṁ tasyaiva ca vaśe sthitāḥ // 198 //

***

By reciting it two lacs of times he can control all persons—they come to him as freely as women go to a pilgrimage. They give him all that they possess, and remain always under his control.

tribhirlakṣais tathā japtair maṇḍalīkāḥ samaṇḍalāḥ /
vaśam āyānti te sarve nātra kāryā vicāraṇā // 199 //

By reciting this *Mantra* three lacs of times, all the deities presiding over the spheres as well as the spheres, are brought under his dominion.

ṣaḍbhirlakṣair mahīpālaḥ sabhṛtyabalavāhanaḥ // 200 //

By reciting this six lacs of times, he becomes the vehicle of power—yea, the protector of the world—surrounded by servants.

lakṣair dvādaśabhir japtair yakṣarakṣorageśvarāḥ /
vaśam āyānti te sarve ājñāṁ kurvanti nityaśaḥ // 201 //

By reciting this twelve *lacs* of times, the lords of Yakṣas, Rākṣasas and Nāgas come under his control; all obey his command constantly.

tripañcalakṣajaptais tu sādhakendrasya dhīmataḥ /
siddhavidyādharāś caiva gandharvāpsaraso gaṇāḥ //
vaśam āyānti te sarve nātra kāryā vicāraṇā /
haṭhāc chravaṇavijñānaṁ sarvajñatvaṁ prajāyate // 202 //

By reciting this fifteen *lacs* of times, Siddhas, Vidyādharas, Gandharvas, Apsarās come under the control of the Yogī. There is no doubt of it. He attains immediately the knowledge of all audition and thus all-knowinghood.

tathāṣṭādaśabhir lakṣair dehenānena sādhakaḥ /
uttiṣthen medinīṁ tyaktvā divyadehas tu jāyate //
bhramate svecchayā loke chidrāṁ paśyati medinīm // 203 //

By reciting this eighteen lacs of times, he, in this body, can rise from the ground; he attains verily a luminous body; he goes all over the universe, wherever he likes; he sees the pores of the earth, i.e., he sees the interspaces and the molecules of this solid earth.

aṣṭāviṁśatibhir lakṣair vidyādharapatir bhavet /
sādhakas tu bhaved dhīmān kāmarūpo mahābalaḥ //
triṁśallakṣais tathājaptair brahmaviṣṇusamo bhavet /
rudratvaṁ ṣaṣṭibhir lakṣair amaratvam aśītibhiḥ //
koṭyaikayā mahāyogī līyate parame pade /
sādhakas tu bhaved yogī trailokye so'tidurlabhaḥ // 204 //

By reciting this twenty-eight lacs of times, he becomes the lord of Vidyādharas; the wise Yogī becomes *kāmarūpī* (i.e., can assume whatever form he desires). By reciting these thirty lacs of times he becomes equal to Brahmā and Viṣṇu. He becomes Rudra by sixty lac recitations; by eighty lac recitations he becomes all-enjoyer; by reciting one crore of times, the great Yogī is absorbed in Parama Brahma. Such a practitioner is hardly to be found throughout the three worlds.

tripure tripurantvekaṁ śivaṁ paramakāraṇam /
akṣayaṁ tatpadaṁ śāntaṁ aprameyam anāmayam //
labhate' sau na sandeho dhīmān sarvam abhīpsitam // 205 //

O Goddess! Śiva, the destroyer of Tripura, is the one first and highest cause. The wise one attains him, who is unchanging, undecaying, all-peace, immeasureable and free from all ills—the Highest Goal.

śivavidyā mahāvidyā guptā cāgre maheśvarī /
madbhāṣitam idaṁ śāstraṁ gopanīyam ato budhaiḥ // 206 //

O great Goddess! This science of Śiva is a great science *(mahāvidyā);* it has always been kept secret. Therefore, this science revealed by me, the wise should keep secret.

haṭhavidyā paraṁ gopyā yoginā siddhim icchatā /
bhaved vīryavatī guptā nirvīryā ca prakāśitā // 207 //

A Yogī, desirous of success, should keep the Haṭha Yoga as a great secret. It becomes fruitful while kept secret; revealed it loses its power.

ya idaṁ paṭhate nityam ādyopāntaṁ vicakṣaṇaḥ /
yogasiddhir bhavet tasya krameṇaiva na saṁśayaḥ //
sa mokṣaṁ labhate dhīmān ya idaṁ nityam arcayet // 208 //

The wise one, who reads it daily from beginning to end, undoubtedly, gradually obtains success in Yoga. He attains emancipation who honors it daily.

mokṣārthibhyaś ca sarvebhyaḥ sādhubhyaḥ śrāvayed api /
kriyāyuktasya siddhiḥ syād akriyasya kathaṁ bhavet // 209 //

Let this science be recited to all holy men, who desire emancipation. By practice success is obtained; without it how can success follow.

tasmāt kriyāvidhānena kartavyā yogipuṅgavaiḥ /
yadṛcchālābhasantuṣṭaḥ santyaktāntarasañjñakaḥ //
gṛhasthaś cāpyanāsaktaḥ sa mukto yogasādhanāt // 210 //

Therefore, the Yogīs should perform Yoga according to the rules of practice. He who is contented with what he gets, who restrains his senses, being a householder, who is not absorbed in the household duties, certainly attains emancipation by the practice of Yoga.

gṛhasthānāṁ bhavet siddhir īśvarāṇāṁ japena vai /
yogakriyābhiyuktānāṁ tasmāt saṁyatate gṛhī // 211 //

Even the lordly householders obtain success by *Japa,* if they perform the duties of Yoga properly. Let, therefore, a householder also exert in Yoga (his wealth and condition of life are no obstacles in this).

gehe sthitvā putradārādipūrṇo
saṅgaṁ tyaktvā cāntare yogamārge /
siddheś cinhaṁ vīkṣya paścād gṛhasthaḥ
krīḍet so vai me matam sādhayitvā // 212 //

Living in the house amidst wife and children, but being free from attachment to them, practising Yoga in secrecy, a householder even finds marks of success (slowly crowning his efforts), and thus following this teaching of mine, he ever lives in blissful happiness.

iti śrīśivasaṁhitāyāṁ yogaśāstre
īśvarapārvatīsaṁvāde pañcamaḥ paṭalaḥ //5//

End of chapter 5 on Kinds of Yoga.

Glossary of Key Sanskrit Terms

abhyāsa	practice.
ācārya	teacher.
ādhāra	foundation, support.
adharma	unrighteousness.
Ādinātha, Ādīśvara	Primal Lord (a title of Śiva).
advaita	non-dual.
Āgama	'coming near to'; a revealed text, particularly in the Śaiva tradition.
Agni	fire; fire-deity; gastric fire.
ahaṁkāra	'I-maker'; faculty of egoity.
ahiṁsā	non-injury, harmlessness.
ājñā	order, command.
ājñā cakra	mystic center between the eyebrows.
ākāśa	space; sky; ether (cf.*kha, vyoman*).
amṛta	the nectar of immortality.
anāhata	unstruck (sound).
ānanda	unbroken bliss; happiness.
ananta	unending, infinite.
aṅga	limb, part.
aṅgula	finger, toe; a finger's breadth.
antaḥkaraṇa	inner instrument, inner activator, i.e. the mind comprising buddhi, ahaṁkāra and manas.
apāna	downward-flowing prāṇa, one of the vital airs.
aparigraha	non-grasping, non-covetousness.
asamprajñāta-samādhi	supracognitive samādhi, samādhi without congitive support (syn.: *nirvikalpa-samādhi*).
āsana	posture; seat.
asmitā	'I-am-ness'; egoity.

āśrama	a dwelling or hermitage; stage of life.
aṣṭāṅga yoga	eight-limbed yoga
asteya	non-stealing.
ātman	self or Self.
ātma-samarpaṇa	self-surrender.
avasthā	state; stage.
avidyā	spiritual ignorance (opposite of vidyā); nescience
avyakta	unmanifest prakṛti.
bandha	lock; binding; bodily contraction.
basti	one of the six cleansing acts, resembling enema.
Bhairava	fierce, ferocious; a form of Siva, or a son of Śiva and Pārvatī.
bhakti	devotion.
bheda, vedha	piercing, penetration.
bīja	seed; saṃskāra; somtimes a synonym of *bindu*.
bindu	a point, dot, spot; seed; mystic essence of seminal fluid.
Brahmā	the creative aspect of Timūrti.
brahmacārin	'one who moves in Brahman', is intent upon Brahman; a spiritual student.
brahmacarya	'moving in Brahman', being internt upon Brahman; chastity.
Brahman	the Absolute.
Brahmānanda	'bliss of Brahman'; name of a sage, author of *Jyotsnā,* a commentary on *Haṭhayoga-Pradīpikā.*
brahmāṇḍa	cosmos (macro-or micro-cosm).
brahmarandhra	'hollow of Brahman', a mystic aperture in the crown of the head.
buddhi	mind, intellect, reflective consciousness.
cakra	wheel; vital or mystic centre.
Candra	moon; iḍā-nāḍī.
Citrā	another name of Suṣumṇā
citta	the entire mind-field, reflective screen of consciousness.
citta-vṛtti	modification of the mind.

darśana	true vision; spiritually uplifting sight of a guru or deity; philosophical viewpoint.
deha	body (syn.: *kāyā, piṇḍa, śarīra)*.
deva	being of light, deity, spirit.
Devī	Goddess, Śakti.
dhāraṇā	fixing the mind on a point, concentration.
dharma	law; nature; order; virtue; truth.
dhauti	cleansing of the upper digestive tract.
dhvani	sound.
dhyāna	meditation.
doṣa	a humour of the body.
draṣṭṛ	the Seer, i.e. the Self.
duḥkha	pain.
ghaṭa	pot, vessel, container.
ghaṭastha-yoga	yoga of the vessel (a synonym of *haṭha-yoga* used in *Gheraṇḍa-Saṁhitā* 1.2).
ghaṭikā	a unit of time (24 minutes).
Gorakṣa (-nātha)	(Hindī: Gorakhnāth) 'cow-protector'; the name of a legendary Haṭha-yogin.
granthi	knot.
guṇa	strand; quality (cf. *triguṇa*).
guru	'weighty one', dispeller of darkness, spiritual teacher.
Hara	Śiva.
Hari	Viṣṇu.
haṭha	forceful, firm, persistent; union of 'sun' *(ha)* and 'moon' *(ṭha)*.
haṭha-yoga, -vidyā	a specific soteriological system of physical and mental discipline; the state (of being and knowledge) achieved by means of that system.
haṭha-yogin	a practitioner of haṭh-yoga.
hṛd, hṛdaya	heart; seat of emotion.
iḍā-nāḍī	'refreshing channel'; nāḍī to the left of Suṣumṇā.
Īśvara	God: Lord; Śiva.
Īśvara-praṇidhāna	devotion to Īśvara.

jālandhara	one of the three main bandhas.
japa	repetition, recitation (of a mantra).
jīva	living being.
jīvanmukta	one who has attained jīvanmukti.
jīvanmukti	living/embodied freedom, liberation while still living.
jīvātman	living/embodied self.
jñāna	knowledge, wisdom.
kaivalya, kevalatva	absoluteness, aloneness, liberation.
Kapālin	'skull-bearer'; an epithet of Śiva in his Bhairava form.
karma	action, deed; ritual act.
kāya	body (syn.: *deha, piṇḍa, śarīra*).
kāya-sādhana	bodily perfection (disciplines).
kāya-siddhi	perfection of the body.
kha	sky; space; atmosphere; ether (cf. *ākāśa, vyoman*).
khecarī	'moving in space'; a particular kind of mudrā.
kleśa	affliction.
kriyā	action, performance; (cleansing) act.
kumbhaka	retention (of prāṇa).
Kuṇḍalinī (-śakti)	'she who is coiled'; serpent power.
laya, pralaya	dissolution, absorption.
liṅga	sign, mark; phallus; symbol of Śiva.
mahābhūta	gross element.
mahat	'the great'; cosmic aspect of buddhi.
manas	mind, cognitive faculty.
maṇipūra, maṇipūraka	'jewel-filled', a mystic centre located at the navel.
mantra	thought-power; sacred sound; chanted syllable, word or phrase.
maṭha, maṭhikā	hermitage.
Matsyendra (-nātha)	'Lord of fish'; name of a sage, reputed guru of Gorakṣa.
māyā	(special) power of Brahman which 'veils' or conceals the ultimate reality.
mokṣa, mukti	liberation, release.
mudrā	seal; circuit-forming gesture.

mūla bandha	one of the three main bandhas.
mūlādhāra	a mystic centre located at the base of the spine
nāda	mystic sound (cf. *śabda, vāk*).
nādānusandhāna	contemplation of the nāda.
nāḍī	mystic channel
Naṭarāja	Dancing Lord (a form of Śiva).
nātha	a particular sect of devotees of Gorakṣa.
neti	cleansing of the upper respiratory tract.
nirguṇa, niṣkala	without parts, without attributes, indivisible (as distinct from *saguṇa, sakala*).
nirodha	dissolution; control; restraint
nirvikalpa-samādhi	samādhi-without-distinction (syn: *asaṁprajñāta-samādhi*).
niyama	observance, the second stage of the eight-limbed yoga.
ojas	vitality, life-energy, reservoir of prāṇa.
pāda	foot; part, chapter (of a book).
padma	lotus.
parama, parā	highest, supreme.
paramātman	supreme Self.
Pārvatī	'daughter of the mountain'; a name of Śakti, Śiva's consort.
Pātañjala-yoga, - darśana,	the yoga of Patañjali, as described in the *Yoga-Sūtra;* one of the six main āstika darśanas.
piṇḍa	body (syn.: *deha, kāya, śarīra*).
Piṅgalā-nāḍī	'tawny chnnel'; nāḍī to the right of Suṣumṇā.
pīṭha	temple, shrine, place of pilgrimage.
Pradhāna	primal substance, prakṛti.
prakṛti	primal substance, the ground of all psychophysical manifestation, constituted by triguṇa.
prāṇa	air, breath, vital force, organisational principle of life (syn.: *vāyu*).
praṇava	the syllable *om.*
prāṇāyāma	breath-control.
prasāda	grace.

pratyāhāra	withdrawal (of senses).
pratyakṣa	perception.
pṛthivī	earth.
pūraka	filling; inhalation.
purāṇa	ancient; mythico-philosophical treatise.
puruṣa	male; person; self; principle of consciousness (in Sāṁkhya).
rāga	attachment.
rāja	radiant, splendid; king, regal, royal.
rajas	impulsion, movement; an aspect of triguṇa; also female sexual fluid.
rāja-yoga	the 'royal yoga'; the eight-limbed yoga.
recaka	exhalation.
ṛṣi	seer, sage.
Rudra	'roarer'; a Vedic deity; an epithet of Śiva.
rūpa	form; beauty.
śabda	word, sound (cf. *nāda, vāk*).
ṣaḍaṅga	six-limbed, sixfold.
sādhana	'that which leads to the goal'; spiritual path.
saguṇa	(Brahman) with attributes
sahasrāra-padma	thousand-petalled lotus (a mystic psychic centre in the crown).
Śaiva	associated with Śiva; one who worships Śiva.
sakala	with parts (as distinct from *niṣkala*).
Śākta	associated with Śakti; one who worships Śakti.
Śakti	power; the consort of Śiva.
samādhi, samāpatti	superconscious state (the goal of yoga).
samāna	one of the vital airs which function in digestion.
samarpaṇa	surrender, giving (oneself) (cf. *ātma-samarpaṇa*)
Śāmbhavī	of a particular kind of mudrā.
Saṁhitā	collection (of verses)
Śāṁkhya	one of the six main Āstika Darśanas.
saṁnyāsa	renunciation.
saṁnyāsin	renunciant.

saṁprajñāta-samādhi congnitive samādhi, samādhi-with-cognitive support (syn: *savikalpa-samādhi*).

saṁsāra 'wandering'; the cycle of life, death and rebirth.

saṁskāra residual mental impression, subliminal activator.

saṁtoṣa contentment.

saṁyama intense concentrative meditation; the combined practice of dhāraṇā, dhyāna, and samādhi.

Sanātana-dharma eternal law or truth: a name of the Vedic religion.

Sarasvatī 'the flowing one'; power and female consort of Brahmā; name of a river in ancient India; Suṣumṇā-nāḍī.

śāstra doctrine, teaching.

śataka a set of one hundred (verses).

ṣaṭ-karmāṇi six (cleansing) acts.

satsaṅga 'in the presence of truth'; assembly before a guru.

sattva 'realness'; illumination, purity, lucidity; an aspect of triguṇa.

sāttvika pure, good, lucid, of the nature of sattva.

satya truth, truthfulness.

śauca purification, cleanliness.

savikalpa-samādhi samādhi-distinction (syn.: *saṃprajñātasamādhi*)

Siddha adept, one who has attained perfection.

Siddhi attainment, perfection, paranormal power.

śiṣya student, disciple, spiritual aspirant.

Śiva the Absolute (according to Śaivism); a personification of the Absolute; the aspect of trimūrti responsible for dissolution or absorption.

śloka stanza.

smṛti memory, recollection; that which is remembered, i.e. teachings that are based upon śruti but are not themselves direct revelations of truth.

śodhana cleansing, purification.

Soma	moon; moon-detiy, divine nectar.
spanda	vibration.
Śrī	beautiful, radiant, splendid; name of Lakṣmī, consort of Viṣṇu; an honorific.
śruti	'that which is heard'; revealed scripture, comprising Saṃhitā, Brāhmaṇa, Āraṇyaka, and Upaniṣad.
sthira	steady.
sthūla	gross, physical.
sukha	easy, pleasant, comfortable, agreeable.
sūkṣma	subtle, refined.
śūnya	space without form; void, empty.
Sūrya	sun; sun-deity; Piṅgalā-nāḍī.
suṣumṇā-nāḍī	'gracious channel'; the central nāḍī in the spinal region, running from mūlādhāra-cakra to sahasrāra-padma.
sūtra	thread; that which sews; a terse written statement; a text composed of such statements.
Svadharma	own duty, own nature.
svādhiṣṭhāna	a mystic centre located at the root of genitals.
svādhyāya	study (of the scriptures).
svara	sound; breath.
Svātmārāma (Yogin, Yogīndra)	the name of a sage, previously known as Cintāmaṇi; author of the *Haṭha-Yoga-Pradīpikā*.
tamas	darkness; inertia: an aspect of triguṇa.
tāṇḍava	dance, sp. of Śiva.
tammātra	subtle element.
Tantra	web, warp; ritual; doctrinal theory; literary exposition; a school of philosophy involving esoteric practices.
Tāntrika	Tantric; related to, or in accordance with, the Tantras; one who follows such teachings.
Tapas	heat, heating, burning; zeal.
tarka	contemplation (cr. *vitarka*).
tattva	'that-ness'; existent principle, truth.

tejas	fire.
triguṇa	the 'three strands' of prakṛti, namely *sattva, rajas* and *tamas*.
trimūrti	'three faces'; the three aspects of Brahman's power, represented as Brahmā, Viṣṇu and Śiva.
Udāna	one of the vital airs controlling intake of food and air.
uḍḍīyāna	'flying up'; one of the three main bandhas.
ujjāyī	uplifting; victorious.
upadeśa	chapter, lesson, instruction.
upādhi	limitation, veil, disguise.
Upaniṣad	secret teaching; a text belonging to the fourth category of śruti.
vāda	view, theory, doctrine.
Vaidika	Vedic; related to, or in accordance, with, the Vedas; one who follows such teachings (cf. *āstika*).
vairāgya	non-attachment.
vajra	thunderbolt; adamantine; diamond.
vajrolī	a particular kind of mudrā.
vāk	word, speech (cf. *nāda, śabda*).
vasti	basti
vāta	wind, air; one of the three doṣas.
vāyu	air, wind, breath (syn.: *prāṇa*).
Veda	revelation, true vision; ancient text, comprising hymns, ritual instructions, mystical and philosophical expositions, etc.
Vedānta	end of (or final part of) the Veda', i.e. the Upaniṣads; one of the six main āstika darśanas.
vibhūti	special power; manifestation; gift, blessing.
vicāra	refined vitarka; 'special movement' of the mind, subtle perception.
vidyā	vision, knowledge.
vijñāna	special or discriminatory knowledge (syn.: *viveka*); consciousness, intelligence.

viśeṣa	particularised; distinction.
Viṣṇu	the Absolute (according to Vaiṣṇavism); a personification of the Absolute; the aspect of Trimūrti responsible for existence and preservation.
viśuddha	a mystic centre located at the throat.
vitarka	special or intense contemplation.
viveka	discernment, discriminatory knowledge (syn.: *vijñāna*).
vṛtti	whirl, vortex, wave, modification, turning, version.
vyakta	manifest.
vyāna	one of the vital airs permeating the whole body.
Vyāsa	'compiler'; the name of a sage, purposed author of the *Yoga Bhāṣya* and *Mahābhārata*.
vyoman	space; sky; atmosphere; ether (cf. *ākāśa, kha*).
yama	restraint; ethical precept (cf. *niyama*), the first stage in Rājayoga.
yantra	device, mechine, tool; symbol.
yoga	union, Self-realisation; the mehtod of achieving that goal.
Yoga darśana	[see Pātañjala-yoga].
yogin	a practitioner of yoga.
yoni	womb, vulva; perineum; source, origin.
yuga	age, epoch.
yukta	joined, connected, united.

Bibliography

PRIMARY SOURCES

A. Editions and translations of principal Haṭha-yoga texts

Gheraṇḍa-Saṁhitā of Gheraṇḍa

Vasu, Śrīś Chandra, trans. 1895. *The Gheraṇḍa Saṁhitā: A Treatise on Haṭha Yoga*. Adyar: Theosophical Publishing House.

Gorakṣa-Śataka attributed to Gorakṣa

Briggs, George Weston. 1973. *Gorakhnāth and the Kānphaṭa Yogīs* (Chapter 14). Delhi: Motilal Banarsidass.

Haṭha-Yoga-Pradīpikā of Svātmārāma Yogin

Iyangar, Srinivasa, trans. 1972. *The Haṭhayogapradīpikā with the Commentary Jyotsnā of Brahmānanda and English Translation.* [Trans. revised by Radha Burnier and A.A. Ramanathan.] Adyar: The Adyar Library and Research Centre/The Theosophical Society.

Rieker, Hans-Ulrich. 1989. *The Yoga of Light: Hatha Yoga Pradipika.* New edn., trans. Elsy Becherer. London: Unwin.

Vishnudevananda, Swami, trans. 1997 *Hatha Yoga Pradipika.* New York: Om Lotus.

Śiva-Saṁhitā

Vasu, Rai Bahadur Srisa Chandra, trans. 1996. *The Siva Samhita:* New Delhi: Mushiram Manoharlal.

Śiva Saṁhitā, Kaivalya Dhāma, Lonawala, Pune.

B. Other related Tāntrika material

Ṣaṭ-Cakra-Nirūpaṇa of Pūrṇānanda-Svāmī, and commentary by Kālīcaraṇa

Avalon, Arthur (Sir John Woodroffe). 1974. *The Serpent Power: The Secrets of Tantric and Shaktic Yoga.* New York: Dover Publications.

[This is a republication of the seventh edition. The first edition, published in 1919 by Luzac & Co., London, has also been referred to.]

Śiva-Svarodaya

Muktibodhananda Saraswati, Swami. 1984. *Swara Yoga; The Tantric Science of Brain Breathing.* Munger, Bihar: Bihar School of Yoga.

C. Principal Sāṁkhya and Yoga texts

Sāṁkhya-Kārikā of Īśvara Kṛṣṇa and its commentaries

Jha, Ganganatha, trans. 1934. *Sāṁkhya-kārikā* of Īśvara Kṛṣṇa, with the *Tattva-kaumudī* of Vācaspati Miśra. 2nd edn. rev. Poona: The Oriental Book Agency.

Sastri, S. S. Suryanarayana, ed. and trans. 1953. *The Sāṅkhya-kārikā of Īśvara Kṛṣṇa.* Madras: University of Madras.

Yoga-Sūtra of Patañjali and its commentaries

Arya, Pandit Usharbudh. 1986. *Yoga-sūtras of Patañjali with the Exposition of Vyāsa.* Trans. and commentary. Vol. 1:*Samādhi-pāda.* Honesdale, Pennsylvania: The Himalayan International Institute of Yoga Science and Philosophy.

Baba, Bangali. 1976. *The Yogasūtra of Patañjali with the Commentary of Vyāsa.* Tr. with additional notes. Delhi:Motilal Banarsidass.

Miller, Barbara Stoler. 1996. *Yoga: Discipline of Freedom.* Berkeley, California: University of California Press.

Satchidananda, Sri, Swami. 1984. *The Yoga Sutras of Patanjali.* Revised edn. Yogaville, Virginia: Integral Yoga Publications.

Shastri, Dhundhiraja, ed. 1930 *Pātañjalayogadarśana,* with the *Rāja Mārttaṇḍa* of Bhoja Rāja, *Pradīpikā* of Bhāvāgaṇeśa, *Vṛtti* of Nāgojī Bhaṭṭa, *Maṇiprabhā* of Rāmānanda Yati, *Pada-Cadrikā* of Ananta-Deva Pandit, and *Yoga-Sudhākara* of Sadāśivendra Sarasvatī. Varanasi: Chowkhambā.

Secondary Sources

Anand, B.K. and G.S. Chhina. 1961. 'Investigations on Yogis Claiming to Stop Their Heart Beats'. *Indian Journal of Medical Research* 49:90-94.

Arya, Pandit Usharbudh. 1985. *Philosophy of Hatha Yoga.* 2nd edn. Honesdale, Pennsylvania: The Himalayan International Institute.

Aurobindo, Sri. 1956. *On the Veda*. Pondicherry: Sri Aurobindo Ashram.

—1970. *The Synthesis of Yoga*. Pondicherry: Sri Aurobindo Ashram.

—1970-76 *The Collected Works*. Pondicherry: Sri Autobindo Ashram.

Bagchi, B.K. and M. A. Wenger. 1958. 'Simultaneous EEG and Other Recordings During Some Yogic Practices'. *Electroencephalography and Clinical Neuro-physiology* 10:193.

Bagchi, Prabodha Chandra, ed. 1986 *Kaulajñāna-nirṇaya of the School of Matsyendranātha*. Trans. Michael Magee. Varanasi: Prachya Prakashan.

Balasubramanian, R. 1990. 'Advaita Vedānta: Its Unity with Other Systems and Its Contemporary Relevance'. *Indian Philosophical Systems* [various authors]. Calcutta: The Ramakrishna Mission Institute of Culture.

Banerjea, Akshaya Kumar. 1962. *Philosophy of Gorakhnath, with Goraksha-Vacana-Sangraha*. Delhi: Motilal Banarsidass.

Barnett, Lionel D. 1905. *Bhagavad-Gītā or the Lord's Song*. London: J. M. Dent & Sons.

Bernard, Theos. 1968. *Haṭha Yoga: the Report of a Personal Experience*. London: Rider & Company.

Bhole, M. V. and P.V. Karambelkar. 1971. 'Water Suction in Internal Cavities During Uddiyana and Nauli'. *Yoga-Mimamsa* 13.4:26-32.

—1971. 'Effect of Yoga Training of Vital Capacity and Breath-Holding Time—A Study'. *Yoga-Mimamsa* 14.3, 4: 19-26.

Birch, Beryl Bender. 1995. *Power Yoga: The Total Strength and Flexibility Workout*. New York: Simon & Schuster.

Brent, Peter. 1972. *Godmen of India*. Middlesex: Penguin.

Briggs, George W. 1938. *Gorakhnāth and the Kānphaṭa Yogīs*. Delhi: Motilal Banarsidass.

Buddhanada, Chela (under the guidance of swami Satyananda Saraswati). 1984. *Moola Bandha: the Master Key*. 2nd edn. Munger, Bihar: Bihar School of Yoga.

Bühler, George. 1886. *The Laws of Manu*. Oxford: Clarendon Press.

Buhrman, Sarasvati. 1998. 'Leaving Depression Behind: The Yogic Way Out'. *Yoga International* 40: 26-33.

Burley, Mikel 2000, *Hath-Yoga*, Motilal Banarsidass, Delhi.

Conze, Edward. 1962. *Buddhist Thought in India*. London.

Das, Maya. 1990. 'Indian Philosophical Systems: Their Basic Unity and Relevance Today'. *Indian Philosophical Systems* [Various authors]. Calcutta: Ramakrishna Mission.

Das, N. N. and H. Gastaut. 1955. 'Variations in the Electrical Activity of the Brain, Heart, Skeletal Muscles During Meditation and Trance'. *Electroencephalography and Clinical Neurophysiology 6:* 211-19

Datey, K.K., S. Deshmukh, C. Dalvi and S. L. Vinekar. 1969. 'Shavasan: A Yogic Exercise in the Management of Hypertension'. *Angiology* 20: 325-33.

Dennett, Daniel C. 1991. *Consciousness Explained:* London: Penguin.

Desikachar. T. K. V. 1995. *The Heart of Yoga: Developing a Personal Practice.* Rochester, Vermont: Inner Traditions International.

Deussen, Paul. 1906. *The Philosophy of the Upanishads.* English trans. A. S. Geden. Edinburgh: T & T Clark.

Dimmitt, Cornelia and J. A. B. van Buitenen. 1978. *Classical Hindu Mythology: A Reader in the Sanskrit Purāṇas* Philadelphia: Temple University Press.

Easwaran, Eknath. 1988. *The Upanishads.* London: Penguin.

Edgerton, Franklin. 1965. *The Beginnings of Indian Philosophy: Selections from the Rig Veda, Atharva Veda, Upaniṣads, and Mahābhārata.* London: George Allen & Unwin.

Eliade, Mircea. 1969. *Yoga: Immortality and Freedom.* Trans. from the French by Willard . Trask. London: Routledge & Kegan Paul, —, ed. in chief. 1987. *The Encyclopedia of Religion.* Vol. 14. New York: Macmillan Publishing Company.

Feuerstein, Georg. 1974a. *Introduction to the Bhagavád-Gītā: Its Philosophy and Cultural Setting*. London: Rider and Company.

—.1974. *The Essence of Yoga: A Contribution to the Psychohistory of Indian Civilisation.* London: Rider and Company.

—.1979. *The Yoga-Sūtra of Patañjali: An Exercise in the Methodology of Textual Analysis.* New Delhi: Arnold- Heinemann.

—.1980. *The Philosophy of Classical Yoga.* Manchester: Manchester University Press.

—.1990a. *Encylopedic Dictionary of Yoga.* London: Unwin.

—. 1990 b *Yoga: The Technology of Ecstasy.* Wellingborough, Northamptonshire: Crucible/Thorsons.

—, trans. and ed. 1997. *Teachings of Yoga.* Boston & London: Shambhala.

—, Subhash Kak and David Frawley. 1995. *In Search of the Cradle of Civilization: New Light on Ancient India*. Wheaton, Illinois: Quest Books/Theosophical Publishing House.

— and Jeanine Miller. 1971. *A Reappraisal of Yoga: Essays in Indian Philosophy.* London: Rider and Company.

Frawley, David. 1993. *Gods, Sages and Kings: Vedic Light on Ancient Civilization.* New Delhi: Motilal Banarsidass.

—.1994. *The Myth of the Aryan Invasion of India.* New Delhi. Voice of India.

Funderburk, James. 1977. *Science Studies Yoga: A Review of Physiological Data.* Honesdale, Pennsylvania: The Himalayan International Institute.

Gandhi, Mohandas K. 1960. *Discourses on the Gita.* Ahmedabad: Navajivan Publishing House.

Garbe, Richard. 1990. 'On the Voluntary Trance of Indian Fakirs'. *The Monist* 10:492-500.

Gelblum, Tuvia. 1992. 'On "the Meaning of Life" and the *Bhagavad Gītā. Asian Philosophy* 2.2:121-30.

Gerson, Scott. 1993. *Ayurveda: The Ancient Indian Healing Art.* Shaftesbury, Dorset: Element Books.

Gharote, M. L. 1973. 'Effect of Yogic Training on Physical Fitness'. *Yoga-Mimamsa* 154:31-35.

Ghosh, Jajneswar. 1977. Introduction to: Swāmī H. Āraṇya, *The Sāṁkhya-sūtras of Pañcaśikha* and *The Sāṁkhyatattvāloka.* Delhi: Motilal Banarsidass.

Gopal, K. S., V. Anantharaman, S. Balachander and S. D. Nishith. 1973. 'The Cardiorespiratory Adjustments in "Pranayama," with and without "Bandhas," in "Vajrasana". *Indian Journal of Medical Science* 27.9: 686-92.

Govindan, Marshall. 1991. *Babaji and the 18 Siddha Kriya Yoga Tradition.* Montreal: Kriya Yoga Publications.

Goyandaka, Jayadayal, trans, 1943. *The Bhagavadgītā, or the Song Divine.* Gorakhpur: Gita Press.

Harshananda, Swami, 1981. *Hindu Gods and Goddesses.* Madras: Sri Ramakrishna Math.

Hewitt, James. 1987. *The Complete Yoga Book: The Yoga of Breathing, Posture, and Meditation.* London: Rider.

Hocking, M. G. 1993. *Exploring the Subconscious Using New Technology.* London: CMC Ltd.

Iyengar, B. K. S. 1981. *Light on Prāṇāyāma.* London: George Allen & Unwin.

—. 1988. *The Tree of Yoga.* London: Aquarian Press.

—. 1991. *Light on Yoga.* London: Aquarian Press.

Johari, Harish. 1986. *Tools for Tantra.* Rochester, Vermont: Inner Traditions India.

—. 1987. *Chakras: Energy Centers of Transformation.* Rochester, Vermont: Destiny Books/Inner Traditions.

Karambelkar, P.V., M. V. Bhole, and M. L. Gharote. 1969. 'Muscle Activity in Some Asanas'. *Yoga-Minamsa* 12.1:1-13.

Kirtan: Sivananda Chantbook. 1989. International Sivananda Yoga Vedanta Centres.

Koelman, Gaspar M. 1970. *Pātañjala Yoga : From Related Ego to Absolute Self.* Poona: Papal Anthenaeum.

Kramrisch, Stella. 1981. *The Presence of Śiva.* Princeton. New Jersey: Princeton University Press.

Krishna, Gopi. 1976. *Kundalini: Path to Higher Consciousness.* New Delhi: Orient Paperbacks.

—. 1992. *Kundalini –The Secret of Yoga.* New Delhi: UBSPD.

—. 1993. *The Purpose of Yoga.* New Delhi: UBSPD.

Larson, Gerald J. and Ram Shankar Bhattacharya, Eds. 1987. *Encyclopedia of Indian Philosophies.* Vol.4: *Sāṃkhya: A Dualist Tradition in Indian Philosophy.* Delhi: Motilal Banarsidass.

Leadbeater, C.W. 1968. *The Chakras: A Monograph:* 8th edn. Adyar: Theosophical Publishing House.

Lipner, Julius. 1998. *Hindus: Their Religious Beliefs and Practices.* London: Routledge.

Lott, Eric. 1980. *Vedantic Approaches to God.* London: Macmillan Press.

Marshall, P. J., ed. 1970. *The British Discovery of Hinduism in the Eighteenth Century.* Cambridge: Cambridge University Press.

Mitra, Vihari-Lála, trans. 1891. *The Yoga-Vásishtha-Maharamáyana of Válmiki.*3 vols. Calcutta: Bonnerjee And Co.

Monier-Williams, Monier. 1963. *A Sanskrit-Englilsh Dictionary* Delhi: Motilal Banarsidass.

Murphy, Michael. 1992. *The Future of the Body: Explorations Into the Further Evolution of Human Nature.* New York: G.P. Putnam's Sons.

Murray, Muz. 1986. *Sharing the Quest.* Shaftesbury, Dorset: Element Books.

Nikhilānanda, Swāmi, trans. 1994. *Māṇḍūkyopanishad with Gauḍapāda's Kārikā and Śaṅkara's Commentary.* Mysore: Sri Ramakrishna Ashrama.

O' Flaherty, Wendy D. 1973. *Śiva: The Erotic Ascetic.* Oxford: Oxford University Press.

Ozaniec, Naomi. 1990. *The Chakras.* Shaftesbury, Dorset: Element Books.

Potter, Karl H., gen ed. 1977-96. *The Encyclopedia of India Philosophies.* Vol.2: *Indian Metaphysics and Epistemology: The Tradition of Nyāya-Vaiśeṣika up to Gaṅgeśa.* Vol.6: *Indian Philosophical Analysis: Nyāya-Vaiśeṣika from Gaṅgeśa to Reghunātha Siromani.* Delhi: Motilal Banarsidass.

Radha, Swami Sivananda. 1993 *Kundalini Yoga for the West.* Spokane, Washington: Timeless Books.

Radhakrishna, Sarvepalli. 1928. *The Vedānta According to Śaṁkara and Rāmānuja.* London: George Allen & Unwin.

—, trans. 1953. *The Principal Upaniṣads.* Delhi: Oxford University Press.

— and Charles A. Moore, eds. 1957. *A Sourcebook in Indian Philosophy.* Princeton, New Jersey: Princeton University Press.

Rajaram, Navaratna S. 1993. *Aryan Iṅvasio of India. The Myth and the Truth.* New Delhi: Voice of India.

Raju, P.T. 1985. *Structural Depths of India Thought.* New York: State University of New York Press.

Rama, Swami. 1986 *Path of Fire and Light.* Vol. 1: *Advanced Practices of Yoga.* Honesdale, Pennsylvania: The Himalayan International Institute.

—, R. Ballentine, and Swami Ajaya. 1976. *Yoga and Psychotherapy: The Evolution of Conciousness.* Honesdale, Pennsylvania: The Himalayan International Institute.

Śaṅkarācārya. Srī. 1992. *Vivekacūḍāmaṇi.* 13th impression. Trans. Swāmī Mādhavānanda. Calcutta. Advaita Ashrama.

Sannella, Lee. 1987. *The Kundalini Experience: Psychosis or Transcendence?* Lower Lake, California: Integral Publishing.

Sastri, Dewan Bahadur K. S. Ramaswami, 1953. *Sivananda: A Modern World-Prophet.* Rishikesh: The Yoga-Vedanta Forest University.

Satyasangananda Saraswati, Swami. 1984 *Light on the Guru and Disciple Relationship.* Munger, Bihar: Bihar School of Yoga.

Scott, Mary. 1983. *Kundalini in the Physical World.* London: Routledge & Kegan Paul.

Schweizer, Paul. 1993. 'Mind/Consciousness Dualsim in Sāṅkhya Yoga Philosophy' *Philosophy and Phenomenological Research* 53.4:845-59.

Sharma, Chandrahar. 1960. *A Critical Survey of Indian Philosophy.* Varanasi: Motilal Banarsidass.

Shastri, D. C. B. 1990. 'The Indian Philosophical Systems: Their Basic Unity and Relevance Today'. *Indian Philosophical Systems* [Various authors]. Calcutta: Ramakrishna Mission.

Singh, Jaideva. 1979. *Śiva Sūtras: The Yoga of Supreme Identity*. Delhi: Motilal Banarsidass.

Sivananda, Sri Swami. 1955a. *Tantra Yoga, Nada Yoga and Kriya Yoga*. Rishikesh: The Yoga-Vedanta Froest University.

—, 1955b. *The Yoga- Vedanta Sutras*. Rishikesh: The Yoga Vedanta Forest University.

Svoboda, Robert E. 1998. 'A Question of Vision: The Relationship Between Ayurveda and Modern Medicine'. *Yoga International* 40: 34-41.

The Holy Bible, Containing the Old and New Testaments. 1901. Oxford: Oxford University Press.

Thomas, Edward J. 1927. *The Life of Buddha as Legend and History* New York: Alfred A. Knopf.

Thoreau, Henry David. 1992. *Walden, or Life in the Woods: Selections from the American Classic*. Boston: Shambhala.

Upupa, K. N., R. H. Singh and R. M. Settiwar. 1971. 'Studies on Physiological, Endocrine and Metabolic Response to the Practice of Yoga in Young Normal Volunteers'. *Journal of Research in Indian Medicine* 6.3:345-53.

Warren, H. C., trans. 1915. *Buddhism in Translations*. Harvard Oriental Series, Vol. 3, 6th edn. Cambridge, Mass. Harvard University Press.

Wenger, M. A. and B. K. Bagchi. 1961. 'Studies of Autonomic Functions in Practitioners of Yoga in India'. *Behavioural Science* 6: 312-23.

Whicher, Ian R. 1992 [unpublished Ph. D. thesis]. *A Study of Patañjali's Definitions of Yoga: Uniting Theory and Practice in the* Yoga-Sūtras. University of Cambridge.

—,1995. 'Cessation and Integration in Classical Yoga'. *Asian Philosophy* 5.1:47-58.

—,1998. *The Integrity of the Yoga Darśana: A Reconsidration of Classical Yoga*. New York: State University of New York Press.

Wood, Ernest. 1959. *Yoga*. Middlesex: Penguin.

Yogananda, Paramahansa, 1981. *Autobiography of a Yogi*. 12th edn. California: Self-Realization Fellowship.

Zaehner, R. C., ed. and trans. 1966. *Hindu Scriptures*. London: Dent.

—, trans. 1969. *The Bhagavad-Gītā*. Oxford: Clarendon Press.

Zvelebil, Kamil V. 1996. *The Siddha Quest for Immortality*. Oxford: Mandrake.

Index

Q

R

S

T

U

V

W

Y

COPYRIGHT, DISCLAIMER & INTENT

DISCLAIMER

The author is not a SEBI-registered investment advisor.
This book is based on personal experience and independent research and is intended solely for educational purposes.
General considerations of inflation, taxation, and long-term economic factors have been taken into account; however, individual circumstances may vary.
Readers are encouraged to conduct their own research and consult a qualified professional before making investment decisions.
Investment outcomes depend on market conditions and are not guaranteed.

AUTHOR'S INTENT

This book is written with the belief that wealth creation is achievable for individuals from all financial backgrounds.
Through discipline, consistency, patience, and a long-term mindset, financial growth can be built over time- regardless of the size of the starting capital.
For those who believe that time and patience build wealth.

Publisher: Built By Time
Author: Piyush Mittal
ISBN: 978-93-5777-837-4
First Edition 2026
Printed in India

Designed Across Horizons